The Rhetoric of Outrage

The
Rhetoric
of Outrage

Why Social Media
Is Making Us Angry

Jeff Rice

THE UNIVERSITY OF
SOUTH CAROLINA PRESS

© 2023 University of South Carolina

Published by the University of South Carolina Press
Columbia, South Carolina 29208

uscpress.com

Printed in the United States of America

Library of Congress Cataloging-in-Publication Data
can be found at http://catalog.loc.gov/.

ISBN: 978-1-64336-396-7 (hardcover)
ISBN: 978-1-64336-397-4 (paperback)
ISBN: 978-1-64336-398-1 (ebook)

To Vered and Judah.
You bring me only joy and love.
Never outrage.

Contents

Acknowledgments

The Rhetoric of Outrage was influenced by two theoretical mentors I never met: Vilém Flusser and Roland Barthes. Their ideas regarding aggregation and technical images shape a great deal of how I see this world, whether I am writing about outrage or another topic. Barthes, in particular, is my theoretical mentor. All of our lives and the components of our lives, as I have learned from him, are "icities": love, hate, disillusionment, travel, professionalism, and so on. We aggregate into our lives the images that make meaning, superficial or not, for us. For this book, I have focused on what I feel has become a major aggregated component of digital discourse and social media: outrage.

Too often, we blame social media for the discourse that humans create and disseminate. Those who share ideas online have agency. Those who share ideas online spread ideas, even when they are not aware of where such ideas originate or how such ideas are embedded within other, previous ideas. This book is my attempt to explore this rhetorical phenomenon. I acknowledge that it is not the software that generates outrage, but us.

I wrote this book with the generous support of the Martha B. Reynolds endowed professorship I hold at the University of Kentucky.

I thank Aurora Bell for her incredible support for this project. I also thank the two anonymous reviewers for their constructive and helpful feedback. I thank those who supported previous talks whose content, in different iterations, eventually made its way into this manuscript: Scott Barnes and Justin Hodgson for inviting me to speak and participate in the Indiana Digital Rhetoric Symposium, as well as those who attended related talks at Bar-Ilan University, Rhetoric Society of America, Rhetoric Society 7 in Ghent, Belgium, the Conference on College Composition and Communication, Society for Literature, Science and the Arts, and the National Communication Society. This book was written at various moments in Lexington, Kentucky, and Tel Aviv, Israel. I thank my close friends Bradley Dilger and Thomas Rickert for listening to me talk about this project even if they didn't realize they were helping me think ideas through or that I was even talking about a book. I also thank them for being there for my own personal outrage at the pitfalls of life, what occurred as I was writing this book.

Finally, I thank my children, Judah and Vered, who, whether they realize it or not, calm all around me and give my life meaning. They let me rap in public (well, they don't really), eat my food, eat the food I discover for us, and travel with me to small towns in Kentucky or other countries so that we can eat even more food. I thank them for being in my life. And I thank Lev, my Australian Shepherd, who was too crazy for the farm where he previously lived, and whose oddness should provoke outrage in me, yet it doesn't. I'm sure he doesn't understand what "thank you" means anyway.

Introduction

On any given day, at any given hour, across the various platforms that constitute what we call social media, someone is angry. Facebook. Instagram. Twitter. Reddit. 4Chan. These are but a few of the numerous online spaces where users comment on a political, popular culture, local, personal, economic, visual, professional, or other issue because something angers them. Somewhere across the Internet a post or tweet occurs, and somewhere that post or tweet reflects anger. We are angry at police brutality in Ferguson, Missouri; Waller County, Texas; and Minneapolis, Minnesota. We are angry at the Counselor to the President for putting her feet up on the couch during a visit by presidents of historically Black colleges and universities. We are angry at a president for telling citizens to drink Lysol as a way to ward off the coronavirus. We are angry at publicized breaches of consumer data at companies like Target, Marriott, or Facebook. We are angry at polluted water in a northern Michigan town and the government's failure to solve the problem. We are angry at the decision to tear gas asylum seekers on the Mexican border and put Central American and Mexican children in cages, separated from their families. We are angry at an NFL quarterback for kneeling during the national anthem, or we are angry at the NFL for blacklisting him. We are angry at a body wash ad for its racist suggestion that washing removes "black" and replaces it with "white." The list goes on.

Anger is all around us. Everything, it seems, sucks today, and we need some way out of this situation. One yoga studio offers "rage yoga" as means for coping with our current climate of outrage. One instructor explains the benefits of rage yoga: "We are all angry about something and we all have been holding onto an "F"-bomb for a little bit too long. So that's what this does—is—it allows you to have a safe space to let go of your and frustration and rage in a healthy way . . . and then also wash it all away with some ice cold beer" (Pygas).

Has there ever in our history been an age of such widespread discontent? The *Atlantic* noted that the 2019 Democratic party had adopted anger as "the ethic of the moment" (Garber). Even forgotten cartoons set us off. In November 2018, outrage occurred over a forty-five-year-old *Peanuts* cartoon. Suddenly, even though the cartoon had been in circulation for almost half a century, viewers felt that the Charlie Brown Thanksgiving Day special was racist.

> Critics are slamming ABC's "A Charlie Brown Thanksgiving" for seating its only black character, Franklin, alone on one side of the holiday table—in a rickety old lawn chair.
>
> Meanwhile, white friends—including Peppermint Patty, Charlie Brown, Sally and even Snoop—were all seated across from him in real chairs as they feasted, Twitter users pointed out. (O'Neill)

If not *Peanuts*, then politics. Did we elect Donald Trump because of anger? "According to exit polls and endless postmortems," Casey Cep writes, "many people were so furious about immigration, the economy, the election of a Black president, the potential for a female one, Black Lives Matter, the War on Christmas, and any number of other real and phantasmagorical issues that they voted for Trump. Was there ever a better example of blind rage?"

"As far as I am concerned, anger is okay," Donald Trump noted early in 2016, prior to his election. "Anger and energy is what this country needs" (qtd. in Duhigg). Indeed, Bob Woodward's book about Donald Trump is titled *Rage*. Anger overtakes us, but is it, really what we need? "For a frightening amount of people," Heather Wilhelm writes, "the art of being offended by everything—or, even better, loudly and publicly complaining about being offended by everything—is pursued with alarming dedication. For some, being offended is practically a credo and an all-encompassing way of life." In 2019, the phrase "OK, boomer" sparked offense for how it dismissed a phase of life: middle age. Angry at this phrase addressed toward those born just after World War II, radio host Bob Lonsberry tweeted that "boomer" is "the n-word of ageism" (Sung). Yuki Noguchi called #okboomer's presence on Twitter a way to "convey a fundamental disconnect between younger generations and baby boomers who cling to outdated, off-base ideas." Outdated ideas, as figure 0.1 shows, offend. On any given day, the hashtag #offended generates a massive return of tweets dealing with outdated ideas about college mascots, white waiters in Indian restaurants, body shaming, and Starbucks, among others.

Maybe anger is what we need after all, whether we are discussing *Peanuts*, the president, racism, or some other issue. It certainly has become the most dominant digital reaction to how awful the world has become. In response to this state, anger may be a contemporary way of life. *Slate* declared 2014 "the year of outrage." In the *Slate* special issue, Julia Turner wrote, "Over the past decade or so, outrage has become the default mode for politicians, pundits, critics and, with the rise of social media, the rest of us." In response, *Slate* constructed the "rage-a-day calendar," a tracking of daily rage at a variety of events and moments. According to the calendar, on August 6, Ann Coulter called a doctor

Fig. 0.1.
#offended tweet.

who fought Ebola in Liberia idiotic. On September 22, *Jeopardy* winner Ken Jennings tweeted "Nothing sadder than a hot person in a wheelchair." And on December 9, the CIA reported to the Senate that for four years prisoners were tortured without then–President Bush's knowledge. Each of these moments produced public outrage. Diverse topics, similar anger.

"Anger is the most viral emotion on the Internet," Helen Popkin writes. Anger is often a reflection of real-world events, and it is often a reflection of emotional frustration in general. Anger is directed at popular culture as much as it is directed against economic or foreign policy, police brutality, racism, sexism, and other serious issues. As Sarah Ahmed writes, anger and outrage can stem from an overall lack of cultural and personal happiness: "Your rage might be directed against the object that fails to deliver its promise, or it might spill out toward those who promised you happiness through the elevation of some things as good. Anger can fill the gap between the promise of a feeling and the feeling of a feeling. We become strangers, or affect aliens, in such moments" (*The Promise* 42). As affect aliens, many of us direct our anger at individuals and at institutions. Anger and outrage are not always the same affective response to cultural, political, or personal issues, but when read together, they reflect a trend worthy of attention because of its place within cultural expression. My focus is on outrage more than on anger. In particular, my focus is on the digital rhetorics and logics that construct outrage.

As I will argue in this book, outrage comprises several traits. Outrage is an affective response, an image, a technology, an aggregation, a medium, and a form of communication; that is, it is rhetorical. These characteristics often appear simultaneously, but throughout this book I will focus on specific aspects of digital outrage in order to better articulate and understand how outrage functions in the age of social media. My principal argument is that outrage typically lacks a referent—that is, an object of reference. It relies, instead, on aggregations and ideological algorithms, and what Vilém Flusser calls the technical image. My intent is not to deny the very specific and important racial, gendered, or class-based perspectives that may shape a moment of outrage, nor do I mean to conflate serious issues with the trivial. Instead, my purpose is to shift overall focus on outrage to the digital rhetorical roles of aggregation and algorithms in contemporary social media outrage. Key to this work will be Flusser's concept of the technical image and Roland Barthes's theory of aggregation.

Because of aggregations and algorithmic thinking, *The Rhetoric of Outrage* argues, much of our culture lives continuously in moments tied to moments tied to other moments. I will call this process in later chapters "layering." With layering, collected moments are assumed to be singular representations; that assumption often sparks immediate anger. I will break down this collection as the logic of aggregations and algorithms. *The Rhetoric of Outrage* is about digital outrage, but it is also about the specific rhetorical logics that lead to and perpetuate such outrage, logics not always obvious to either the angered or to the respondents to anger.

Facebook, one of the most prominent social media spaces helping to spread outrage, is often included in these logics. Writing in the *Guardian*, Zoe Williams describes the daily anger she observes regularly on Facebook, an anger algorithmically pushed across her newsfeed: "It's the private finance initiative, or the degradation of the biosphere, or someone on a train with a loud voice, or a perfume called Psychoanalysis, or a helicopter. From people you know, anger is endearing: vaudeville, passionate, playful, hyperbolic, bonding, amusing to watch. In people you don't know, it is alienating: recognizing neither the subtleties that temper it, nor the subtext that humanizes it, all you can see is its denaturing effect." Facebook, like a news reader or a series of online publications, shares information. Facebook, though, with its billion users connected to each other in obvious and abstract ways, is also an information sharing machine. Social media platforms like Facebook help translate the sharing of information into outrage because we don't just read online, we share and comment. Sharing and commenting continues outrage, spreading it further outward, increasing the algorithm's effects. Teddy Wayne summarizes just a few of his own observations regarding such digital anger, considering the ways social media prompts its spread: "Certainly, outrage can function as a corrective or anguished expression of helplessness, punishing the offending party if he, she or it has not been given any official penalty; think of George Zimmerman. Moreover, it can double as effective activism, forcing a response from the powers that be, as in the case of Ms. Sacco, whom IAC fired the day after her post went viral and who inspired someone to create a website with her name that redirects visitors to the nonprofit alliance Aid for Africa."

Outrage is definitional, or it is causal. News media, as projected via Twitter, Facebook, and other platforms, reminds us of this. Indeed, media outlets are aware of both the content of outrage and their own meta-relationship to such outrage. Headlines define the cultural status as such. "Why is Everyone on the Internet so Angry?" a *Scientific American* headline asks. "Why Social Media is Making You Miserable," *Cosmopolitan* explains. "Maybe It's Time for Everyone to Give Up on Social Media," The *New York Post* declares. "Think You're Angrier Lately? You Probably Are and Your Facebook Feed is to Blame," the *Philadelphia Inquirer* states. Many of us may be emotional activists, but we are, as these headlines pronounce, succumbing to beliefs online that may only sink us deeper into despair. Even if social media creates unhappiness, many remain engaged with social media, spreading someone else's anger via a retweet or like. Most of us at some point will use social media to, in the words of *The Simpsons* character Comic Book Guy, go on the Internet within minutes to register our disgust with the world. Facebook, of course, offers an angry emoji option if the "like" doesn't suffice; yes, it is also possible to be iconically angry.

The problem with digital anger and outrage, as many observe, is that it often reduces complex and possibly contradictory situations to headlines, immediacy, or emotional gut impulses. Complexity yields to a post's or tweet's immediate impact, and that impact is typically based on our first reactions rather than reflection or thoughtful consideration, or even acknowledgement that what we are reading or viewing is not singular but instead a gathering of previous iterations and images. Upworthy and Buzzfeed are popularly known for reducing ideas and events to catchy headlines, but most information shared online depends on the immediate, instinctual response to a headline embedded in a tweet or post or image. Headlines generate inferences, and inferences can lead to emotional outbursts. "By now," Maria Konnikova states, "everyone knows that a headline determines how many people will read a piece particularly in this era of social media." Headlines mislead, she adds, and can distort how one reads the accompanying writing. "Misinformation appears to cause more damage when it's subtle than when it's blatant. We see through the latter and correct for it as we go. The former is much more insidious and persistent" (Konnikov). Persistent because first impressions regarding information can shape one's overall view of any situation. Subtlety demands reflection and thought. It often receives neither.

If the public sphere was meant to be a place of deliberate discussion and debate, as proponents of democratic exchange and the public sphere contend, digital outrage has eliminated that role. When we are angry online, Ephrat Livni explains, "Complex issues are simplified to fit in a tweet or headline and the messages make us feel good, even while they make us mad. The simplification creates an illusion that problems are easier to solve than they are, indeed that all problems would be solved if only they (whoever they are) thought like us."

Anger, in other words, reflects and reinforces our certainty that what we believe is wrong is actually wrong the moment we read about it, and that it is our responsibility to point out such wrongs in the world to everyone else. Being angry online makes us feels as if we are solving or at least addressing a problem, particularly if we are responding to a headline or brief social media post. Because social media connects us to so many people, it is the perfect platform for such emotional activism. Activism needs impulse and condensed information to rile up emotions on social media.

A few brief examples may allow me to better introduce this topic, moments I feel exemplify the emotional aspect dominant in online outrage. One facet of digital outrage that I will detail in chapter 2 is affect. Affect, as a preemotional state, often relies on assumption. As this book will demonstrate, assumptions, which are components of aggregations, play a role in forming associations among disparate events or actors. When University of Tampa adjunct professor Kenneth Storey tweeted in 2017 that Hurricane Harvey's destruction in Texas was a justified response to Republicans, he was likely performing digital outrage activism based on particular, political assumptions formed from associations. Responding to a snippet of news (hurricane hits Texas), Storey likely believed that his own snippet, a tweet, would shame a political party whose policies he disagreed with. Headlines helped this process.

Underlying Storey's tweet was the assumption that Harvey victims were all Republicans (because they lived in Texas, a largely red state), supporters of a political party that often denies climate change and creates policy that can, in fact, exacerbate climate change. Storey condemned victims for their political affiliation in the hope that tragedy would change their perspective, even though hurricanes do not target political groups. In doing so, Storey formed what I will later describe as an aggregation, or a profile based on variety of already held beliefs, in this case about a state and a political party. "I don't believe in instant karma but this kinda feels like it for Texas," he tweeted. "Hopefully this will help them realize the GOP doesn't care about them." A tweet, Storey assumed, would right a wrong (such as changing people's political affiliations).

What made Storey feel obligated to tweet after a natural disaster that killed twelve people? What made Storey feel the need to associate Republican politics (and those likely aligned with Donald Trump and his supporters) with a disaster in Texas? Anger. Not anger at a hurricane, of course, but anger at the assumed climate-related positions of Texans, whom he assumed were all Republicans and, therefore, supporters of Trump and his denial of climate change, which had been documented in many headlines, tweets, posts, and other snippets of information online. Storey formed an emotional association between two unrelated objects—a hurricane and Republican politics—and that association transformed online into digital outrage.

Storey, of course is not alone. There are numerous instances online of these kinds of associative moments of anger based on a glimpse or impression of information, whether in digital format or even in a face-to-face encounter. After visiting a restaurant in New York's Harlem, for example, Rutgers University history professor James Livingston posted to Facebook the following expression of outrage: "OK, officially, I now hate white people. I am a white people, for God's sake, but can we keep them—us—us out of my neighborhood?" Livingston used Facebook to voice his outrage over perceived gentrification of a Black neighborhood by perceived white interlopers, a wrong, he suggests, that demands a right. His perception was based on a headline-like snippet: a visit to a restaurant. Despite being a white man eating in a Black restaurant, Livingston was angered at, it seems, a significant presence of other white people also eating in a Black restaurant. A wrong, his post argues, has been committed (where white people in New York opt to eat or spend their money), and Livingston felt prompted to correct that wrong by arguing for no more white people in his neighborhood (except, maybe, himself).

Facebook, in response, removed his post as a violation of community standards. Rutgers launched an investigation to determine if the post violated the university's Policy Prohibiting Discrimination and Harassment. Like Storey, Livingston formed an emotional association as digital outrage: anger over historical and current gentrification of neighborhoods where racial minorities reside, juxtaposed with broader anger at white actions that supposedly limit Black residents' ability to remain in neighborhoods when white people move in, buy property at higher prices, and contribute to higher property taxes. Like Story's anger over a hurricane, a complex issue—the shifting racial and ethnic demographics of neighborhoods and associated economic development—was reduced to a headline-based social media post.

It is thus not uncommon for associations between historic injustices and current events to foster digital outrage. Our reasons may be political; they may be based on popular culture; or they may arise from the perception of personal attack even if we are not the focus of a representation. Consider, for example, Gillette's January 2019 razor blade commercial entitled "We Believe." The commercial draws an association between shaving and "an introspective reflection on toxic masculinity very much of this cultural moment" (Dreyfuss). Historically and culturally, toxic masculinity has been ignored by many, particularly the very men creating toxic masculinity and causing damage to both men and women. The ad, by tapping into this past and the various imagery associated with male toxicity, asked men to consider how toxic masculinity endangers our culture by teaching young boys to engage with girls and women, as well as with each other, through aggression, insensitivity, and violence. What should be a fairly safe position—masculinity can exist without sexual harassment or aggression—became a controversial focal point of public outrage because of personal associations. "The assault on traditional masculinity is an assault on their very natures," celebrity Piers Morgan angrily wrote, as if he was the personal target of the advertisement. "The subliminal message is clear: men, ALL men, are bad, shameful people who need to be directed in how to be better people." Morgan, like other men, promised to never buy Gillette razors again. The association (likely with one's own selfhood) was emotional for those who objected. Protesters posted online videos of themselves destroying already purchased Gillette products in response. The hell they'd be told they were supporting toxic masculinity. In response to this "absurd" claim regarding male anger, they became outraged.

I find Morgan's and others' responses to the ad preposterous. The ad is not threatening. The ad is a response to a cultural condition. But I also wonder how various images, what Vilém Flusser calls "technical images," have aggregated a layered image called "toxic masculinity," which challenges and threatens some people's notions of gender. What is layered within "toxic masculinity" that threatens Morgan and others, and why would they stop using a razor because of that perceived threat? The association between a razor (a commercial) and a state of being caused an outrage uproar, but why? I wonder similarly about many circulated images.

In this book, the examples I discuss are drawn from politics and popular culture. They may be visual, educational, or banal. Eating horse? Donald Trump? A campus presidency gone awry? A dead lion? Professors online? Pepper spray? Israel? These are a few of the topics I touch upon because of how their layered imagery evokes outrage among specific audiences. I specifically avoid certain political issues as sources of outrage if they have a long history of dominating public discourse. For instance, abortion rights and gun control are familiar topics driving anger and protest, as those who feel deeply about these issues (on either side) take to various platforms and outlets to voice their positions. These topics' presence in our current outrage culture, though, is not shaped by our interactions within social media. They precede digital culture. So, I leave such issues aside.

While I have written previously about social media and have taught it for years, I am not a social media expert when it comes to issues of data analytics, search engine optimization, data visualization, or other technical matters that have a great deal in common with computer science. I am a rhetorician who studies digital culture. Instead of exploring the technical aspects of algorithms or the complicated back-end mechanics of various social media platforms, then, in this book, I concentrate on rhetorical logics in social media. In particular, I focus on what I understand as specifically relevant to the creation and fostering of digital outrage across social media as its communication functions.

Other times in this book, I touch upon specific political issues or movements, such as Obamacare's "death panels" or the Occupy Movement or Black Lives Matter, but only as their circulation pertains to social media, not because of what I believe. A variety of texts and images that circulate across social media platforms evoke digital outrage. I cannot capture every moment that leads to outrage, but I can focus on a few selected moments for how they specifically operate within larger rhetorical contexts where different types of aggregation occur. This book proposes a theory for how and why social media generates outrage.

This book is not a history of outrage, nor is it a documentation of every single instance of outrage or the pundits who often spread it, nor is it a literature review of outrage in digital scholarship. Nor is this a book about a specific political outlook or party. This book proposes a theory for how and why social media generates outrage. Chapter 1 outlines the theories I draw from in order to discuss digital outrage. Chapter 2 discusses outrage as affective. Chapter 3 demonstrates outrage as a technology as well as form of communication. Chapter 4 outlines the notion of digital outragicity by focusing on the case of a lion's killing by a dentist. Chapter 5 studies the ways photography embeds multiple meanings via a well-publicized pepper spray incident. Chapter 6 continues with two examples of outrage shaped by ideologically embedded algorithms. Chapter 7 offers two digital outrage case studies as informed by enthymemic rhetoric. Chapter 8 continues with two more case studies as informed by epideictic rhetoric. Finally, I conclude with the killing of George Floyd by a Minnesota police officer in order to consider the intersection of many of these ideas within a singular person's image.

My overall purpose is not to stop us from being angry or to propose some utopian state of social media usage where "we all just get along" and overcome the lure and attraction of outrage. Nor is it to change Facebook, Twitter, or any other social media platform. Instead, I am interested in unravelling, even if just a little bit, the complex yarn that produces a network of interactions driving outrage. Whatever the end result of this unravelling may be—understanding, observation, critique, awareness—I cannot say. At the least, however, this is a project, like a typical Bruno Latour breakdown of objects of study, of making the invisible somewhat visible. This is a project of outlining and presenting a theoretical lens that can explain some of the ways outrage functions in social media. This is a project toward understanding, in some way, digital outrage.

One

Outrage Theory

Digital outrage, I contend, is both a medium and a technology. It depends on modern communicative technologies to act as its media. In this chapter, I explain the theoretical principles I draw from in order to make that claim. Early Greek poetry offered the technology of persuasion via a different medium, oration. Anger, as well, can be found in this technology. The first line of Homer's *The Iliad* begins with outrage: "Sing, Goddess, Achilles' rage."[1] Peter Sloterdijk explains Homer's turn to rage accordingly: "To sing of rage means to make rage noteworthy, to make it worthy of being thought (*denkwürdig*). However, what is noteworthy is in proximity to what is impressive and permanently praiseworthy—we could always say: it is close to the Good. These valuations are so thoroughly opposed to modern ways of thinking and feeling that one probably has to admit that an authentic access to the intimate meaning of the Homeric understanding of rage will remain closed off to us" (3). To be angry, in this case, is to be good. This good derives from some ideal state, or even from the gods. "Rage," Sloterdijk adds in his reading of this line, "which blazes up in intervals, is an energetic supplement to the heroic psyche, not a mere personal trait or intimate feature" (11). A hero doesn't just get angry. To be heroic, one must already have rage; it is part of the hero's automatic psyche and profile, just as a media form might be part of one's communicative act. One interacts with rage as one would with any other force that is part of one's being. This view of rage, Sloterdijk seems to bemoan, no longer exists.

Or does it? Outrage, as I will explain in this chapter, stems not from one moment, but from a serious of layered moments that individuals or collectives experience over time and repeated exposure. Outrage moments shared on social media may feel immediate and singular (the result of one person posting one image or idea), but they are, in fact, the result of many types of interactions, whether these interactions are with complex profiles, stereotypes, historical memory, or imagery. In this way, outrage becomes built into contemporary methods of communication because individuals carry such experiences into each new engagement. My task in this chapter is to explicate my theoretical understandings of digital outrage, and of the specific types of networks that transform moments into outrage, so that I can offer specific and more elaborate examples in the following chapters. Digital outrage is not from the gods nor part of the heroic psyche, but it has been integrated fully into digital communication as a form of communication largely dependent on contemporary technologies such as social media.

Throughout the rest of this book, two theories will greatly inform my understandings of digital outrage, neither of which originates with social media but both of which I feel speak greatly to social media. The first comes from German media theorist Vilém Flusser, who describes images that capture a number of moments or ideas within one space as "technical images." Flusser theorizes the ways representations are constructed out of other elements, though they appear to be singular to generic audiences, who typically focus on the immediacy of the image's delivery and its supposed meaning. "Information is a synthesis of prior information," Flusser argues. "This holds true not only for the information that constitutes the world but also for man-made information" (*Into the Universe* 89). While this statement may resonate as a recognition of appropriation and influence, it speaks more to the ways information creates information. Flusser was responding to the oversaturation of circulated information generated by the digital age (before the proliferation of social media to the extent we see it today) and how this abundance of information shapes culture—often for the worse, because ideas generated out of previously circulated ideas can elude critical thought or even recognition of their origins. This notion runs counter to positive instances of idea-building, such as creativity and the arts, that openly reflect on appropriation and influence.

Rather than focus on artistic appropriation (which is often recognized by its audience as such), I borrow from Flusser the technical image to better understand cultural knowledge and its valuation. Flusser does not make a claim for textual connectivity, intertextuality, or similar theoretical understandings of how texts relate to other texts. Instead he theorizes information's construction as ideologically embedded, yet promoted by the rise of digital culture. While the digital age presents us with more information than any previous time period, it continues to build off of previous iterations of news, ideas, beliefs, imagery, and ideology, and it presents—or its audience presents—these iterations as new. These items are layered, Flusser argues, and not new, although audiences assume they are: "When images supplant texts, we experience, perceive, and value the world and ourselves differently, no longer in a one-dimensional, linear, process-oriented, historical way but rather in a two-dimensional way, as surface, context, scene. And our behavior changes; it is no longer dramatic but embedded in fields of relationships" (*Into the Universe* 5). This dramatic shift, Flusser argues, is based on a dichotomy of "linear" predigital texts and contemporary layered, multifaced digital texts he calls technical images.

Technical images, for Flusser, are digitally based. They are indications that "the universe . . . for the past few decades has been making use of photographs, films, videos, television screens, and computer terminals to take over the task formerly served by linear texts, that is, the task of transmitting information crucial to society and to individuals" (*Into the Universe* 5). The technical image, Flusser insists, is a computation—or what he terms a "computational concept" situated within a given digital image. Technical images, Flusser explains, are not "observations of objects" but are "computations of concepts" (*Into the Universe* 10). Whereas imagery is generally perceived to be a representation captured by a camera, television, or computer, Flusser asks us to consider imagery as generically conceptual and technical. As Thomas Hauer argues regarding technical images, "The human observer is deceived into thinking the technical image is closer to reality or the physical world, when in fact the image is farther away from nature than ever before, due to the mathematical nature of the apparatus" (44). Whatever the image represents, it does so not by a direct capture of the thing itself but via the computations *viewers make* when viewing the image. These computations are based on past interactions with the image, related imagery, associations with the image, and so on. The singularity of a given image typically is not questioned or challenged by viewers because of general assumptions regarding reception as a singular viewer activity. Reception can instead be thought of as a computation, a process of computing internal algorithmic code in order to evaluate, understand, critique, or comment. Reception, then, is a computer-based process, only it occurs ideologically rather than on a machine.

Audience ideology and experience project other images within the audience's reception. In that sense, computations for Flusser are not Photoshop layering or other software manipulations but rather ideological. These computations show "relationships among things that no one would otherwise suspect." Flusser argues that "technical images don't depict anything; they project something" (*Into the Universe* 48). He suggests that a technical image is not a representation of an actual thing but a projection of an already held belief. In such projection, an assumed referent and an established ideology can be conflated. "A technical image changes symbolic reality, it changes meanings, but as reality becomes reality only after meanings are assigned to it, a technical picture changes reality itself" (Hauer 43). As someone who opposed his presidency, when I engage with a Donald Trump image, I may project my already held negative views regarding his presidency or personality long before I consider the specific thing he is addressing or proposing. I may miss meaning as a consequence, or I may not. In a projection, either possibility exists. My projection, though, is performing computations (Donald Trump is a jerk / Donald Trump is a sexist / Donald Trump doesn't know what he is doing / Donald Trump is a racist . . .). I make a reality out of meanings (aggregated over time) I have assigned to the image.

"Ontologically," Flusser claims, "traditional images signify phenomena whereas technical images signify concepts" (*Toward* 14). Technical images, then, are not necessarily digitally constructed representations. Instead, they are the result of a digital logic; that is, whatever medium the image is within (and images may also be textual representations which, as well, function as imagery), its logic is digital. To say an image is digital, therefore, does not necessarily mean it is a technical construction within a web browser or TV screen, for instance. This is a McLuhanist approach to digital culture and technological influence. McLuhan argues that technology shapes logics, practices, and identities, whether we recognize the influence or use technological tools. Media is an environment, and we live within that environment. Our senses depend on the environments that encompass us, our understandings and knowledge, and our interactions. "Any understanding," McLuhan wrote, "of social and cultural change is impossible without a knowledge of the way media work as environments" (*Medium* 26).

Within the given environment, we engage and become involved based on technology's shaping of that environment. But as John Durham Peters argues, "The old idea that media are environments can be flipped; environments are also media" (3). Durham Peters focuses on the natural environment as media: water, sky, clouds, fire. We can also, however, add the various topics and events I explore in the following chapters, events that occur around us but that also function as environments fostering outrage-based communication. Donald Trump, in that case, would be an environment as much as a person. A professor's angry tweet, as we'll see, can be understood as an environment supporting image projection and not just as an off-the-cuff remark. Within these environments exist various layered representations (that is, technical images) also helping to produce some semblance of meaning for both the writer/speaker and the assumed audience. For McLuhan, the question of media involvement is also one of control; audience reception can be influenced by a medium's cool or hot status, each status having the potential to facilitate or impede interaction. For Flusser, however, the environment is layered no matter what medium is chosen for communication. He suggests our engagements within that layered environment can be problematic when we fail to understand the computations at work and thus transform the projection into a given reality.

Flusser, like McLuhan's concept of the environment, argues that technical images are not isolated imagery we may occasionally interact with, but rather environments within which we understand the world. "The magical fascination of technical images can be observed all over the place: the way in which they put a magic spell on life, the way in which we experience, know, evaluate and act as a function of these images" (*Toward* 16). That magic allows the technical image to act as a network, aggregating a variety of experiences, moments, nostalgias, times, documents, and perspectives that encompass daily life, thereby offering meaning-based relationships that one representation on its own cannot offer. The problem, however, is that these items typically are read as fragments, not as historical processes or even as environments from which meaning is generated. Images for Flusser, whether in film or video, are not singular pieces of imagery. They are sequenced over time and space: "We experience the environment not as a process, but as a sequence of scenes. For we are able to cut and paste the rows; not acting historically, but magically. Certainly the photograph has succeeded in carrying the image into history; but in doing so, it has interrupted the stream of history. Photographs are dams placed in the way of the stream of history, jamming historical happenings" (*Writings* 128). By focusing on the interruptive nature of imagery, Flusser also draws attention to how technical images can generate inaccuracy. The window onto the past may not look out at a moment that occurred, but at, instead, pieces of that moment, or at the pieces we select (or not) to bring into the current moment. Or the past imagery we engage with may be erroneous.

This point is central to my extended examples of outrage in the following chapters (particularly the example of Israel and dams). The image, repeated over and over, leads to a programming of historical reflection and possibly false notions that prompt outrage. Anger at specific imagery (text or visual) acts as if it has grasped the environment of the imagery from which our interaction with the image exists. Technical images, Flusser adds, can be treated as if they are windows onto past imagery, "through which the receiver, having been driven into his corner, can observe things that are happening outside, and as if these images could always renew themselves because new things are always happening and because the sources on which they draw (past history) could never be exhausted. On closer inspection, however, both the windowlike character of technical images and the inexhaustibility of history oriented to past and future turn out to be in error" (*Into the Universe* 56). The error Flusser highlights is the receiver's treatment of technical images as representation. The moment captured in an image and the chain of associations it draws upon do not represent a historical past so much as they network already held imagery. While networked relationships might be considered positively for forging unseen relationships, for Flusser, such networking can be problematic for the types of anticipated meaning produced by audience responses as collective memory is networked. The anticipated meaning might shut down other, important meanings, meanings that go unexplored when the networked anticipation prompts an expected meaning.

In the next chapter, I cite critiques of profiling at Facebook and other platforms, and their dependence on stereotypes for predictive action. I also highlight the role of anticipated meanings. A social media profile might lead to a specific behavior (such as buying shoes or voting for a particular party), but the

anticipation that *it will lead* to a specific behavior is problematic. That anticipation is a projection based on items aggregated into a technical image. Profiling argues that an individual who likes X and Y will buy Z or will engage in
a behavior reflective of A, who shares similar likes. For this reason, as I noted
in the Introduction, Storey condemns Texas residents suffering from a natural
disaster. He anticipated their behavior via an aggregated and projected profile,
both of a state and of membership in a political party. Maybe those residents
have contributed to climate change through their voting patterns. Maybe not.
Anticipated meanings, though, argue in the affirmative. A culture of algorithmic computing argues in the affirmative as well. The algorithm anticipates. With
anticipated meanings, technical images, too, can be algorithmic, computing predictive responses of outrage.

When I write algorithm, I also write programmatic belief. Flusser compli-
cates the notion of a networked chain of concepts within the image by proposing
the technical image as an act of programming, not a connotative or denotative
moment of meaning that strengthens or weakens understanding. By claiming
that the image is programmed, Flusser changes our overall understanding of the
representations we interact with, which typically are assumed to be "natural."
When critics speak of Facebook privacy violations, a topic I will also explore
in the next chapter, they often do not speak of one specific violation—or even a
series of violations—on a platform or of the "natural" state of privacy as something to protect, but rather they speak of a programmed understanding that privacy is important and should not be violated. While the idea of privacy as a good
may sound natural (nobody should violate my privacy), it is in fact a learned
concept, learned from our interactions with publications, proclamations, images, and reports regarding violations of, concerns about, and the importance of
privacy. This learning programs our understanding over time. Facebook, in particular, adds to the *privacy should not be violated* image because of the many reports of its own violations. Facebook, too, when confronted with outrage, would
not be understood as a singular platform offering its users the ability to connect
to one another while simultaneously providing information to potential advertisers; as a programmed image, it would be read as a layered image of meanings
drawing on previous notions of privacy, advertising, social media generally, specific social media platforms such as Friendster or MySpace, consumerism, and
much more. Each layered image adds to the programmed privacy image. Recognizing this larger network of embedded meaning does not necessarily lead to a
critique, nor does it automatically confer an ability to overcome a given problem
or issue, but it can greatly affect how we read imagery overall and the conclusions we draw from the images we encounter. Recognizing this network—which
following chapters will do for different examples—can alleviate some of the concerns we should have with reception assumptions.

But with critique, particularly with Facebook critique, that is not always the case. Assumptions tend to prevail over the recognition of layering and programming. One popular critique of Facebook allows for a brief look at how Facebook as a technical image is not typically addressed. Siva Vaidhyanathan's book-length diatribe about Facebook, *Anti-Social Media: How Facebook Disconnects Us and Undermines Democracy,* depends largely on the assumption that Facebook is a singular image deserving of critique for its contributions to various widescale problems. For Vaidhyanathan, Facebook is a singular company with its own agency, or it is a platform of users with agency who act in a singular fashion. Either way, Facebook is never described as an aggregation of various forces, pasts, practices, or beliefs which may complement or even contradict one another. Facebook, as Vaidhyanathan characterizes it, causes racism, discrimination, mob mentality, genocide, and other atrocities. There is, for Vaidhyanathan, a singular image called Facebook that has, by itself, agency and is therefore responsible for bad actions. I say "image" in order to draw attention to things, people, places, and ideas that are the items their taxonomies declare, but that are also images as well. The image of Facebook drives much of Vaidhyanathan's critique. Facebook, of course, is a social media platform. Facebook, as well, is a technical image. Facebook is a company with employees. Facebook depends on users. Facebook is advertising. Facebook is a database of writings and images. It is not singular even if discussed or projected as a singular entity. An understanding like Vaidhyanathan's is automatic in its programmed critique, which follows other similar critiques regarding social media, tech companies, corporations, or search engines (including Google, the subject of Vaidhyanathan's previous book), critiques which are based on the singular image under question. With each singular image, we often hear familiar critiques regarding business practices because of how the image is read. Whether the companies in question do good or bad is inconsequential to the question of programming. Programming, as Flusser argues, is a reflection of the type of response produced and how it has been produced.

Typically, if I engage with a platform, the platform is a singular image I conceptualize. That conceptualization tells me: "Facebook is a social media platform. Facebook is making the world worse than it used to be." Vaidhyanathan draws that conclusion. This, Flusser might argue, is an automatic understanding of an image's meaning: if I see a singular entity, then it must in fact be singular, and such singularities have agency. "For this is, in fact, the definition of *automation*: a self-governing computation of accidental events, excluding human intervention and stopping at a situation that human beings have determined to be informative" (*Into The Universe* 19). Within Vaidhyanathan's image of Facebook, the only human beings who appear to exist are Mark Zuckerberg—and maybe some of the engineers who design the software. Any other human or non-human activity within the larger network we can call Facebook is ignored. There is only Facebook the actor/agent. Of course, in reality that is not the case; Facebook is an aggregation of many types of uses and users.

While most of us do not want our privacy violated, and while it feels correct to be angry at Facebook for continuing to allow privacy violations, this image, what Flusser would call a technical image, is automated and programmed because this belief regarding privacy has been "determined to be informative" without question. We automatically assume certain criteria about another technical image called privacy. If that is the case, and if automatic assumptions are problematic, should we question the overall notion of privacy in order to determine that maybe privacy violations are not so bad? Not exactly, according to Flusser. Privacy can be a technical image, but critiquing that image (revealing the layers) doesn't stop privacy from being a technical image. It will still be so whether we critique it or not. Critique won't reverse the process. Instead, Flusser advocates examining the programmed nature of technical images. "To decode a technical image is not to decode what it shows but to read how it is programmed" (*Into the Universe* 48).

Programming, therefore, is a key notion to the overall argument I am making in this book. If an image is programmed, as Flusser claims, then it is beneficial to understand the nature of that particular programming—how we can believe something to be what we think it is. We can trace Vaidhyanathan's critique via other critiques that perform similarly and see the programming as it plays out temporally. Such understandings don't, however, generate deprogramming. They do, however, reveal rhetorical practice at the level of repetition or pattern formation, or what is sometimes referred to as doxa, whereas opinion is presented as singular and not as repeated or programmed. Takis Poulakos turned to Isocrates' notion of doxa to understand the shaping of opinion, political or otherwise, a notion to which a contemporary critique of Facebook as singular image might belong. "Deliberation," Poulakos writes, "calls for the pronouncement of a judgment in the uncertain world of politics, a conjecture that aims to hit the mark. And this is exactly what Isocrates conveys through the term *doxa*" (71). Roland Barthes's response was to posit a different understanding of doxa, defining it in terms of repetition. One attempts to critique or "demystify," as Barthes names the process, "but then the demystification is immobilized in repetition, it must be displaced" (*Roland Barthes* 71). Recognizing the role of technical images in outrage can be a type of displacement. That recognition does not hit a judgmental mark but instead recognizes the programming of an image.

Repetition plays into programming. Flusser declares, "We don't live dramatically anymore; rather we live programmatically" (*Does Writing Have a Future?* 135). Drama, of course, exists online, as is evident in everything I am calling the rhetoric of outrage. In the next chapter, I will explore affect as a type of dramatic formation. But drama is not, for Flusser, what drives audience response as much as programming is. When an image is read and interpreted as representation, that reading could, of course, reveal programming; however, for Flusser (and consequently for me) many digital moments regarding the political tend to represent a programmed moment as a moment of *the text being read*. Vaidhyanathan reads Facebook across many examples. He reads Facebook and determines it is evil (drama). But he doesn't view Facebook as an image programmed. If Facebook is programmed, as Flusser might claim, then our responses to it are as well; Facebook is read as a singular privacy moment online and not as part of a larger network of interactions regarding privacy. This does not mean that what we read is correct or incorrect; but it does suggest an inability to look beyond the surface of the image and a preference to settle on a type of immediate critique.

Another example might help, one that is different from Facebook but speaks to the same issue of programming: public scandal, too, is programmed. In 2019, for instance, Virginia governor Ralph Northam came under public scrutiny for a 1984 medical school yearbook photograph of two individuals, one in blackface and one dressed like a Klansman. The circulation of the photograph across televised news and social media produced a dramatic moment of outrage directed at Northman's extremely poor choice made in medical school. Northam admitted, then denied, being in the photograph, but also confessed that he had once dressed in blackface in a different situation. When the state's attorney general Mark Herring admitted a few days later that he, too, had once dressed in blackface during a 1980 costume party, the drama continued. If we read these incidents not as singular moments of racist behavior which generate public contempt, but instead as technical images, we might identify the drama as programmed. A history of racist blackface portrayals, mostly in entertainment, have, over time, programmed outrage at their depiction in any context. The outraged is programmed both individually and collectively. Anytime we witness blackface now, *we must* become angry. Even if the governor and his attorney general's blackface moments occurred more than twenty years earlier and received no attention at that time, dramatic engagement demands response now. The audience has been programmed to understand blackface as offensive, whether or not one is aware of blackface's layered problematic history within American culture (post–Civil War entertainment, minstrel theater, *Amos and Andy*, *The Jazz Singer*, a demeaning practice of depiction, infantilizing Black Americans, creating an image of inferiority, etc.). I, too, object to blackface as racist. But I also identify a programmed response in my own and others' immediate objection. Identifying that programmed response does not mean I think the response is unwarranted. It means there exists a network of interactions that make me believe the response is warranted. According to Hauer, "This is what technical images are used for— putting reality together again. Our new arrangement of the world, new after the end of the age of linear writing, depends on two things—on apparatuses and on their programmes" (Hauer 41). Untangling the programming might allow for a better understanding as to why a photograph that has gone ignored for twenty years now generates more anger online than the actual political positions or acts in which such politicians may have participated more recently.

What is presented as an interpreted moment where meaning is mediated is, in fact, a moment of programming. A program is a script. To be more outraged at twenty-year-old photographs than at current policy is to follow a script of anger. We do not deny the offensive nature of the photograph simply by acknowledging this script. Even if we *should* be outraged (and I, too, am outraged by blackface depictions), our belief that we should be arises from what Flusser calls programming. Programming offers anticipated meaning. One should anticipate outrage at photographs of politicians in blackface. When Facebook critics point to the platform's privacy violations, they also focus on an anticipated meaning: privacy should be protected at any cost. Programming is meant to be predictive. For Flusser, programming results from an overall conflation of private meaning (this is what I think) and public meaning (this is what I have been exposed to) where the two become one yet are often treated as separate. For Flusser, technology has "blended political with private space and made all inherited conceptions of discourse superfluous" (*Into the Universe* 30). The technical image provides a starting point for understanding why our reactions begin as dramatic when that drama, too, is programmed.

-ICITY

Despite Roland Barthes's claim that "it is not very accurate to talk of a civilization of the image," Flusser's technical image is not too far removed from Barthes's complex examination of the rhetoric of the image ("Rhetoric" 38). The relationship between the technical image and the rhetoric of the image depends on aggregation in visual spaces. In "The Rhetoric of the Image," Barthes explains the concept of aggregation without ever using that term. In the essay's canonical discussion of advertising, Barthes describes the image as the "message without a code" (36) because of the connotations and associations viewers bring to its reception (154). Our readings are coded, Barthes claims, not the image itself. Barthes does not use the word "aggregation," but his definition closely resembles aggregating practices. Barthes, like Flusser, attempts to demythologize the supposed naturalness of visual communication. "We never encounter an image in a pure state" (42). Barthes adds that "the absence of a code clearly reinforces the myth of photographic 'naturalness': the scene is *there*, captured mechanically, not humanly" (44). For Barthes, we often read imagery (and again, I will use the term "image" for both visual and textual representations) as a natural occurrence, and not as an aggregation. Elsewhere, Barthes described this process as "mythology," the reading of messages as natural and not as coded constructions.

In "The Rhetoric of the Image," Barthes isolates an Italian advertisement in order to exemplify the types of readings viewers bring to its iconic display. Reading an advertisement for a line of Italian Panzani products, Barthes calls such a message "Italianicity" for the way the ad's display of ingredients—a tomato, pasta, onions, mushrooms, garlic in a string bag; the dominating colors yellow, red, and green—produce a sentiment of being Italian even if one does not know how to use the ingredients to make Italian food. Knowledge *of being Italian* already exists in the aggregated objects because of the audience's assembled preexisting cultural stereotype or profile of Italian food. Italian cuisine consists of far more than these ingredients, but this does not matter to the ad's average reader. Viewers feel that this aggregation is Italian because of their past exposure to each item within a particular context named Italian. The ad's focus is predictive and, we might add, programmed. A viewer should make an association between the displayed food and some place called Italy, and they should then want to purchase the products based on the presented aggregation. Italianicity, therefore, is not too far removed from a typical social media aggregation across Amazon or Facebook. It depends greatly on stereotypes, profiles, aggregations, and the ability to predict future behaviors such as consumption.

The advertisement Barthes focuses on does not represent Italian food as it may actually exist in Italy. The advertisement is not a referent for Italian food in the sense that it is an actual representation of what Italians eat. "An Italian would barely perceive the connotation of the name [Panzani], no more probably than he would the Italianicity of tomato and pepper" ("Rhetoric" 34). Barthes continues: "Italianicity is not Italy, it is the condensed essence of everything that could be Italian, from spaghetti to painting" ("Rhetoric" 48). Despite this disclaimer, the profile of something called "Italian" exists for many people when they read such ads. That profile includes specific colors and objects as well as assumptions regarding what these colors and objects represent. One expects this aggregation when eating Italian food (most Italian restaurants follow the aggregation's rules because of their predictive stance regarding what customers desire) or wanting Italian food. "The perceptual message and the cultural message" are assembled by the viewer of the ad so that a sense of what is Italian is understood (36) even if that sense is not representational. This is why I briefly drew attention to Vaidhyanathan's critique of Facebook, for instance, a critique that treats the image as representational of some actual entity. *Facebookicity*, it seems, is more responsible for our perception of privacy and networked communication than the company itself (which is also not representational of the thousands of bodies that constitute its being) or the many other forces within it. Barthes never claims the ad is an exact representation of being Italian. Just as he will compose Japan in *Empire of Signs*, Barthes explains how aggregations—the assemblage of stereotypes, assumptions, beliefs, preset values, and so on—create *an idea* of what something is. An aggregation, in other words, reflects not what something actually is (whatever that may be), but what we believe it is. The central function of any -icity is its aggregation, not its representation.

This aggregation—not the actual thing called "Italian" or "Facebook," but Italianicity or Facebookicity—offers insight into other versions of -icity when we look at social media moments as they circulate across platforms. My reason for introducing the Barthes example is not to focus on Italian food and its supposed authenticity in advertising, but to draw attention to an overall -icity of the many aggregations we encounter and respond to online, and to the question of a referent's existence. Within the concept of *-icity* Barthes emphasizes the ways imagery is not static but moving in meaning, depending on user background and interaction. "All images are polysemous," Barthes declares. "They imply, underlying their signifiers, a 'floating chain' of signifieds" ("Rhetoric" 156). But where do such signifieds come from? And why do they float or change with our textual and visual interactions? As with the technical image, they come from our previous interactions and beliefs, and these two items can greatly alter the meaning of any text or image.

In *Mythologies*, Barthes calls such images "myths," what he also refers to as a form of speech (i.e., a type of communicative system) in which "we are dealing with *this* particular image, which is given for this particular signification. Mythical speech is made of a material which has *already* been worked on so as to make it suitable for communication" (110). While the image may appear natural or unmanipulated, it, indeed, has been worked on by us, the viewers who then use it to further communication (as I argued for outrage in the previous chapter). We see what we already have seen. We share what we already have seen. "The meaning is *already* complete, it postulates a kind of knowledge, a past, a memory, a comparative order of facts, ideas, decisions" (117). In doing so, myth "transforms history into nature," Barthes argues (129). The image feels natural or historical ("this really occurred," "this represents a real problematic act"), but it isn't. "Myth is constituted by the loss of the historical quality of things: in it, things lose the memory that they were once made" (*Mythologies* 142).

What anchors the viewer in the image is the given signified the viewer fixates on, such as what one imagines Italian food to be or what an audience might assume death panels entail. Lloyd Bitzer calls these interactions and beliefs "constraints." Bitzer argues, "Every rhetorical situation contains a set of constraints made up of persons, events, objects, and relations which are parts of the situation because they have the power to constrain decision and action needed to modify the exigence" ("Rhetorical Situation" 8). An assumption regarding

Italian culture serves as a constraint when reading an Italian advertisement or its various contemporary imagery: a Fazoli's or Olive Garden advertisement, for instance, relies upon the same aggregations to foster consumer understanding of Italian food. As Barthes argues, "in the total image [connotations] constitute discontinuous or better still scattered traits" ("Rhetoric" 162). Our connotations are our constraints. "This common domain of the signifieds of connotation," Barthes claims, "is that of ideology" ("Rhetoric" 49). This point is vital to any understanding of digital outrage. Most outrage is directed at representation—such as a comedian's homophobic tweets or a company's improper approach to a product's sale or the collection of personal data within a popular platform. But the real question for Barthes or anyone interested in aggregation should be ideology, not singular representations spread virally or via headlines, or even the isolated acts themselves. Ideology, itself a constraint, acts as an aggregation of various connotations assembled into a given image. Slavoj Žižek argues, "The very concept of ideology implies a kind of basic, constitutive naïveté: the misrecognition of its own presuppositions, of its own effective conditions, a distance, a divergence between so-called social reality and our distorted representation, our false consciousness of it" (28). A reader may identify the ad, image, representation, or headline as communicative naturalness, but ideology blinds readers to their own internal aggregations.

The Italian ad is a profile, much like what one encounters on Facebook, where interests, photographs, moments, and tastes are aggregated into one image—the user. A profile, therefore, is a variation of Barthes's -icity. Whatever aggregation is assembled by an advertiser, data company, or pollster, it reflects the polysemous floating chain of signifieds Barthes identified in moments of visuality. These signifieds could be labeled "lexia," as Barthes does briefly in "Rhetoric of the Image" (and more completely in a different reading in S/Z). Lexia are small units or fragments of communication which, assembled, create the semblance of a unified image or idea. "What gives this system its originality is that the number of readings of the same lexical unit or lexia (of the same image) varies according to individuals" ("Rhetoric of the Image" 46). Barthes clarifies lexia, however, as denotations, not literal representative meanings. "The variation in readings is not, however, anarchic; it depends on the different kinds of knowledge—practical, national, cultural, aesthetic—invested in the image" (46). Consternation over any Facebook privacy violation is typically focused on the loss of personal, though shared, information. The assumption is that gathered information is "me." But all a company, advertiser, or government agency is left with is an -icity or a profilicity. That aggregation of data is and is not me. It is a meicity. "There is a sort of paradigmatic condensation at the level of the connotations (that is, broadly speaking, of the symbols), which are strong signs, scattered, 'reified' on the other a syntagmatic 'flow' at the level of the denotation" (51).

Most critics believe in the connotations associated with what I call profilicity (violation of privacy is wrong, an abuse of power, etc.). But for Barthes, the profiles gathered and employed for algorithmic activities are denotations whose meanings change with usage. These public aggregations do not have human referents as we might expect a "strong sign" to have. Instead, they are capturing floating chains of signifieds, stereotypes, images, beliefs, habits, and so on, that supposedly build a representation when aggregated but that really do not. Barthes's Japan is not Japan. The advertisement's Italy is not Italy. A Facebook profile is not a person. Barthes, like Flusser, draws our attention away from imagery as singular. By redirecting us to consider the layered, networked, polysemous make-up of imagery, Barthes and Flusser foreground ideology. Imagery is, as we know, ideological.

I make this point in order to foreground how outrage fixates on the perception of singular imagery or natural imagery, even though that imagery is anything but singular. "We are here dealing with a normal system whose signs are drawn from a cultural code" ("Rhetoric of the Image" 46). Elsewhere, Barthes uses the phrase "image reservoir" to explain this process. The image reservoir is described as a "second language" that is "also a reservoir of images" (*Roland Barthes* 124). Every act or belief or moment of identity is constituted out of such a reservoir. The reservoir is cultural and political. "Philosophy, then," Barthes writes, "is no more than a reservoir of particular images, of ideal fiction (he borrows objects, not reasonings)" (99). When we approach examples of outrage, it is also helpful to focus on a variety of ideological aggregations, whether they be ours in the image's initial perception or what others might have embedded in the image.

I return to the example of blackface imagery once more because of its power to spark outrage and because it depends greatly on an image reservoir to do so. In 2018 on her show *Meghan Kelly Today*, talk show host Meghan Kelly expressed her lack of understanding of blackface controversies in the news: "'But what is racist?' Kelly asked. 'Because you do get in trouble if you are a white person who puts on blackface on Halloween, or a black person who puts on whiteface for Halloween. Back when I was a kid that was OK, as long as you were dressing up as, like, a character'" (Kaur). After public outrage erupted over this comment, her show was cancelled. In this example, one could argue either that Kelly is racist and is excusing blackface, or that she is unaware of the aggregations behind the practice of a racist, hyperbolic performance of Black identity, or even that she is unaware of the programmed response to blackface in contemporary culture which should have deterred her from making this comment in the first place. Or all of the above.

For those who understand the aggregations which construct blackface, such a claim of ignorance can feel absurd. The history of racism in America, which includes blackface performances, should be obvious. Any problematic image, we believe, should be obvious. Blackface's offensiveness belongs with the aggregation of previous problematic images, such as the "Mammy" and "Sambo" images circulated throughout popular culture and consumer products and extends into oppressive practices and humiliation. Indeed, *it should be* obvious; it's programmed to be obvious. Yet, Kelly's response mirrors many of the responses I outline in this book. Kelly naturalizes the image into a singular representation— Halloween costume. She is not the only one to do so. Within "Halloween costume" exist these other meanings which make up the overall image reservoir she understands.

To understand that blackface is not just a Halloween costume but an aggregation of racist practices means being educated (as many critics suggested), but it also means unveiling some of the programming that led to blackface's inappropriateness. Some of that programming involves a holiday in which people dress up in costumes. Some costume choices, for whatever reason, involve performing race. "Halloween is around the corner and guess what that means? Someone will metaphorically step in it with an insensitive or straight up racist costume," Leila Fadel wrote in 2019. She stressed the racist aggregation that occurs during Halloween. "The shelves of most costume stores still stock the "Arab Sheikh" outfit complete with the sinister mustache. Or you can order the "Ride a Camel Adult Male Costume." There are the "Mexican" costumes: wide sombreros, ponchos, handlebar mustaches. There are the people who darken their skin to pose as a black or brown person, although many people now understand the degrading and dehumanizing history of blackface now" (Fadel).

"Without fail," David Dennis comments, "every October, Facebook, Instagram and Twitter are loaded with 'controversial' pictures of people donning blackface for Halloween costumes." Stereo Williams echoes that comment: "Every October, across America, white people don blackface. And every October, white people act like they don't know that there is a problem with blackface." Halloween is presented as singular by many (harmless day in which people put on costumes), but is, in fact, an aggregation (every Halloween, people dress up as other races, and it is offensive). "It's possible to dress up for Halloween without being racist," Sade Carpenter writes. "But this year—and let's face it, next year, too—I'll head out to a party and brace myself for offensive costumes masqueraded as jokes. When I speak up, my feelings will be disregarded and I'll be told to lighten up." Adam Harris expands this notion of not being aware of aggregations. "This is a common refrain after a racist or offensive costume is donned," Harris notes. "*It didn't occur to me that it was wrong* . . . The 'it didn't occur to me' argument is more common—despite an annual cycle (2017, 2016, 2015, 2014, 2013, and so on) of offenses, apologies, and claims of unawareness. And on campuses, regardless of routine efforts by administrators and fellow students alike to nip any offensive costume ideas in the bud, the incidents are guaranteed to happen anyway. News outlets may just as well have a skeleton post titled 'College Student Facing Discipline After Blackface Incident' prewritten and waiting on Halloween" (Harris.)

While critics show an understanding of the programming at work, costume wearers often don't, as evident in the "it didn't occur to me" argument. Kelly's own ideological stance prevents her from seeing that programming at work when she declares a Halloween costume to be a neutral and natural term. In this case, the ideological aggregation is one that directs our attention to racism as opposed to Halloween garb. There is, however, a larger issue here regarding outrage, one I will work through in following chapters. Racist costumes are not the only image we may assume as natural and not an aggregation, and racists who put on blackface and think it's acceptable are not the only people who fail to understand the programming at work in a given image. In the next several examples, I will focus on the aggregation make-up of other technical images and -icities, but I also draw attention to how the stickiness or spreadability of these images is assisted by such aggregated ideologies as claiming ignorance, assuming a "natural" state of an image, or being insensitive. Technical image is my preferred classification, but I could, as well, borrow Barthes's image reservoir or -*icity* to make a similar claim about the examples I will discuss. Each concept informs my thinking and what I will call digital outragicity. First, however, I draw attention to the importance of affect to digital outrage and the theorization I have now introduced.

Note

1. I thank John Muckelbauer for reminding me of this line.

Two

Affective Outrage

In *The Promise of Happiness*, Sarah Ahmed notes that "to be affected by some-thing is to evaluate that thing" (23). Outrage, of course, encourages evaluation. Something is wrong, upsetting, damaging, unending, and a public evaluation or response is warranted. The question of evaluation is my rationale for turning to Flusser and Barthes for theories that might better understand the how and why of digital outrage. Within these two guiding ideas—the technical image and aggregation—we also find affect. After all, an immediate response to an aggrega-tion of items within an Italian advertisement is also an affective response: some-where inside one's body, one *feels* the presence of Italianicity even if a supposedly accurate Italian representation is absent. The affective elements of outrage, I'll argue in this chapter, "work not through 'meanings' per se," as Kathleen Stewart writes regarding what she terms "ordinary affects," "but rather in the way that they pick up density and texture as they move through bodies, dreams, dramas, and social worldings of all kinds" (3).

Affect, what Brian Massumi calls "the virtual as point of view" (35), is the bodily reaction to a moment, event, person, situation, or something else. Emo-tion, Massumi argues, is only one type of affective stance, but for the purpose of this chapter's exploration of outrage, it serves as an important one. Outrage feels emotional. With outrage, it is easy to dismiss those trivial moments which aggregate various associations and assumptions for a public audience at an emo-tional level. Expression in the popular sphere (music, art, television, social me-dia, comics, journalism, etc.), however, demonstrates a trajectory from historical and political injustice to what appears to be inconsequential, but is, in fact, de-monstrative of rhetorical phenomenon. Because I am exploring digital rhetoric and reception, the two cannot be read separately. Popular culture, where a great deal of expression occurs, helps understand the role of affect in outrage. In this chapter, I will interweave political, digital, and popular culture moments as I try to understand the affective dimension of outrage and how it functions as part of aggregation and response to technical images.

Writing about Ronald Reagan, Massumi identifies the role affect played in Reagan's reception by arguing that "Reagan's incipience was prolonged by technologies of image transmission" (41). Massumi writes that "Reagan was many things to many people, but always within a framework of affective jingoism" (42). Image transmission and a type of affective jingoism have worked similarly on the reception of Donald Trump. Trump's racist criticisms of racial and ethnic groups generate in his opponents an immediate affective outrage, as well as what Massumi might also identify as a virtual point of view. As the Heath Brothers note regarding emotion and association, however, a great deal of public anger at Trump is also based on associations, those Trump makes and those made in the reception of Trump. That is, an association, too, can be a virtual point of view. Associations can be affective; as Massumi writes, "relation is immediately perceived as *such*" (231). Or as Lauren Berlant writes, "the present is perceived, first, affectively" (4). An association is a present-like (of the moment) response to a person, event, or controversy.

In one such instance, Trump draws an association *as such* between a concept he has popularized, called "fake news," and an established TV news source, CNN. This association, for those who follow Trump, contributes to an anger that is directed at the news *as such,* since CNN represents the misinformation supposedly circulating in various news outlets. Hearing "fake news" evokes outrage among a Trump audience. CNN, as some read its assumed profile, serves as a stereotype, a profile aggregation. CNN is a generalization of the failure of news as an accurate source of information for those who support Trump and are angry. These viewers associate the news network with lies and falsehoods. The same type of rhetorical logic, though, occurs for those angry at Trump. Just as CNN serves as a stereotype for critics of mainstream news organizations, Trump becomes a stereotype for critique. He attracts and contains various stereotypical associations within his image that allow for a fairly predictive and programmed response, one often affective in nature. These associations often revolve around predictable, programmed associations because the associations are based on profile assumptions, a topic of importance for understanding affective outrage. Assumptions and profiles feel immediate. They feel *as such.* But they are aggregations within a technical image.

For example, outrage can rely on heavily circulated stereotypes, such as Hitler stereotypes, in order to tap into affective assumptions. The Hitler stereotypes often allows for any object of scorn to be attractive to a specific audience profile. When a group or individual is angry at a country, policy, government action, and so on, they often draw upon Hitler as a marker of reference and association. Whatever attributes Hitler had, they become aggregated into another image. Trump and his profile have been no exception to this rule. For example, one popular social media meme equates Donald Trump with Adolf Hitler. Comparisons are based on the appearance of similarity as such; similarity suggests equation.

Fig. 2.1. (above) A popular Trump/ Hitler meme.

Fig. 2.2. Trump angry online.

Whereas Trump popularizes the outrage-based phrase "fake news" in speeches and interviews, for instance, Hitler is seen using the phrase "lying press." The two, therefore, are calculated as equal. If an image captures Donald Trump raising his arm as if in salute, one can find Hitler making the Sieg Heil salute. If Trump drinks from a glass of water and a photograph depicts Hitler drinking from a glass of water, public outrage determines the two figures as equal. Profile assumptions suggest equality just as stereotypes make distinct objects the same. "Metaphors can be based on similarities," George Lakoff and Mark Johnson write, "though in many cases these similarities are themselves based on conventional metaphors that are not based on similarities" (153). The generic metaphor that drives one aspect of Trump outrage is "fascism" or "dictatorship," which, regardless of any anti-Trump feelings one may hold, is not itself a similarity between Trump and Hitler. At least up until the time of this writing, Trump has not created a dictatorship, started a world war that devastated most of the planet, conquered most of Europe, or orchestrated the genocide of six million Jews. Trump's profile, though, is aggregated as Hitler based on the collection and computation of collected Trump moments that affectively suggest the Hitler profile. Lakoff and Johnson also argue, "the only kind of similarities relevant to metaphors are *experiential*, not *objective*, similarities" (154). Experiential evidence can also be emotional. Because of this aggregation I read, I *feel* that Trump is Hitler. Thus, he is. After all, I just experienced it. Such affective logic will continue throughout the examples I explore in later chapters. "Being precedes cognition," Massumi writes (231). Such logic is based on profiles and their aggregations, but also how individuals read such aggregations.

EATING HORSE

I don't support Trump. But I also don't think he is Hitler. I also am not angry on social media (at Trump or others). I seldom participate in the circulation of anger, but I am fascinated by it no matter who or what it is directed at. Whether we are angry at the president's stupidity or an advertiser's visual insensitivity or a quarterback's refusal to stand for the national anthem (the subject of a later chapter), we are angry because of the circulation of stereotypes online. Stereotypes, as in Barthes's aggregations, can be affective. Politics allows for one type of stereotype. Lifestyle choices (such as diet) can allow for others. Association needs these stereotypes to be rhetorically effective.

There are many types of associations that drive affective outrage because of aggregations internalized by viewers into specific technical images. Several years ago, I began posting on Facebook statements about wanting to eat horse. On November 3, 2011, for example, I shared a Chow.com article with the headline, "They Eat Horses, Don't They?" The short piece I linked to outlined some of the American aversion to eating horses by placing this disgust within the context of an impending Congressional bill to ban horse slaughtering for consumption. The piece noted that while horse meat appears exotic to many in the United States, even humble and boring Canadians enjoy eating horse. By sharing a link to the article, my intent was to see what kinds of responses my post would evoke. I assumed that readers of my Facebook page would aggregate the shared article into previous ideas they held regarding eating horse, which, for most people, are based on an associative feeling of disgust (they lack experiential evidence of taste). Those ideas, I assumed, would be based on past concerns about animal welfare, perception of horses, opinions on which animals are or are not appropriate to eat, popular culture representations of horses such as Black Beauty or The Pie from *National Velvet*, and so on.

Part trolling, part experiment in audience reaction, my post was meant to satisfy my curiosity as to how my more than nine hundred Facebook friends would react to the desire to consume this animal. The answer was: not well. Most people who responded to my post did so out of anger. They were disgusted with me. They were angry with me. How dare I! Yet I had not eaten horse. I had only expressed an interest in eating horse. Eating horse evokes outrage even if no horse is being consumed or being offered up for consumption. Karine Nahon and Jeff Hemsley call media moments that users focus on in such ways *remarkable*. "By this we mean that they exhibit qualities such that people want to make a remark about them" (98). Remarkable moments are affective. I hadn't eaten horse, but others wanted to remark on my post about eating horse because of an internal profile that they suddenly composed for me and assumed was me.

Where I live in Lexington, Kentucky, there is no shortage of horses because of the very large and prosperous horse racing industry. Even with all these horses in our state (and many horse farms are just a few miles down the road from where I used to live), there are no restaurants devoted to eating horse. This feels like a contradiction to me, but it is a point of outrage to those who followed my post on Facebook. If one feels that eating a horse is deplorable and inhumane, however, why doesn't one feel the same (or why does one?) about running a horse around a track for the purpose of gambling, or about breeding an animal only so that it can create other genetically superior animals?

The response to any of these questions—whether the topic is eating or racing—is largely affectively algorithmic. In this last example, we react the way we do based on how we have previously internalized favorable or romanticized imagery of horses, ideas regarding the domestication of horses, ideas regarding meat consumption, ideas about animals and sports, or even ideas about animals in general, and from these ideas we form associations. Media offer up the knowledge that some people eat horses in Belgium, Canada, Japan, and elsewhere. Chow.com helps facilitate our knowing, as indicated via my shared link. In *Strange Foods,* after a historical overview of nations that have eaten horse, Jerry Hopkins also extends that knowledge by providing a recipe for horse tartare (10), noting that horse meat "is particularly suited for raw dishes" (12). The Travel Channel helps circulate this knowledge as well. Andrew Zimmern, host of the popular *Bizarre Foods* television show, demonstrated the suitability of raw horse meat in the show's Toronto episode when he ate horse tartare at the now closed Black Hoof restaurant.

When Zimmern focuses on the consumption of horse, he displays a *remarkable* moment. Viewers are expected to respond to that moment by tweeting it, linking to its hosted YouTube videos, and commenting on Facebook (as I did as well), thus helping aggregate the moment further. Remarkable moments are meant to be shared. Remarkable moments, however, are not arbitrary social media projections, nor do they form out of a simple moment of shared fascination or interest. Instead, remarkable moments are shared with socially connected groups in order to continue expediting the specific knowledge and affective positioning at stake when the main channels of media communication (book, website, travel show) cannot on their own distribute the moment. Remarkable moments, such as eating horse (or Trump doing something that resembles something Hitler did), can produce digital outrage. The individual who happily gambles on horses at Keeneland racetrack in Lexington or Churchill Downs in Louisville and abhors the thought of eating a horse does so because of a specific aggregated profile that individual has built over time for herself. Eating horse is remarkable despite her other problematic horse-based activities (or problematic for some and not for her), which are not remarkable. Social media makes these algorithmic aggregations (race a horse / eat a horse) circulate widely. It does so by tapping into our visible and invisible profiles, which, in turn, trigger affective responses.

PROFILES

Consider the following image (fig. 2.3) posted on Twitter in 2019 by a journalist covering Iowa Democratic campaigning. More than four hundred users tweeted critical responses to the journalist's criticism of how to slice a pizza—square slices supposedly symbolizing an offensive act to foodies and pizza lovers. Another almost four hundred people liked the tweet. The main focus, an individual running for his party's nomination, vanished. Whatever convictions Twitter followers felt about pizza, its history, its style, and how it should be sliced, they brought those convictions to this tweet and condemned the author. In turn, the journalist blocked anyone who lambasted his knowledge of pizza slicing. Is

Fig. 2.3. Pizza outrage.

Twitter at fault? Is social media? Or is some other rhetorical force at play? What affective force ignores a political campaign in favor of outrage regarding how a pizza is prepared? Is this a question of an assumed pizza profile evoking digital outrage?

Profiles, whether of a pizza or a president, are based on data collection. It is common to blame Facebook or Twitter as evil or deceitful for collecting data that builds aggregations of profiles for a variety of purposes. I bracket the ethics of such practices in favor of understanding the *why* and *how* of aggregation and what I will call later call algorithmic outrage. We build our own profiles and the profiles of objects, places, events, and controversies over time based on the aggregations we create and believe in as fixed images or realities. These aggregations circulate and transform, online and offline, as affect sticks to them.

Consider in the next paragraph the aggregation of outrage as a profile spread out and circulated across various popular culture moments. In these moments, disparate items aggregate into a larger profile called outrage based on a trajectory of their occurrence. As Kathleen Stewart writes, "Affects are not so much forms of signification or units of knowledge, as they are expressions of ideas or problems performed as a kind of involuntary and powerful learning and participation" (40). I identify some of these expressions accordingly, not for their forms of signification but for how they perform, when viewed together, a type of cultural participation. Pizza and political campaigning are only one such moment. Others follow.

"They are making *Ghostbusters* with only women! What's going on?" Donald Trump angrily exclaimed in a 2016 posted video.[1] When comedian Norm McDonald attempted to express sympathy for the MeToo movement on *The Howard Stern Show*, his comment that "you'd have to have Down syndrome" not to feel sorry for sexual abuse victims drew public outrage. Even though *The Simpsons* had been on the air for almost thirty years, in 2018, the show's Indian stereotype character Apu suddenly drew public outrage as a racist representation. In 2019, YouTube star Logan Paul created outrage on Twitter when he promised to "go gay for just one month" as a New Year's resolution (Dugan). Celebrities reading angry tweets about themselves has become a popular video meme. Jimmy Kimmel has hosted such readings on his late night show, where Julia Roberts, Mindy Kaling, Courtney Cox and many others read tweets about how awful they are. "Don Rickles looks like Yoda," Don Rickles reads in the seventh iteration of this skit. "Matthew McConaughey is a dick turd," the actor Matthew McConaughey reads. "What the fuck's a dick turd?" he asks. Whatever it may be, it expresses some Twitter user's rage at McConaughey, his acting, or simply celebrities in general. There are dick turds and there are actors. An angry association joins the two.

Digital outrage often brings the past into the present. "The perpetual outrage machine must be fed," *Reason's* Robby Soave declared after comedian Kevin Hart was forced to resign from hosting the 2019 Academy Awards due to homophobic tweets he had made ten years earlier. Social media, by its very nature as a database-driven genre, always remembers, always archives, always is available for revisiting and retweeting. Hart could not escape that archive. Once Hart was named the event's host, people responded with anger over the comedian's history of homophobic jokes; others responded with anger over Hart's inability to actually apologize for telling homophobic jokes. In this case, anger arose not over a social issue or public gaffe over a natural disaster, but over who may host a show that honors filmic narrative, entertainment, and celebrity culture in what is often a trivial and superficial manner. Even though Hollywood has produced numerous homophobic films, and even though racist films and racist actors have won Oscars, the Academy Awards show projects a celebrated status of glamor within a specific public base (just as professors might represent a specific educated status within conservative or liberal audiences).

Writing in *Variety*, Owen Glieberman made such a point clear when, in his argument against Hart, he emphasized the importance of the Academy Awards as a symbolic text within American culture: "Some might argue that the high council of identity politics now demands too much. In this case, however, the real question was whether a comedian whose mocking reactionary spirit led him to write off a segment of our citizens in the most demeaning way possible was the person we wanted in 2019 to symbolize, on global television, the spirit of Hollywood." Death. Assault. Hollywood. The spirit of what we value. These are distinct cultural markers—entertainment vs. politics—whose commonality within the public imagination seems to be based on emotion. That emotion places current values within an individual's previous timeline of public discourse when such values may or may not have been present.

Hart's situation is not the only example of past tweets returning and sparking outrage. In 2019, twenty-four-year-old Carson King, caught in the background of an ESPN GameDay broadcast, held up a sign that read "Busch Light Supply Needs Replenished" along with his Vemmo handle. He raised one million dollars after the image went viral. His decision to donate the money to a local Iowa children's hospital resulted in a matching donation from Busch and a profile of King in the *Des Moines Register*. The reporter who wrote the profile, however, discovered racist tweets written by King when he was sixteen years old. In response, Busch backtracked on some of their commitments to King, and a local festival cancelled its decision to serve Busch beer. But the main outrage over the incident occurred when the reporter, Aaron Calvin, too, was discovered to have made racist and homophobic tweets between 2010 and 2013, as figure 2.4

Fig. 2.4. Twitter reaction to *Des Moines Register.*

documents, and he was fired. The present is outraged in ways the past is not. Time fosters associations. After all, these tweets, like Hart's, did not receive attention when initially posted.

When we become equally angry over a political party's platform as we do over who gets to host the Academy Awards or what a sixteen-year-old once tweeted, we have transformed outrage from an emotional response over a serious issue, or at least an issue interpreted as serious, into a medium of expression. Outrage is *how* we share thought. In this sense, its affective quality is not only response, as a great deal of affect theory professes, but also expression. Marshall McLuhan famously noted that the content of media is less important than the medium itself. Outrage, too, exemplifies this position. Outrage depends greatly on the associative and the symbolic in order to function as a medium of expression. These acts of symbolization are definitional. Keven Hart's ten-year-old tweets mean . . . they mean something because they define a state of the world that the Hollywood symbolic, as at least one critic noted, resists. Defining the world around us often means translating that world into symbols, and symbols can be affective and provocative. As Kenneth Burke argued, "Inasmuch as definition is a symbolic act, it must begin by explicitly recognizing its formal grounding in the *principle* of definition as an act" (*Language as Symbolic Action* 14). Definitional acts are often emotional acts. Emotions, Burke also writes, are channeled into symbols. "The symbol becomes a generative force, a relationship to be repeated in varying details, and thus makes for one aspect of technical form" (*Counter Statement* 61). Facebook can serve as one example of this process.

FACEBOOK OUTRAGE

While politicians and comedians attract public outrage, Facebook is a symbolic target and proponent of digital outrage across the Internet. That outrage may be generic and generalizing, as in Siva Vaidhyanathan's critique regarding Facebook's destruction of the very fabric of our lives. As I noted in chapter 1, Vaidhyanathan's outrage, like that of other social media critics who form similar positions about their objects of study, does not convey the same tone of a professor expressing happiness over a disaster's victims, but what Vaidhyanathan conveys is clearly outrage. Facebook upsets Vaidhyanathan for its role in supposedly propagating problematic beliefs and violence across the globe through its circulation of fake news, improper innuendo, wrong-headed political beliefs, privacy violations, unwanted advertising, and other injustices. Vaidhyanathan's argument is that Facebook is the centerpiece of everything wrong online. Facebook, Vaidhyanathan argues, "increasingly serves us news content, or content that purports to be news. It is the most powerful and successful advertising system in the history of the world. It's increasingly the medium of choice for political propaganda" (101). Facebook pretends. It is powerful. It spreads propaganda.

Though he is short on evidence regarding Facebook's maliciousness, Vaidhyanathan's prose is highly emotional and full of outrage. "We are collectively worse off because of Facebook," Vaidhyanathan declares (19). "Facebook manipulates us" (33). "The dominance of Facebook on our screens, in our lives, and over our minds has many dangerous aspects" (5). As the largest social media platform, Facebook both serves as a target of digital outrage and is accused of promoting digital outrage. Facebook is ubiquitous. Facebook networks individuals, commerce, politics, humor, the banal, imagery, advertising, and so on. Anything we engage with regularly can easily become the focus of outrage since diverse positions will isolate these moments differently but share them widely. In that isolation, and at the core of social media, is sharing. "Yes, we should be outraged about Facebook," the *Washington Post* declares (Dionne). "Facebook's Crisis Management Algorithm Runs on Outrage," a *Bloomberg* headline reads (Frier). We should be outraged because sharing supposedly encourages the support of injustice, wrongdoing, incitement, and other activities we are upset with. Vaidhyanathan's anger, like the *Post's*, stems from specific quotidian moments associated with Facebook that have created larger, more vocal moments of outrage online once shared.

Often, as the *Washington Post* and Vaidhyanathan show, these moments are associated with the very emotionally charged subject of privacy. Privacy, as a technical image, is affective. Facebook, which encourages the social, organically lacks privacy, and that point angers a general public. Dionne argues, "We also need to confront conflicts between the public interest and the ways that social media companies make their profits. Where do privacy rights come in? Are they unduly blocking transparency about how political campaigns are conducted and who is financing them? Were they indifferent to their manipulation by foreign powers?" Privacy is a flashpoint for digital outrage. Such a concern, however, is not new. Privacy is layered with emotional meaning.

Privacy, Helen Nissenbaum writes, has long been a cultural concern and "is one of the most enduring social issues associated with information technologies" (101). Nissenbaum traces American privacy fears to a number of legislative acts and their legacy within the American consciousness: "Examples include the Family Educational Rights and Privacy Act of 1974, which recognizes information about students as deserving protection; the Right to Financial Privacy Act of 1978, which accords special status to information about people's financial holdings; the Video Privacy Protection Act of 1988, which protects against unconstrained dissemination of video rental records; and the Health Insurance Portability and Accountability Act of 1996 (HIPAA), which set a deadline for adoption of privacy rules governing health and medical information by the US Department of Health and Human Services" (111). Nissenbaum's concept of contextual integrity, which situates "norms" as the guiding force of our privacy expectations, outlines a rationale for why we may accept privacy violations in one situation but not in another—such as giving our zip code to a cashier in one instance, but being furious about a free social media platform's business practices which depend on monetizing the information it gathers (as the cashier's store does as well). Nissenbaum writes: "A central tenet of contextual integrity is that there are no arenas of life not governed by norms of information flow, no information or spheres of life for which 'anything goes.' Almost everything—things that we do, events that occur, transactions that take place—happens in a context not only of place but of politics, convention, and cultural expectation" (119). "I posit two types of informational norms," she adds, "norms of appropriateness, and norms of flow or distribution. Contextual integrity is maintained when both types of norms are upheld, and it is violated when either of the norms is violated" (120).

One norm of appropriateness might, for instance, include the right to attend a university without one's records being freely shared (as they were when I was an undergraduate student in the 1980s, and grades were posted outside classrooms with our social security numbers displayed). Another norm of appropriateness might be that one's medical history cannot be put online for anyone to look at. Another might be that it's OK for me to share on social media what my son did today, what my thoughts on the Middle East are, how much I hate the president, or what I had for dinner, but it's not OK for the platform I shared that on to share it further with another entity I have not preapproved. Norms of flow are the expectations that certain forms of information, such as a professor's public tweet or news of a comedian's past homophobia, can be released and shared. Where, then, does Facebook, described by some as a public utility and by others as a private social media platform, fit within contextual integrity? How much have past legislation and norms, such as those traced by Nissenbaum, affected or influenced our current outrage over Facebook privacy violations (a major focus of Vaidhyanathan's outrage)? Do we base our emotional responses to the highly charged term "privacy" on current moments or on previous moments (i.e., aggregations) we have been exposed to or heard about over time? Outrage, as I will write about at length in the following chapters, does not emerge from a vacuum. It is influenced by previous exposure, by technical images. Our previous exposure regarding privacy includes the points Nissenbaum raises.

Outrage is typically shaped by the imagery we have long encountered in various situations. Contextual integrity, too, becomes shaped by this same process. One image, such as privacy, is often layered with previous, related, or associated imagery. In fact, every image we encounter is layered. This simple concept is the focal point of this book.

Consider a prominent example of privacy violation that fueled public outrage. In 2012, Facebook—working with Cornell University and University of California—secretly ran an experiment in which the platform's algorithms manipulated users' newsfeeds in order to generate emotional responses. Based on how many negative stories a user posts, for instance, Facebook would measure the likelihood such a user would write a negative post (or the reverse regarding positive posts). Entitled "Experimental Evidence of Massive-scale Emotional Contagion Through Social Networks," the study examined the virality of emotion. Emotions spread. Emotions spread quickly. Emotions are contagious. Emotions stick, as Sarah Ahmed argues. What she calls "stickiness" is "an effect of the histories of contact between bodies, objects, and signs" (*Cultural Politics of Emotion* 90). She adds, "Stickiness then is about what objects do to other objects—it involves a transference of affect" (91). Facebook, with its specific histories and circulated signs, obviously affectively sticks to outrage, as the Cornell example suggests and the Cambridge Analytica example will also demonstrate.

Dan and Chip Heath also argue that emotions are sticky. Stickiness, a form of persuasion the Heath brothers outline and examine as a replicable practice across a number of professions and moments, depends not on creating emotional connections from scratch, but from tapping into existing, circulating emotional states, or on the emotional generic associations we often make. "The most basic way to make people care is to form an association between something they don't yet care about and something they do care about" (Heath and Heath 173). In many ways, the Facebook study did just that. It formed associations between already held beliefs (issues we feel good or bad about) and related items not yet in one's reservoir of emotion. From this experiment, the study examined how emotions transfer from one person to another across social networks. If I am angry, in other words, can it be because of anger my contacts have shared with me? This type of stickiness often results from social comparisons, in which, Sigal Barsade writes, "people compare their moods with those of others in their environment and then respond according to what seems appropriate for the situation" (648). One kind of emotional contagion, Barsade investigates, is anger, or what she calls "unpleasant" emotions. "When people try to determine their affective state through social comparisons, cues about negative rather than positive emotions have been found to be more relevant to them" (Barsade 649).

Determination stems from connectivity. Facebook, like other social media platforms, depends on users' interactions with known contacts (strong ties) and unknown contacts (weak ties). The experiment sought to trace and track these connections and their ability to affect ties' emotional responses to posts and likes. In some ways, the study reinforces the water cooler effect; gathering around a workplace water cooler offers the sharing of information, but typically in a way that corroborates what each worker already feels (I hate my job, this political party is crooked, that country is doing wrong, taxes are too high, government is irresponsible, we don't have privacy, etc.).

Similarity is contagious. Likeminded beliefs lead to the circulation of the same likeminded beliefs when individuals assume everyone thinks identically. If I think Republicans deserve a natural disaster because they supported Trump, I tweet this idea believing everyone else feels the same. "Living in bubbles is the natural state of affairs for human beings," Derek Thompson writes in the *Atlantic*. Facebook's study confirmed this point. As its authors write, its purpose was to test "whether exposure to emotions led people to change their own posting behaviors, in particular whether exposure to emotional content led people to post content that was consistent with the exposure—thereby testing whether exposure to verbal affective expressions leads to similar verbal expressions, a form of emotional contagion" (Kramer et al.). The Facebook study's objectives were not the focus of users' rage and public outcry. After all, emotional stickiness is hardly a novel or a threatening concept. Instead, the dominant feeling of privacy violation—which Vaidhyanathan largely focuses on as well—sparked public anger. How could Facebook, many asked, manipulate users' posts and feeds without permission?

Facebook and privacy have long been a focal point of online anger, and even though many users have abandoned the platform over privacy fears, over a billion people still maintain Facebook accounts despite knowing that their privacy is always in question. Whether or not privacy can ever exist in a platform based on the logic of connectivity and sharing is debatable. The emotional fear of a violation, however, is powerful even if we willingly yield private information when we like, share, comment, or simply post. "This," Charlie Warzel wrote in *Buzzfeed* about the issue, "it bears repeating, is a privacy disaster." He continues, "The possible fallout for affected users is potentially staggering; Some of the exposed data (location, recent search history) is invasively personal. Even more concerning is how it might be abused in the aggregate. Facebook is arguably the internet's most sought-after advertising engine largely because of its ability to assemble very targeted data profiles for its users" (Warzel). This fear of Facebook privacy violations is sticky regardless of what we responded to or what we posted. A privacy violation suggests overall personal violation. A privacy violation suggests intrusion. Privacy is associative. As soon as users felt violated, they voiced their anger. Were they subjects of the study? Maybe. Maybe not. It never was clear who unwittingly participated in the emotional examination or whether anyone was manipulated in a way harmful to their health or wellbeing. Usernames were not released. The fact that the violation occurred was enough to spark outrage. The violation is, as well, a technical image generating an affective response.

CAMBRIDGE ANALYTICA

In 2018, Facebook again found itself immersed in a similar privacy controversy, the sharing of 50 million Facebook users' information with the private company Cambridge Analytica. Via third-party apps, Facebook allowed Cambridge Analytica to gather information on users and, via users' Facebook friends lists, information on their contacts. A personality quiz app, thisisyourdigitallife, was allegedly used to gather this data. More than 270,000 people took the quiz, but because the app had access to each user's contacts, it is estimated that 50 million accounts were breached. As with the previous example, the Cambridge Analytica moment demonstrated the power of contacts—and of public outrage when contacts are accessed without permission. The purpose of the information gathering, it appears, was to construct user profiles from all of the gathered data that could then be exploited for advertising or possibly political purposes. Like the Facebook study controversy, the Cambridge Analytica case involves the usage of data in order to emotionally persuade. This, too, is not a novel act. Companies, universities, the government, advertising agencies, retail operations, credit agencies, and other organizations have long compiled data on their users, customers, or participants in order to develop persuasive strategies. For instance, we are asked for our zip code or phone number when we shop at Home Depot or Crate and Barrel—the data will allow the companies to send us catalogs and encourage further shopping.

Once a company can construct emotional or psychological profiles of users, such a company can also build networked associations based on already held beliefs and practices. Profiles have long been central to Facebook and other so-cial media platforms' structure. Profiles and their aggregations, I will later argue, are central to digital outrage. Joining Facebook has always meant providing per-sonal information—relationship status, name, email, where one went to school, where one lives, what movies or books one likes, and so on. Every time one posts to Facebook (or any social media platform), one adds to Facebook's data-base of information. One also typically shares personal information: a personal photograph, where one is having dinner, an opinion, a news story one is inter-ested in, a mundane thought, a child's birthday, one's own birthday, a joke. This information can be aggregated and shared beyond the user's initial rationale for sharing.

Facebook's Social Graph search was meant to allow access to user profiles—people who speak German, people who like *Rocky* movies, people who prac-tice yoga, people who love cats—and generate aggregations of those profiles for a variety of search-based purposes, advertising chief among them. "We are building a Web where the default is social," Mark Zuckerberg declared when Social Graph was introduced (qtd. in Schonfeld). Social is the key word. So-cial Graph was always meant to share personal information. With Social Graph, Facebook users became data. Data gets aggregated. Aggregations are used to inform or persuade. When Facebook introduced the Social Graph–based ad-dition called Timeline, it openly demonstrated how user profiles can quickly be accessed and, by way of aggregation, transformed into a common narrative. This point was evident in Facebook's "Introducing Timeline" video, which high-lighted the familiar narrative of growing up, going to high school, graduating from college, getting married, and having a child via the types of activities a typical Facebook user would engage with and record via Social Graph by post-ing pictures and other updates.[2] A profile, then, can be personal (what I like, what I do), but it just as easily can be an aggregation or stereotype (the narrative of growing up, getting married, and having children that is relatable to many users of the platform).

It's never been a secret that profiles on Facebook are aggregations of what most people consider private ("my child's birth should not be a public event"). Still, the Cambridge Analytica violation sparked great outrage. Social Graph was the API that Cambridge Analytica used to acquire the information, suggest-ing that Facebook's infrastructure was designed to exploit the user profile. This is a feature of Facebook, many critics noted, not a bug. As one *New York Times* article covering Facebook's privacy issues pointed out, "According to Facebook, each of the outside companies acted as an extension of the social network. Any information a user shared with friends on Facebook, the company argues, could be shared with these partner companies without additional consent" (Confes-sore et al.).

Rather than focus on the ethics of the Facebook study or the potential criminality of the Cambridge Analytica breach, I offer these examples in order to draw initial attention to the role of the network in aggregating emotions, associations, and profiles into online outrage. Facebook has long been a pivotal network element of digital outrage. Saying "Facebook" among certain social critics, even those who are active on Facebook, such as Vaidhyanathan (who I am Facebook friends with), can generate immediate anger. Why? There exist keywords and concepts that, over time, as they circulate from one informational source to another, have become aggregated into a generalized Facebook image; privacy offers one major example I'm briefly outlining. Deceit may be another. Advertising yet another. These two moments tap into the ways deeply entangled fears and concerns can connect and contribute to the proliferation of further fears. These fears and concerns are generated over time and image exposure.

Facebook is a network. Networks connect. Networks, as Bruno Latour has argued, are fluid and not "things" you simply isolate. A network shifts and becomes altered depending on the relationships it builds and disconnects from. Everything we encounter—an office space, a library, a public restroom, a meal, a beer, a family member, a news headline, a social media platform, and so on—is a network. Each object or person or place consists of any number of visible or invisible relationships that allow that object or person or place to exist. Remove a relationship, and the network changes. Facebook exists because of its members, but within that network exist many other objects such as advertising campaigns, politics, news, false information, images, and even concerns over privacy. Some of these items are accepted as is (friends); some are highly emotional when brought to light (privacy).

The Facebook study identifies ways social networks, via human and textual connections, allow emotions to travel from one space to another: "Emotional manipulation is a touchstone that enables the manipulation of what someone thinks, believes, and does—even who they are. The personal significance of emotions ups the stakes significantly, such that the experiment is understood as manipulating not only user experience, but also the very identity of the user" (Hallinan et al. 1,084). When a node in that network, such as privacy, is activated, anger erupts. Yet even that node—privacy—also is a network. Privacy, or how we understand privacy, is a series of relationships formed between humans, things, emotions, beliefs, past legal decisions, current legal decisions, notions of individuality vs. communality, and so on. Privacy is an affective technical image. Understanding that point, I contend, can help us better comprehend the power of networks to evoke outrage. When we better visualize the network's many relations, we may realize the singular concepts making us angry are, in fact, layered, multiple meanings which are affecting us.

This book is an extension of the Facebook emotion study. Unlike the study, I have not attempted to manipulate social media users' emotions without their knowledge. I am more interested in the ways connections within larger networks of meaning (whether textual or image based; computer or non-computer based) foster outrage. My interests are theoretical. Like the study, though, I am interested in understanding how and why our emotions travel so eagerly, so quickly, so seductively, so stickily, and so successfully. A social media platform that is built on an openly acknowledged lack of privacy, and whose users happily give it their personal information, can still evoke tremendous anger when a privacy violation occurs. To me, that is fascinating. We already yielded our profiles to Facebook, for instance, when we joined its platform and participated in the act of posting. We contributed to the Facebook network, we helped build it through our posts, uploaded images, check-ins, and comments, and we became a part of that network by choice and desire. We share our lives with our connected friends (and often with unconnected friends). We can stop posting on Facebook any time. We can stop providing Facebook with personal information. Many of us don't. Yet, many individuals are angry when their profiles are shared without their knowledge despite the fact that they have been sharing these profiles all along—to both known users (strong ties) and unknown users (weak ties). A profile, too, is a network, a complex network vulnerable to emotional manipulation and particularly to outrage.

DATA

The affective nature of digital outrage is not limited to one subject, such as privacy, but occurs over a variety of interests and concerns, whether the issue is popular culture representation or social injustice. A professor. A Facebook privacy violation. A president. An awards show. We are angry about everything because of the specific profiles aggregated across our information universe that direct us toward this emotional response. Profiles are a basis of the Facebook experience. Some studies might trace profiles and affect by utilizing a computing framework that incorporates data visualization or other digital tools commonly used for social media analysis.

Aggregation, both as software activity and as rhetorical logic, plays a major role in the affective element of digital outrage. Networks aggregate. They gather. They assemble into single spaces disparate materials that otherwise may not have connected. When that occurs, as Marshall McLuhan famously stated, the results are startling and effective. Aggregation, whether via a Google news feed, a gathering of *Huffington Post* articles, a medical database, a Reddit discussion, Yelp restaurant recommendations, credit card purchases, Amazon purchases, RSS, and so on, dominates digital life. Aggregation supports how news is gathered, consumerism functions, and politics spreads. Aggregation, Michael McFarland writes, transforms our lives into databases. What we visualize. What we understand. How we respond. What we buy. Where we go. These have become database-driven actions. Our digital lives, which also include our non-digital lives since the two are forever coupled, are database lives: "Now a single database can have information not only on what searches one has done, but also all of one's emails and voicemails, what videos one has watched, one's photos and who is in them, where one has been, what meetings and events one has attended, who one is in touch with and what information they have shared, what purchases one has made and a myriad of other details, and can compile and analyze them to produce an intricate profile that includes every aspect of one's life, including the most intimate details" (McFarland). Database living is predictive. All of this material is collected in order to predict behavior and attitude. Databases support pattern identification. Thus, social media users became outraged over Facebook's privacy violations as the violations suggested the manipulation of personal data—such as shopping or voting—for predictive purposes generated out of patterns. There are, however, other predictive behaviors I will claim database living fosters, often focusing on political and ideological beliefs, including the expectation of privacy as one particular predictive state. While we maintain human agency to make decisions and choices, a great deal of emotion, interest, movement, and habit is computed and, in its own way, as Flusser argues and I will discuss in more detail, programmed. The computations emerge from our various life and media aggregations. One does not need a MacBook or PC to perform these computations. They are occurring all around us during every moment of our lives. Whether that means, as some critics argue, our lives are controlled by Facebook or Twitter is debatable. It does mean, I contend, that an information age is recognizable as a space of endless visual and textual computations occurring within our own individual databases and the collective databases we actively engage with. It means that our networked engagements help shape such computations. These computations generate beliefs and practices. The computations occur on platforms such as Facebook, but also in headlines, shared imagery, news updates, and other information actors within our networked engagements.

One danger of such computations, Lori Andrews argues, is the stereotype. Cambridge Analytica, after all, was compiling information in order to form stereotypes of either consumption or political leaning so that predictive action could occur. A stereotype is affective. A stereotype is an assumption. Assumptions aggregate information and experience into the singular, projected image in order to generalize a person, group, job, place, or situation (all Texans are Republicans who deserve nature's wrath). These generalizations do not strive for authenticity or accuracy; they are sketches of tendency or similarity. "Automatic, stereotyped behavior is prevalent in much of human action" (Cialdini 7). These generalizations can have predictive consequences that go beyond *what we want*; but often include, instead, what others believe we want or who we are. They are profiles. A racist stereotype, for instance, is merely an aggregation of prejudices, incorrect assumptions, visualities, misreadings of others, generalizations, conflations, and so on. Other stereotypes allow for different kinds of aggregations. Some of these stereotypes are built upon group affinities. "Group norms (and other distinctive group properties such as stereotypes) reflect the comparative relations within which the group defines itself, as well as, and as much as, they reflect attributes of group members" (Oakes et al. 82). These stereotypes build up over time as the aggregations increase, are shared, and settle into a singular image.

Andrews focuses on how aggregations that rely on forming stereotypes can lead to life hardship: "Stereotyping is alive and well in data aggregation. Your application for credit could be declined not on the basis of your own finances or credit history, but on the basis of aggregate data—what other people whose likes and dislikes are similar to yours have done. If guitar players or divorcing couples are more likely to renege on their credit-card bills, then the fact that you've looked at guitar ads or sent an e-mail to a divorce lawyer might cause a data aggregator to classify you as less credit-worthy." Stereotypes, too, are predictive. If enough information is gathered on generic behaviors and individuals, the thinking concludes, an action can be predicted. One will vote for Trump. One will buy a pair of boots. One will travel to Jamaica. Amazon's algorithmic ability to predict a consumer's interest in a book based on other similar consumers' interests in other books (i.e., aggregations) was, at first, novel and intriguing. The algorithm stereotyped consumption habits but did so in a way that sold more books. Today, many find it creepy, particularly when—via a computer's cookies which aggregate across your web browser—that book you saw on Amazon is now an ad on your Facebook feed. All of this activity is sticky. The database's "objects" form relations within an image that stick and lead to outrage.

Databases are not only assembled online. Contests. Promotions. Sweepstakes. Such items allow companies to collect information, information voluntarily yielded on the promise of winning a prize or getting a discount, so that the information can be used to build a profile based on a stereotype. A free Facebook quiz or game downloaded from the Apple store gathers data (as Cambridge Analytica demonstrated). But so do many other sources. These database aggregations, online or offline, build profiles; they turn casual social media users into marketable categories. As Julia Angwin, Surya Mattu, and Terry Parris Jr., write, "Facebook uses algorithms not only to determine the news and advertisements that it displays to users, but also to categorize its users in tens of thousands of micro-targetable groups." Such is Steven Rosenfeld's conclusion regarding Google: "Google's mission, detailed in its patents, stands apart. Its business is based on analyzing user metrics with ever-growing precision, and selling those insights to advertisers." Again, I am less interested in the ethics of the profile or stereotype and more interested in the *aggregation of profiles* and how profiles contribute to outrage.

Profiles—human and non-human—are constantly being formed out of stereotypes and assumptions. Profiles generate something akin to what Sarah Ahmed calls "conditions of arrival." She writes, "The object is 'brought forth' as a thing that is 'itself' only insofar as it is cut off from its own arrival. So it becomes that which we have presented to us, only if we forget how it arrived, as a history that involves multiple forms of contact between others. Objects appear by being cut off from such histories of arrival, as histories that involve multiple generations, and the 'work' of bodies, which is of course the work of some bodies more than others" (*Queer Phenomenology* 41–42). The profile is a "thing that is itself" in the sense that its arrival is typically not received by a specific public as arriving with a recognized history. The Facebook profile, like other profiles, hides those items aggregated within it. Ahmed also describes conditions of arrival as the reception of not just the object but what surrounds it: "To experience an object as being affective or sensational is to be directed not only toward an object but to what is around that object, which includes what is behind the object, the conditions of its arrival" (*Promise* 25). What is behind the object, a profile or something else, is also aggregated within the object. The profiles of Facebook users hide those items aggregated within them; we may see what someone likes at a given moment, but not their shopping habits, browsing, total likes and interactions, and so on. As figure 2.5 shows, my own profile—whatever online activities I engage with—is aggregated into a suggestion that has arrived long before I am aware of why or how. The technical image, which I will show in later chapters, is a type of profile in which the user does not recognize what is aggregated within it. To recognize this dimension of outrage is also to ask: What does it mean to profile? To contribute to the profile? To always be aggregating? What are the outrage implications of this kind of computation?

Most of the discussion on privacy and user aggregation, rather than recognize the profile or the technical image, has focused on critique—critique that reveals, condemns, and then, based on these responses, asks us to change our behavior or our level of trust. I won't do that in this book. That work has already been done, and yet, we still have outrage. My interest in Facebook, Google, Twitter, and other algorithmic aggregations is rhetorical, not critical. I want to look further at the ways aggregations network us into a variety of beliefs and positions. I don't blame Facebook. I don't blame Google. I don't blame anyone. In addition to affect, aggregation, as I'll show, is the heart of digital outrage. We

Fig. 2.5. Amazon ad sent to me via Gmail. Aggregation suggestions. I have no idea what I bought to encourage this.

don't need to blame any platform or organization for how we, too, allow aggregation to occur.

"Relations on social media sites," Tero Karppi writes, "are not only connections between people; they also serve as data aggregates and bait to draw users' attention" (11). For the purpose of this book, data and profiles are interchangeable parts of the overall computational culture we live within, and that generates technical images. Data is central to digital outrage. I am data. A news feed is data. An image is data. A headline is data. A credit report is data. A country is data. A university is data. A purchase—online or offline—is data. A like is data. "What are we to do to data and it to us?" ask Lisa Gitelman and Virginia Jackson (1). As we produce and interact with data, we contribute to aggregations which, in turn, contribute to our behaviors and perceptions. Those aggregations scare us, anger us, provoke us, and cause us to believe we can stop contributing to them, but we seldom escape the data universe around us.

Data supposedly helped elect Donald Trump. The controversy over Russian meddling in the 2016 presidential election centered on how data was manipulated to exert influence because of assumed profiles. If companies know their audience's preferences and political leanings, the logic claims, these audiences can be easily manipulated to believe in a fake news story or vote a specific way. Cambridge Analytica, it is also assumed, may have contributed to the ways data pushed voters toward Trump as its collected data may have played a part in voter manipulation. With the suggestion of impropriety, the election of Donald

Trump as president has greatly contributed to social media anger. That anger is directed towards his policies, but also to a possible manipulation of unsuspecting social media users whose collected profiles provided enough stereotypical data that an election could be predictive. That anger is not always at Trump (though it often is), but at the digital process that may have elected him. This is at least the case within my own limited bubble of mostly academic—and some non-academic—online friends, whose daily posts and retweets aggregate a number of anti-Trump positions outlining this logic. Every day during his presidency, my social media friends posted headlines, Twitter screenshots, Trump memes, Trump quotes and online commentary which appeared across my Facebook and Twitter feeds. Trump is sticky. Trump provides a network that does not resemble any other presidential network we recognize based on our past perceptions and aggregations regarding the United States presidency profile. Trump's aggregated profile is neither stereotypical nor expected. His angry tweets. His lack of political knowledge. His insensitivity. His sexism. His racism. His alignment with white supremacists. All of this data aggregates an image not congruent with the profile a president is supposed to have.

Trump, as a data set, reflects anger. Anger is directed at Trump, and Trump showcases the image of anger. The *Atlantic's* Joanne Freeman notes that since Trump's rise to power, "Emotions are rising every day, with social media leading the way." Anger, she writes, "feeds on raw emotions with a primal power: fear, pride, hate, humiliation. And it is contagious, investing the like-minded with a sense of holy cause." On March 17, 2019, for instance, Trump wrote twenty-nine angry tweets that CNN called "Trump's Craziest Day Ever on Twitter." Among his barrage of tweets, Trump called for the FCC to investigate *Saturday Night Live* for mocking him, attacked the late John McCain, expressed support for the controversial television host Tucker Carlson, and retweeted a conspiracy theorist (Cilliza). What are we supposed to feel about contemporary culture if the president of the United States is open about his anger? Should we be different? Shouldn't we be angry, too? Trump generates digital outrage from his own image; Trump supports digital outrage via his online and political activity. He creates a new aggregated profile of himself and the presidency. Trump did not invent digital outrage. But he actively promotes it more than any other presidential figure. He does so because his particular brand of digital outrage taps into an aggregation of outrage such as specific Americans' fears (immigrants), frustrations (jobs), and persistent belief that government is corrupt (drain the swamp). By using Twitter, an extremely popular social media platform, Trump participates directly with the same technology the rest of us do.

Writing in *Newsweek*, Chris Riotta asks, "Does Donald Trump have an anger problem?" Drew Magary writes, "I am angry at Trump being president, and I am angry that I live in a country where tens of millions of people actually thought this was a solid idea." Trump attracts and generates anger. Immigrant children in cages. Cancelled world treaties. Tweets assaulting world leaders, veterans, popular culture stars, members of his cabinet, businesses, CNN and others all have generated a public anger at a president who appears to be anything but presidential. An accompanying image, circulated in newspaper stories and various memes, visualizes Trump's projected anger: finger raised in defiance, teeth clenched down like a beaver's, eyebrows raised. The image aggregates into one visual space what the average angry, anti-Trump social media user likely feels the president embodies because of the collected data. The aggregation is affective, and as I explore in the next chapter, technological.

Notes

1. In Jen Yamato, "Donald Trump's Sexist Anti-'Ghostbusters' Crusade Goes Mainstream," *Daily Beast,* May 19, 2016, https://www.thedailybeast.com/.

2. See "Introducing Timeline—a New Kind of Profile," Facebook, accessed August 12, 2022, https://www.facebook.com/facebook/videos/.

Three

Technological Outrage

One of the most canonical popular culture moments of outrage occurs in the 1976 movie *Network*. Howard Beale, the angry news anchor whose on-the-air rants and threats of suicide have increased ratings at a beleaguered TV station, urges viewers to open their windows and shout to the world: "I'm as mad as hell, and I'm not going to take this anymore." Before he urges this moment of communal outrage, however, Beale sits at his anchor desk, dripping wet from the rain, still in a raincoat, looking flustered and out of place, and preaches to his live viewership: "Everybody's out of work or scared of losing their job. The dollar buys a nickel's worth. Banks are going bust. Shopkeepers keep a gun under the counter. Punks are running wild in the street, and there's nobody anywhere that knows what to do and there's no end to it." Ours, as Beale bemoans, is a time of desperation. Nothing is right anymore. In response to this public frustration, Beale tells his audience to get mad. He urges them to yell out their windows and express their anger with a world that they cannot control. And people do. They open their windows, stand on their fire escapes, and yell, "I'm as mad as hell, and I'm not going to take this anymore." Each person follows the next. A network of rage takes over New York. Outrage builds off of other, similar expressions of outrage. Outrage communicates itself.

Beale is hardly the only one who is mad as hell. When Republican pollster Frank Luntz interviewed several Trump supporters in 2015 about what they were "mad as hell" at and if they were "not going to take it anymore," their answers mimicked *Network*: jobs, taxes, a collapsing economy, and frustration with government (Banicki). *Network's* insight is not mid-1970s rage. *Network* demonstrates the stereotype of public, aggregated rage and its continued circulation. These topics Beale focused on generate a profile of supposed public anger. That profile could be the contemporary situation, an ordinary individual, or a popular figure.

One could easily trace the outrage of *Network*, for instance, to contemporary outrage pundits such as Rush Limbaugh, who said the following on his radio show in 2014:

If you come from a place where you've had no inspiration in your life. If you come from a broken family, which there are more and more of those in this country. If you come from a place where there hasn't been a role model in your life to tell you how good you can be. If you haven't been inspired. If you haven't gone through life learning how good you are. If you haven't gone through life being told that you're capable of much more than you think you are. If you've gone through life thinking that it sucks and that you suck and that there's no hope, then not working for $400 a week is gonna be much more attractive than working for $500 a week, and that's exactly where we are. ("The Shrinking")

One could just as easily be listening to Howard Beale. The economy. Jobs. Wages. These rhetorical markers of public outrage highlighted in *Network's* diegesis continue through contemporary broadcasting to reach large audiences who share similar affinities and opinions. These markers resonate; they build off of aggregated profiles (the struggling American, the unrecognized everyday Joe, the supposedly unfair labor system), and they evoke audience sympathy. If there is something we can all be angry at, it is often our economic situation. Even that point, however, hides the more relevant issue that "economics" is only an image employed to spread outrage itself. The economy, as a generic, rhetorical marker, is an aggregated image of media representations such as those repeated in *Network* or a Rush Limbaugh show or mainstream media outlets. Because of how this technical image poses a representation in its generic state (inequality, individuals struggling to make ends meet, unfair trade issues), anger ensues even if these items are not universal and differ for various parts of the population.

If individuals repeatedly read circulated technical images (such as the economy) that emphasize overall population anger, they believe anger is dominant. A technical image like the economy is just as much a profile as a Facebook profile is. Writing in the *New York Times*, Lynn Vavreck describes her research into the disparity between what voters actually think or experience and how various media aggregate terms like "anger" into news. She draws attention to how ideology can be aggregated into a profile: "Using analytic tools provided by Crimson Hexagon, I calculated the average monthly increase in the share of news articles about the 2016 election with the word 'angry.' Between November 2015 and March 2016, the share of stories about angry voters increased by 200 percent." Charles Duhigg writes, "Watching angry people—as viewers of reality television know—is highly entertaining, so expressing anger is a surefire method for capturing the attention of an otherwise indifferent crowd." Instead of blaming only mainstream outlets such as network or cable news, he also draws attention to social media's circulation of images like the economy or anger itself:

The more recent rise of social media has only further inflamed our emotions. Facebook and Twitter don't create content; they've outsourced that work to their users, who have quickly noticed that extreme statements attract more attention. On social media, the old rewards of anger—recognition of our unhappiness, resolution of our complaints—are replaced with new ones: retweets, likes, more followers, more influence. The targets of our rage, meanwhile, tend to be strangers less inclined to hear us out than to fire back. It's a vicious cycle for users, though a virtuous one for the social-media companies, which profit from our engagement.

What Duhigg refers to as "rewards" are elements of a profile: the unhappy, complaining average individual who believes everything, as Howard Beale might say, is awful and needs an expression outlet. I'm mad as hell. I'm not going to take it anymore.

Outrage, as *Network* shows, is all around us, and it can be media-based. In various media, outrage repeats. "Outrage has become the signature emotion of American public life," Lance Morrow states. "Addiction to outrage is real," the very outraged right-wing pundit Glenn Beck writes, "widespread, and (almost) fully ingrained in our cultural identity" (19). "We must never lose our sense, when appropriate, of outrage," fellow pundit William Bennett claims (69). "When you see a television show that offends your values or morals," Laura Ingraham advises readers, "make a note of the advertisers and take the time to call or write a letter sharing your outrage" (194). Leftists. Right wingers. Racists. Liberals. Conservatives. Newscasters. They are all angry. They use media to spread anger. Outrage, Morrow notes, is not bound to one political position: "On the left, 'stay woke' means 'stay outraged.' Trumpians want to 'lock her up' or 'build a wall.' Outrage is reductive, easy to understand. It is an idiom of childhood—a throwback even to the terrible twos." Outrage translates as anger, as response, as a call to arms, as an aggregated profile of a populace screaming out their windows. But is outrage itself a method of communication beyond its emotional context? That is, can outrage be more than just emotional outburst or dissatisfaction with the state of things as they are, as in many of these interweaved examples I discuss? Is the endgame merely being mad as well? Are there outrage rules and guidelines that those who experience digital outrage, knowingly or not, tend to follow? Is outrage a medium, which I suggest by beginning with the *Network* example?

Jeffrey Berry and Sarah Sobieraj define outrage as a genre: "Outrage discourse involves efforts to provoke emotional responses (e.g., anger fear, moral indignation) from the audience through the use of overgeneralizations, sensationalism, misleading or patently inaccurate information, ad hominem attacks, and belittling ridicule of opponents. Outrage sidesteps the messy nuances of complex political issues in favor of melodrama, misrepresentative exaggeration, mockery and hyperbolic forecasts of immediate doom" (7). Genre suggests rules, guidelines that shape discourse and that allow discourse to shape some form of reality. Without genre, we do not have structure for communication, whether in politics, scholarship, entertainment, or some other expression. In their breakdown of what they call the "outrage industry," Berry and Sobieraj not only set up outrage as genre but also imply that it is a type of rhetoric. Overgeneralization. Sensationalism. Inaccurate information. These sound, as well, like the characteristics of a practice that poses a methodology and that can be replicated. If I want to express outrage, the logic follows, I should embrace these kinds of discursive acts. Such is how rhetoric functions. Rhetoric provides the tool for a variety of communicative acts, and outrage is one.

Outrage is media-based, as *Network* demonstrates. Media engages. "Outrage is also engaging" (Berry and Sobieraj 8). Facebook and outrage allow for simultaneous digital engagement. Facebook, Karppi notes, "needs to expand and intensify: *expand the possibilities* of user engagement and *intensify the existing relations of user engagement*, and the platform is the medium between these two dimensions" (39). Engagement, as Marshall McLuhan theorizes, is a media-generated concept dependent on which medium is used for which communicative purpose. McLuhan's canonical dichotomy of media into hot and cool categories suggests that communication's choice of platform will affect reception depending on whether engagement/involvement does not exist (hot media) or does exist (cool media). "Any hot medium allows for less participation than a cool one," McLuhan argues (*Understanding Media* 23). Depending on one's purpose in shaping opinion or social change, one kind of medium may be more appropriate than the other. McLuhan categorized a number of political and social issues based on the hot/cool dichotomy, attempting to understand audience reception not as content-based but as media-based. The distinction is important because it suggests that content is not the major factor influencing response; medium is. In *Network*, Beale can cause outrage to spread quickly via television because television is the medium. I contend outrage, too, is a medium. Whether affective or technological, it serves a communicative role. Such thinking runs counter to popular understandings regarding outrage where content is assumed to be king. We feel we are outraged over something, not that outrage is spreading outrage.

Media choice, for McLuhan, suggests control (do we want audience engagement, or do we want passive reception?). Media affect response and engagement. A radio debate is different than a televised debate. Film in one country affects audiences differently than radio in another. For McLuhan, television is a favorite tool for creating engagement. He often emphasizes its cool approach to involvement (mostly because of television's predigital role in mass communication).

"Television," McLuhan argues, "demands participation and involvement in depth of the whole being" (*Medium* 125). Howard Beale, following McLuhan, influences an engaged viewership to yell out of their windows because television, according to McLuhan, is cool. It fosters participation through, among other things, identification; viewers identify with Beale's rage and become like him. McLuhan also drew attention to the total effect of such media on our various personal and interpersonal relationships as they are carried out via media influence: "In the merely personal and private sphere we are often reminded of how changes of tone and attitude are demanded of different times and seasons in order to keep situations in hand" (*Understanding Media* 28). Civil rights, technological adaption, and societal roles are among the topics and situations explored in McLuhan's work; outrage is not explicitly addressed. However, under McLuhan's dichotomous framework, outrage is a cool medium. One aggregates into outrage those items not visibly present (i.e., the technical image). That point does not contradict outrage's affective status or evocation via aggregation and technical images. It only helps further explain the process of outrage's ability to communicate outrage.

McLuhan's 1960s isolation of certain types of media (e.g., radio) from others (e.g., television) may not hold up entirely today because of technological changes. Television, in particular, functions differently today than it did when McLuhan based his observations on television's cathode ray tube construction whose broken, projected image lines were reconstructed by the viewer to create a whole image (engagement). The notion of a medium which fosters or inhibits engagement, however, is relevant to any study of digital outrage, especially one focused on the platforms that make up social media. As I've briefly noted, Facebook is central to digital outrage focused on engagement. Outrage can be, by itself, an isolated form of expression (this pisses me off!), but its ability to stimulate engagement and involvement—McLuhan's notion of coolness—also plays a significant role in digital communication, particularly in platforms that promote engagement (if the anchorman is angry, so am I!). Merely being pissed off is not enough to spread engagement in the digital sphere. One must use outrage as a type of medium, the way one would use a piece of paper, a radio broadcast, a website, a video, a newscast, or any other platform in order to convey meaning.

Engagement is central to data-driven social media usage. Facebook, for instance, is based on engagement. Likes. Clicks. Shares. Posts. These items provide the basis of Facebook engagement both for users and for the company, as each post and interaction is tracked and incorporated into an algorithmic logic meant to be predictive. Those predictions are then sold to advertisers and used to prove Facebook's effectiveness (a profile) at generating tailored audiences for goods and services. Facebook defines page engagement as "The total number of actions that people took on your Facebook Page and its posts."[1] "When people like your page," one Facebook promotional video notes for engagement and advertising, "they may see your posts and newsfeeds, the stream of info from their friends, family, and things they like, including your business."[2] In addition, Facebook understands engagement, as the video argues, via location, age, gender, and interests. These categories supposedly foster user engagement through an aggregation into a centralized image called a profile. They help the platform build aggregated profiles to share (much as a newscast builds an aggregated profile of supposed angry voters to share).

McLuhan theorizes that action and engagement are prompted by cool media, in other words, media where the user must fill in what is missing to make sense of the communication. Facebook devotes resources to measuring how a post or shared image does the same. I fill in details regarding where a friend or friend of a friend posts or what she expresses interest in, and I can respond in an engaged way (I want that too; I want to go there; I believe the same). Engagement can mean physically being present or actively purchasing a product, and that has been a central focus for Facebook critics. Cambridge Analytica supposedly can force individuals to feel something and engage (either by shopping or voting). McLuhan, though, suggests emotional involvement as being the overall *feeling* of involvement in a moment, and not necessarily an individual act (such as attending a protest or buying a product). We can add to McLuhan's concerns the question of how layered terms, as well, contribute to this process. Topoi, or commonplaces, generate responses from which individuals become emotional. Being angry at the government (I'm mad as hell) is a circulated topos identifiable in left- and right-wing discourse. This anger becomes layered into various images (text and visual) regarding the economy, government enactment, foreign policy, and so forth. When a user engages with a TV broadcast of that topos, she can become engaged (I'm mad as hell too!). Politics. Shopping. Discrimination. These, too, are topoi for involvement when we are exposed to imagery or headlines. Our networked connectivity to such moments makes us *feel* involved.

Involvement can be associative. Howard Beale or Donald Trump expresses anger, and so do I because I, too, feel their emotional involvement, or because I feel I am involved via support or objection. One of McLuhan's concerns with cool media is its ability to foster said involvement. If one sees police brutality on TV or reads about it online, one may feel involved ("stop that!" or "this must end," or "organize!"). Through shared imagery and video over the network, one sees a man suffocating as police arrest him for illegally selling cigarettes. One sees a woman pulled over by a Texas police officer and then arrested for no reason. One sees a man with his hands up asking for police not to shoot. One sees a man with a police officer's knee pressed into his neck for eight minutes and forty-six seconds. These acts anger for very legitimate reasons; at the most immediate level, we feel anger at the unjust murders of innocent people. Viewers disgusted with these moments may also form historical associations by aggregating into the present offense details such as a history of American discrimination, Jim Crow, civil rights, Black people being arrested for no reason, and political power disparities across race. All of this can be read as the items aggregate over the network and evoke connection, emotional response, and engagement. In turn, the images are shared, commented on, and incorporated into face-to-face conversations; many people will take to the streets, protest, and demand a change.

For this reason, McLuhan punned on message and massage: The engaged message massages. Cool media work us over. Media massage us completely. In *Medium is the Massage*, famously, McLuhan uses the example of a Black woman being arrested outside a movie theater whose marquee reads, "Suspense! Excitement!" (*Medium* 130). The juxtaposition of civil rights with entertainment evokes how specific media can foster engagement. Our involvement, indeed, becomes an extension of entertainment; the suspense of a movie extends into the suspense and excitement of ending discrimination (or, for some, encouraging it). The appeal of Howard Beale's rallying cry extends to our current frustrations. "Participation via television in Freedom Marches, in war, revolution, pollution, and other events is changing everything" (*Medium* 22). Film and television, for McLuhan, are important media. In the 1960s, they helped spread outrage over social injustice by generating involvement. For our current social media moment, outrage itself has become a cool medium. It doesn't matter what the subject matter is—the host of the Academy Awards or a man murdered for selling illegal cigarettes. Outrage is both the message and the medium for expressing that message. Whereas McLuhan, in the 1960s, is interested in materiality as media, today we are dealing with concepts or responses as media.

This chapter breaks down this idea—outrage as media—by providing a brief look at the example of health care and its circulation. Health care circulates as an idea (how it should be provided, who should pay for it, the role of government in providing accessible health care) but health care also circulates as outrage spreading outrage. In doing so, it functions as form of communication, and at times, it functions as more powerful than the subject it represents. I focus on health care, a central, widely circulated topic, to set up later chapters, which will expand some of the concepts I cover in this chapter into further examples.

HEALTH CARE OUTRAGE

Let's consider a brief, emotional example that can help me unpack outrage as a media/technology concept as well as set the stage for subsequent chapters. Like "economy," or other technical images in circulation that, as *Network* demonstrates, spark anger, "health care" works similarly. Despite the incredible importance of health care to a nation, and despite millions of Americans lacking affordable, accessible care, the topic's status within American online discourse often hinges on an engagement with outrage. It is difficult for health care to be reported or discussed without outrage also communicating the issues at stake because health care is often packaged with outrage the way the economy is packaged with anger. "Is The Health Care Ire Part of A Larger Anger?" a 2009 NPR story asks. "Rising Obamacare premiums anger those paying full price," CNN's Virginia Anderson wrote in 2016. In *Forbes*, Peter Ubel writes, "Paying for healthcare is so confusing, patients don't know who to be angry at." CNN reports, "Town Hall Anger Over Health Care Bill" (Kaye). This cumulative, and not exhaustive, discursive outrage drives public engagement and involvement much as Howard Beale prompts people to lean out of their fire escapes and shout. Headlines help layer this anger, but other forces, actors, and moments are layered within as well.

Even when Congress or the White House calls for better access to health care—as Bill Clinton tried and failed to do in 1993—the public becomes incensed from *its own published and disseminated* incensement. In other words, public outrage (medium) fuels further outrage (content and medium). While there is an initial agent—such as a health care proposal—its agency is often overpowered by shared outrage, which spreads from person to person or through media. In Clinton's case and later Barack Obama's as well, the projection of outrage helped generate further outrage, outrage that either killed initiatives or promoted false information. The aggregation of health care imagery across television, in particular, played a major role in this process.

A popular 1993 TV commercial featuring "Harry and Louise," for instance, portrayed the Clinton initiative with stereotypical language meant to generate indignation. The characters of Harry and Louise are stereotypes, generalized images of the average, hardworking American who will lose everything because of a proposed plan to increase access to health care. The commercial highlighted the repetition of expected phrases or words which would foster emotional engagement. These phrases and words are built from profiles, aggregations of what the campaign believed an average, hardworking American might need to feel in order to want to be involved. This includes the commercial's insistence that the plan would lead to "loss" of current coverage and would double insurance rates, and that it would be orchestrated by an inept Congress lacking knowledge of health care issues overall. Loss and government dysfunction are layered topoi aggregated over time into user perception. So is freedom, particularly for American culture. "Having choices we don't like is no choice at all," Louise states as she looks over what a new plan will supposedly change (an assumed buffet of options to nothing). In front of her are piles of what appears to be arcane, confusing paperwork to be filled out and navigated (the bureaucracy profile). These well-placed objects and phrases within the commercial function as media within media (the commercial itself). Seeing all that paperwork, the average viewer must have been as shocked as Louise, thinking, "this will be a nightmare." A profile of an average American, no doubt, would suggest that more paperwork is to be feared. Within this commercial are layered several profiles, in fact, each helping spread user outrage ("how dare they!") along with the media's initial sharing on broadcast television.

This ad's communicative force can be found as well within social media. In an August 7, 2009, Facebook post, Sarah Palin, responding to the proposed Patient Protection and Affordable Health Care Act—otherwise known as "Obamacare"—went further than the Harry and Louise commercial, as it bypassed the loss, paperwork, and dysfunction topoi typically aggregated into users' perspectives, and introduced the highly charged concept of "death panels." Tapping into public fears that socialized health care, or health care programs that draw upon principles publicly associated with socialism, are selective and potentially dangerous to a community's overall care, she asked: "Who will suffer the most when they ration care? The sick, the elderly, and the disabled, of course. The America I know and love is not one in which my parents or my baby with Down syndrome will have to stand in front of Obama's "death panel" so his bureaucrats can decide, based on a subjective judgment of their "level of productivity in society," whether they are worthy of health care. Such a system is downright evil" (Palin). Palin may have been layering into her claim a July 16 remark made by former Lieutenant Governor of New York Betsy McCaughey. On the Fred Thompson radio show, she suggested something like death panels existed in the legislation: "Congress would make it mandatory—absolutely require—that every five years people in Medicare have a required counseling session that will tell them how to end their life sooner" (qtd. in Richard). Palin's readers may or may not have been aware of McCaughey's earlier claim, or of radio host Rush Limbaugh's repetition of McCaughey's claim. Limbaugh combined the death panel idea with the popular topos of privacy: "Mandatory counseling for all seniors at a minimum of every five years, more often if the seasoned citizen is sick or in a nursing home . . . That's an invasion of the right to privacy. We can't have counseling for mothers who are thinking of terminating their pregnancy, but we can go in there and counsel people about to die" (Limbaugh). "The 'death panel' myth," Berry and Sobieraj note, "ricocheted around the Internet and on cable and talk radio with impressive velocity" (199). Ricocheting anger is created by angry people repeating claims. If Palin's readers were aware of the ricocheting that began before her post, these moments I highlight would have contributed to their outrage. The mythological concept of a death panel is based on a provision that would have allowed Medicare to pay doctors who discuss end-of-life care with their patients. The counseling was not mandatory. Its transformation into death panel was a communicative process where each utterance depended on a prior utterance to spread outrage. This layering of claims creates a technical image. That image is not one particular instance of health care but rather an aggregation of many layers into a broader concept.

For now, we can see an initial appropriation of a term over three spaces. This appropriation extends from the fear of one's life being controlled by a government body to an overall fear of the more generic and layered concept called socialism, or of a similar-sounding but completely different political movement, National Socialism. Socialism carries highly negative connotations in certain parts of American culture. Because of its association with Soviet-era oppression and loss of individual freedom (fear of the collective), socialism earns a great deal of anger when it is associated with public policy. The Palin post highlights this fear. Her post depends greatly on previously held beliefs regarding socialism. Add another layer of Nazi-style eugenics—as in Kevin McCullough's argument that "President Obama took a demonstrable step in the shoes, actions, and example of Adolf Hitler," and that Obama "wants doctors to exterminate 'lesser humans' for the purpose of immediate solutions to his social experiment"—and death panel becomes a sticky, repeatable term.

Socialism, with its tropes of equity and equality, in popular discourse must involve "rationing" in order to achieve such equity. In one aggregated profile, that rationing might include who lives and who dies (National Socialism) or an economic rationing; in other words, socialism will take from a generic and symbolic "you" who has earned a decent income and distribute what you have earned to another generic and symbolic "not you" who does not deserve your money. Palin's 2009 post was not the first time she drew upon the socialist trope to generate outrage. In 2008, Palin had brought up the threat of socialism in front of a crowd in Latrobe, Pennsylvania, arguing against Barack Obama's plan to raise taxes. "Now is not the time to experiment with that," she stated. She continued: "They do that in other countries where people are not free and where work ethic is not rewarded. And when an entrepreneurial spirit is absolutely stifled. And that's exactly what his plan will do to Americans and to the children who we are trying to teach work ethic and the reward for hard work" (Bolstad). Socialism has the power to make conversations about other topics, such as health care, threatening.

It's worth tracing some of the connections discourse makes when associative reasoning relies on layered and powerful images like those attached to socialism. Socialism is not a singular image, that is, but rather an image with many other images layered within it by specific audiences. When Trump berated the Democratic party at a February 2019 rally in El Paso Texas, he, too, raised the specter of socialism as Palin had done more than ten years earlier. "Here in the United States, we are alarmed by the new calls to adopt socialism in our country," Trump told the gathered crowd. "America was founded on liberty and independence, and not government coercion, domination and control. We are born free, and we will stay free. Tonight, we renew our resolve that America will never be a socialist country" (Montanaro). Socialism, in other words, is rhetorically presented as antithetical to freedom, democracy, and independence. This is an influential technical image. It is layered with the imagery antithetical to supposed American values.

Trump's statement is not an anomaly. Consider the American Medical Association's early efforts to associate medical care with socialism. Some of this work was done in the 1950s and early 1960s, during the Cold War, when anxiety about socialism was high and doctors feared for their salaries. Julian Zelizer recounts that history: "The A.M.A. women's auxiliary launched Operation Coffee Cup, in which doctors' wives hosted living-room discussions about the dangers of socialized medicine. Ronald Reagan produced a record to be played at these events, 'Ronald Reagan Speaks Out Against Socialized Medicine,' in which he warned that 'one of the traditional methods of imposing statism or socialism on a people has been by way of medicine'" (Zelizer). Reagan, a notable figure in conservative politics (and at that time, an actor), lends ethos to the historical image many have internalized. His recording highlights what I just described as layered imagery. As Reagan states on the 1961 record, when we have socialized health care, "The doctor begins to lose freedoms. . . . first you decide that the doctor can have so many patients; they are equally divided by the government. But then the doctors are equally divided geographically, so a doctor decides he wants to practice in one town and the government has to say to him you can't live in that town. They already have enough doctors. You have to go someplace else. And from here it's only a short step to dictating where he will go" ("Ronald Reagan Speaks Out"). Decisions. Dictating. Control. Notice these very strong topoi layered within the image Reagan creates. Reagan warns of the "precedent" of letting the government make decisions for the populace and "encroachment on individual liberties and freedom." Socialism challenges another accepted image, the individual. In this tradition, Palin framed Obamacare as a "socialist" operation and—evoking for her audience an image of Soviet or Eastern European oppressiveness—circulated the phrase death panel in order to spark fear and outrage over the loss of individual choice and voice.

Conservative talk show hosts and the Tea Party repeated Palin's question, posing it as a central part of the Obamacare legislation and as a legitimate threat to a perceived, free way of life. Consider the Tea Party Patriots Healthcare section of its website, which poses health care as an issue of freedom.

Health care freedom means we can choose our own doctor and health insurance plans, without penalty from government if we do not choose unneeded options. We are capable of making our own choices when it comes to utilizing our hard-earned money to protect and care for our families and ourselves. We have found that across all political groups—Americans place very high importance on the freedom to choose their own doctors, yet, increasingly, they do not feel that this freedom exists. The Affordable Care Act—Obamacare—removes this freedom and also presents perhaps the biggest threat to your money, your job and your opportunity to find a good job, which for many Americans, serves as the starting point for acquiring quality health care coverage.

Four mentions of freedom in this statement emphasize the term's importance to the issue as well as the term's importance simply as a technical image. Lack of freedom implies that a health care plan will usher in a totalitarian government. Suggesting that a health care plan will make life-and-death decisions for the sick, elderly and disabled is also to suggest a Nazi-style Sophie's Choice model of eugenics forced upon the populace (Palin's invocation of her own child's disability makes the association equally powerful).

One Facebook post, however, is not enough for outrage to communicate itself. Palin's post is layered in what precedes her. But her own comments become layered with those that follow her. There are, then, various aggregations occurring that lead to outrage; a history of imagery associated with socialism and nefarious forces, and the furthering of claims Palin and others make from that history. Media, in this instance as news media, play a role. Many news publications promoted Palin's concept in one form or another, each serving as a link within a larger discursive network. "Rationing, death panels, socialism," Stanley Kurtz wrote in *National Review*, "all those nasty old words that helped bring Republicans victory in 2010, and that came to seem so impolite after November of that year. They're back because of IPAB [Independent Payment Advisory Board]." At the end of his critique of Obamacare, Kurtz adds, "The president continues to stealthily consolidate his socialist plans for health care." Writing about Obama in *Politico*, Marion Smith echoes a fairly public tone: "Socialism is not roads, welfare, and free education. Socialism has always had a more ominous goal and shares close historical and ideological connections with more reviled terms: Marxism and communism. Karl Marx took socialism to what he viewed as its natural conclusion: The 'abolition of private property.'" Reminding readers of the importance of the private, as it does in the privacy violation conversation, contributes to the outrage.

Socialism is antiprivacy for many. Privacy will be violated. "In its waning days, the Obama presidency is baring its socialist fangs," Paul Sperry wrote in the *New York Post*. "Besides mimicking some of Lenin's policy strategies, Obama also has adopted Karl Marx's strategies for gradually socializing an economy," Mark Hendrickson wrote in *Forbes*. Socialism, as a public imaginary, is evil. Death panels reflect socialism. A death panel, Ben Cosman argued, "evokes an image of faceless bureaucrats rationing health care and sentencing the elderly and the infirm to death. It's a catch-all term for the ills of Obamacare, and with a little bit of effort, *any* Obama scandal." These are extremely formidable images, drawn from various circulated moments and embedded in a short Facebook post without Palin ever mentioning them. Their appearance depends on public and affective association, on a reader filling in the details (McLuhan's cool media) that have been gathered over years of exposure, discussion, belief, and fear. There is a type of affective accumulation taking place. Obama. Socialism. Death Panels. Private ownership. Freedom. These are at least six images embedded in Palin's post at the associative and affective level. Their public circulation extends, knowingly or not, into the Facebook post, dragging behind them a variety of other related images also associated with a perceived socialist evil.

The Democratic Party should have been able to easily counter the emotional association Palin formed for many voters, since Obamacare did not include any mention of death panels or the destruction of individual liberty. But they couldn't. The phrase was too powerful, too layered with precedent and additional circulation, too affective, and too associative to calm outrage. Health care conveys a dominant image with specific audiences who may struggle to acquire adequate care, but who still fear new health care initiatives because of their other aggregated beliefs regarding private ownership, Capitalism, Cold War politics, eugenics, or even the nation's first Black president.

What is the aggregated profile, then, of someone who believes in death panels? NPR's Don Gonyea summarized an explanation of why the Obama administration and the Democratic Party failed to counter the death panel narrative by focusing on such a profile: "The administration—and Democrats—have been slow to learn: how to talk to white voters who do not have a college education. Those voters were once a key piece of the Democratic base, but [the Center for American Progress's Ruy] Teixeira says they are now too often driven by a core belief that 'the government is up to no good.'" Gonyea assumes a specific audience profiling, and based on that profiling (white, fearful of government, lacking education) believes a counter-position can be created. This, of course, is the position of Facebook and other online platforms regarding the collection of personal data for profiling. Know your audience (i.e., know how generic populations might be aggregated into a profile) and appeal to its beliefs. Such is much of the logic that social media actions rely upon. Profiling does work well for evoking anger (know your audience), but it doesn't always work as well for explaining anger. In other words, even if we know the profile, it might not be sufficient to explain why a person or a group of people have become angry.

The problem with Gonyea's explanation, much like Barthes's example of Italian advertisements, is that it relies on a couple of points that may or may not be true in a given moment of well-circulated outrage (the kairos, or timeliness, of anger may not be connected to the points Gonyea raises). Or Gonyea's list does not account for what, in this case, the assumed white audience knew or experienced prior to the mentioning of "death panels." His list assumes what they know, but how are we sure? Consider Gonyea's assumptions, which function as critical stereotypes (expected conclusions) of a target audience:

1. Only white voters reject proposals for health care reform.
2. A college education acts as a buffer against falling for fake or misleading news and announcements, particularly as they apply to health care.
3. Only those individuals who are suspicious of government and its bureaucracy (itself an associative and well-circulated narrative) are driving the circulation of fake news such as the death panel concept.

While the profile could be used to explain some of the audience, I question whether this profile demonstrates enough and can account for all of the death panel support or health care rejection.

This type of profile offers an easy audience-based explanation (white, uneducated American), but it does not account for many other factors that may cause one to believe that death panels do exist. Being white cannot be the only factor leading to this belief and neither can the believers' level of education. This aggregation is limited. It looks at the surface of audience reception (i.e., white voters) and cannot separate a complex network of meanings, experiences, and emotions many voters bring to an image such as the Palin post. It also cannot distinguish the act of communication occurring over many years through many speakers, communication that arrives with the reading of the technical image under question. If outrage, as I claim, is a communicative medium and not just a concept, it also is layered and networked and not based only on stereotypical profile aggregations.

Sarah Palin, for instance, is college educated. So were many of her followers. Many contemporary Trump supporters are college educated too (and many are not white, and Trump is college educated). Are we sure that all voters who feared death panels were white? Are we sure that only race aggregates across time and circulation when socialism is evoked? When I introduce in later chapters specific outrage examples for unpacking, we'll see that race and education are not the determining factors of belief or profile construction or even major items in most profile aggregations, though critical assumptions often frame these items as central. That point runs counter to a great deal of outrage criticism which, especially concerning topics related to Trump, depends on what I term a *stereotypical aggregation* of audience response (i.e., only white people support Trump, or as I outline in a later chapter, professors act only under the auspice of academic freedom). We'll also see that being antigovernment is not always a prerequisite either. The stereotypical aggregation builds a profile, one that may allow for easy explanation of an outrage moment, but that doesn't explain the other histories viewers/readers layer into the circulated imagery. Voters, like people who buy food, go to horror movies, or enjoy skiing, are aggregated profiles that rely upon stereotypical information, but who also rely on additional items in order to prefer, oppose, get upset, or experience other emotional responses.

One such additional item, as I've briefly shown in my tracings of context, is the headline. The headline, too, is a technical image. Seeing the phrase "death panel" repeated across various media outlets—whether in so-called mainstream publications such as *Forbes*, *Los Angeles Times*, and CNN, or in more fringe outlets such as those supported by Glenn Beck and Rush Limbaugh—reinforces the idea that a death panel actually exists or is being proposed. A headline can confirm reality based on the reader's own profile (what she has read previously across headlines, for instance) or can confirm a reality merely by circulating it widely (if I see the phrase enough, it appears to me to be true). The headline is an extension of outrage as media regardless of what is actually in the text that comes after the headline. Consider the 2016 *Forbes* headline, "Obamacare's Dreaded 'Death Panels' Won't be Triggered This Year" (Mukherjee). Even though there did not exist a death panel, nor coverage for end-of-life counseling, nor even the proposed fifteen-member Independent Payment Advisory Board which would monitor Medicare spending, the mere presence of the phrase in a major publication's headline creates a given reality for some of its reading audience. The headline confirms. It acts as an isolated image projecting a "truth" since one need not read the article to find power in its message, or one may only see the headline in a shared Twitter or Facebook link where the content can only be accessed by clicking through. The headline not only confirms the existence of a death panel by naming it as such, it provides the adjective "dreaded" to suggest that *Forbes* recognizes a horror that awaits. Even NPR, a media outlet often sympathetic with the Obama administration, published the headline "The Truth About Death Panels" (Nangia). The association of "truth" (it's real, not fake) with death panels can confirm a reality for some readers who may not read the article. *U.S. News and World Report* repeated the same headline in 2012 (Lukas). Other outlets did as well. Aggregated reading can transform a headline into a reality. That reality is read across audiences regardless of race. I will write more about headlines in detail in later chapters.

HEALTH CARE CONTINUED

Palin's comments notwithstanding, as my brief outline demonstrates, health care has long been an object of outrage. This is an important point because it indicates the presence in popular vocabulary of a term that already contains various embedded ideas and images meant to provoke anger. Socialism is one of those embedded ideas. Neither Palin nor Obama is the first to direct public attention to health care, its pitfalls, its need for reform, and its failure to help those in need. Let me offer one other brief example that belongs within health care outrage as communicative force.

Adbusters, the predecessor to Kalle Lasn's Occupy Wall Street Movement project, functioned as an art project that often utilized the concept of culture jamming (turning culture back on itself as a form of critique) to target health care issues in stereotypical but angry ways. Fast food, the cigarette industry, alcohol consumption—all were spoofed in order to draw attention to inequities in the country's health care industry and its lack of attention to the forces that cause health issues such as smoking or obesity. The attacks, though, were never subtle. Adbusters depended on stereotypes and remixed imagery to spread its argument to a readership likely already sympathetic to the critique, but even if they were not, they would likely be shocked in response. One Adbusters image of Ronald McDonald, for instance, featured a "grease" sticker fixated over McDonald's mouth. Another spoof depicted a patient being operated on; in the foreground a heart monitor shows the McDonald's Golden Arches in place of the heartbeat measurement. Not everyone will die from eating McDonald's, of course, and most people neither die nor have major health problems from occasionally eating fast food. Instead, like the mentioning of a death panel, Adbusters focused on previously held beliefs about consumer culture, such as the health problems associated with fried food, or corporate business practices associated with the fast-food industry (companies knowingly offer unhealthy options). Exaggeration. Hyperbole. These, too, are relevant rhetorical markers that help spread outrage as they aggregate past belief systems. Whether or not statistics and science indicate McDonald's causes mass death, suggesting such a point to an audience already willing to form such associations does. As Poulakos argues in his reading of Isocrates' notion of doxa, when individuals are presented with information they already believe, they "see the new situation as confirming their traditions and as validating their familiar notions of self, [thus] there is hardly any need for persuasion" (69). Adbusters likely did not convince those who frequent McDonald's to stop doing so, but it likely did appeal to those who already held negative feelings about fast food in the first place.

Adbusters demonstrated outrage via commonplace assumptions. Consumerism. Capitalism. Greed. Inequality. These are the topoi Adbusters aggregated across an image; mockery of them is meant to evoke political awareness and, one assumes, reversal of public policy. Fast food and cigarettes are easy targets because there already exist enough media reporting and public concern regarding these products (just as there already exists a history of objecting to health care reform). An organization like Adbusters can repeat already held concerns in iconic imagery and resurface those concerns for further repetition. One such image, an attack on the Joe Camel cigarette ads, spotlights "Joe Chemo," the iconic camel, lying in a casket, presumably at his funeral. He has, of course, died of cigarette related cancer. If the suggestion of a death panel can rally a populace against a health care initiative, one might assume that a Joe Chemo spoof could rally a populace against smoking cigarettes. Of course, it could not. In the end, Palin was more effective than Adbusters at spreading outrage. Why she was effective depends on how audiences aggregate information and imagery, and how social media facilitates this process by spreading the message. Socialism and death panels contain more public rhetorical history than chemotherapy and cigarettes. "Joe Chemo" was the product of pre–social media circulation.

The most basic reason for this discrepancy involves a number of networked factors I have so far briefly touched upon: networks, profiles, past influences, audience, media, and current influences. Lasn's Occupy Wall Street movement, an extension of his Adbusters project, furthered the Adbusters initiative; but it also directed attention more directly to social inequality, took place largely on social media, and had better, though still limited, success with its attention to precedent. Begun on September 17, 2011, with the takeover of New York's Zuccotti Park across from Wall Street, Occupy contrasted its view of a 1 percent of the population in control of most of the world's finances, and a 99 percent without access to health care, resources, or the ability to get out of debt. In this projection, Occupy presented a digital outrage machine based on an aggregation. In addition to the physical protests across from Wall Street in Zuccotti Park and in other locations across the country (often symbolized as temporary camps), one of Occupy's most potent campaigns was a series of images circulated and repeated across social media. These images, all based on the same template-theme, featured a person holding up a sign. On the sign would be listed a series of traits making up an assumed 99 percent profile, and a list of traits the sign holder felt applied to themselves as well. These signs repeated stereotypes regarding the trope of "the average America" or "the struggling worker," which resembled Howard Beale's rant. Their repetition encouraged further engagement in outrage. "This combination of repetition and variation," Limor Shifman writes, "turns the personal to political: Stories about the sick young woman who is unable to afford medication, the single mom who struggles to provide for her

I am 20 years old and upwards of $275,000 in medical bills from this last year due to a condition I was born with. I can't get insurance because of a "pre-existing condition." I will die before America wakes up. I AM THE 99%. OCCUPY WALL ST. ORG

Fig. 3.1.
An example of 99 percent signage.

son, and the father who cannot send his daughter to college are reframed as particular cases of the same flawed structure. These people's miseries are not just personal problems; they stem from the systemic economic and political illnesses of their habitat" (134). Shifman identifies Occupy's repetitive narratives as content that involves "engaged communication" (59) where "people are encouraged not only to share a certain item, but also to carry other activities related to it" (72). Occupy encouraged people to share a specific genre of protest (holding up a sign with similar content to that shown in fig. 3.1) but at the same time allowed individuals to share their personal outrage over health care, financial stability, and other related matters.

Begun on a Tumblr blog called *We Are the 99 Percent* (but later adopted by Occupy) by an individual only known as "Chris," the campaign asked readers to submit their own images of themselves holding up signs describing their financial hardship. Once readers had the opportunity to read the submission, the content became sticky, and its stickiness led to an increase in submissions by a diverse audience group who found a central, sticky point to identify with and further share. The postings were cool media. Adam Weinstein describes the posts accordingly: "On September 8, the first day he started publishing submissions, there were five posts. Less than a month later, the blog was posting nearly 100 pieces a day: from the 61-year-old who lost her job and moved in with her kids, to the husband of a college professor on WIC and Medicaid to support an infant daughter, to the fiftysomething couple living on tossed-out KFC, to a bevy of youths pummeled by student debt and too poor to visit a dentist" (Weinstein).

The sign posting campaign tapped into specific forms of outrage, but it also allowed outrage to function as a medium of engagement. As a viral or memetic moment, the sign posting became a medium adopted for further communication. As is often the case with viral content, an image that gains circulation (repeated by groups as diverse as a sixty-one-year-old, a husband, a fifty-something couple, young people) does so because the viewer of the initial image experiences a deep emotional reaction as association and then *an impulse to respond.* That response often takes the form of appropriation and sharing. Appropriation is a digital logic of involvement. I become so engaged with the image or text in question that I borrow enough of it to allow myself to become part of the conversation and be recognizable to others within the same conversation. The sign and financial hardship information remains consistent, but I also insert new material to reflect my difference—such as altering some of the financial hardship information or adding new points. Appropriation allows the personal and universal to juxtapose. Many of the 99 percent signs foreground preexisting medical conditions, college debt, losing one's job, not enough income to pay bills, being college educated and struggling financially, high mortgage payments, anger at government bailouts of corporations when individuals don't get such bailouts, and so on. The circulation of the same thematic content allows for identification to occur. *Me too. I know. I have the same problems. I agree. I am that person.* When we identify, we often engage. We feel group affinity. We often engage by borrowing previous positions. The difference between Occupy and *Network* is minimal. Those who yell out their windows in the movie appropriate Howard Beale's anger. They add to his observations their own internal frustrations much as those who hold up "I am the 99 percent" signs do.

An audience, as these brief examples demonstrate, is based on a profile assumption. New York residents are mad as hell. Americans feel disenfranchised for economic reasons. While I chide NPR's Gonyea for relying entirely on audience profiling to draw a political conclusion, the assumption or imagination of an audience is important for outrage to communicate itself. When Sarah Palin invents the notion of a death panel, for instance, she assumes the presence of an audience who will find this term sticky because of its various antigovernment, anti-Socialist, anti-Obama fears gathered over time. She imagines an audience already susceptible to a suggestion of a government conspiracy to eliminate individual freedom, impose Socialism, and kill undesirable citizens as a public might imagine a socialist entity doing. She borrows this language and reapplies it in a Facebook post. Occupy imagines an audience of disenfranchised citizens who struggle financially to make ends meet despite doing everything possible to fulfil the American dream (in contrast to an opposite and more popular narrative—the American self-made man). With imagined profiles, Palin and Occupy can easily provoke people they have never met over a common topic (which is a technical image), health care. As with the Facebook profiles Cambridge Analytica tapped into, one does not have to know an audience to reach it. One has only to imagine it based on various aggregated stereotypes and then appropriate its beliefs in a repeatable communicative moment. The appropriation I note, then, is based both on the message circulated and the audience's assumptions.

Audiences, indeed, are imagined profiles of assumptions and stereotypes. Rhetorical studies treat audience as a rich topic of analysis, and while I won't survey the vast literature in audience analysis or reception, it's worthwhile to highlight a few audience-based positions relevant to the rise of outrage, reflected in Palin's Facebook post and the examples I will later trace out. One theory addresses the assumed passions and beliefs (doxa) audiences carry into rhetorical situations (such as the threatening socialism narrative). Wayne Booth argues that "No rhetorical effort can succeed if it fails to join in the beliefs and passions of the audience addressed, and that almost always requires some 'accommodation,' 'adjustment,' or 'adaption' to the audience's needs and expectations" (*Rhetoric of Rhetoric* 51). Palin, whether she believed in the existence of death panels or not, adapted a specific situation—health care initiatives—with an audience's need to be outraged (at implied socialism or Barack Obama himself). Need, as well, is an assumption. Palin could identify in her assumed audience a specific profile to accommodate with a Facebook post that employs anti-Socialist values.

"For the speaker," Walter Ong writes, "the audience is in front of him. For the writer, the audience is simply further away, in time and space" ("The Writer's Audience" 10). Assumed locations and compositions of audiences will be central to much of the exploration I do in later chapters. Moments of digital outrage are often based on the presumed existence of an audience that is neither present nor easily identifiable except via a preconceived profile. A Facebook audience, indeed, is far away. Yet, Facebook and many users of Facebook can operate as if that audience is not. First of all, one has a group of networked friends one tries to reach with each post. The assumption of connectivity—as friend—puts people in proximity to ideas. A post can assume an audience's profile: my friends are receptive or not receptive to a given idea or image. I make that assumption based on what I know about my friends from personal interaction, but also because of what I know about their jobs, interests, previous likes, previous posts, and so on. Facebook's algorithms tap into these interactions, of course, but so do its various users, such as Sarah Palin. "How does the writer give body to the audience for whom he writes?" Ong asks (10). Ong answers accordingly: "If the writer succeeds in writing, it is generally because he can fictionalize in his imagination an audience he has learned to know not from daily life but from earlier writers who were fictionalizing in their imagination audiences they had learned to know in still earlier writers and so on back to the dawn of written narrative" (11). The speaker (writer, rhetorician, politician, advertiser, social media user, etc.) depends greatly on a history of audience imagination. How have individuals previously responded to X? What kinds of biases and stereotypes do individuals bring to various representations? What interests do these individuals have? What is the history of X's reception?

This series of questions is not too far removed from Facebook's attempts at aggregating audience profiles via basic data entry (what is your favorite movie) or its Social Graph search engine or even Cambridge Analytica's work. It's also not too different from a generic American conservative population hostile to the suggestion of socialism over time. The major difference, if there is one, is the dependence on past interactions and not just overall interests. One is more likely to post about current interests or concerns than one's history of visual and textual interaction. These past interactions, which are not posted online but are embedded in one's informational interactions, become coded, much as "socialism" and its history within American culture served as a code for Palin's supporters. Reading "death panel" on a politician's Facebook post can evoke, for those who carry the socialism code within their internal visualization of economics, outrage. One doesn't have to list "anti-Socialist" in one's Facebook profile the way one would list a favorite movie or where one went to high school. The historical and cultural interaction with a term such as socialism is, however, just as aggregated over time as such information. This is because Palin is not the only author of her Facebook post. She is appropriating past authors and critics whose ideas are already in circulation. As Frank Myers argued, "By evoking cultural stereotypes, symbols, expressions of commitment and other 'codes' implanted with in it, a political speech or act can contain several messages, some of them mutually incompatible, within the framework of a statement crafted by a single author" (58). Palin, as well, found such a strategy useful to provoke an imagined audience. Her post aggregates a series of stereotypes and symbols in a highly effective manner so that they "contain several messages" within their mentioning: big government, bureaucrats, nationalization, a generic concept of evil, and the codes of those supposedly targeted—the sick, the elderly, and the disabled. Her appeal to her own child who was born with Down syndrome combines the initial message of impending danger with her own personal narrative. Death panel, then, is not a singular phrase but an embedded, layered image. It ties into a history of health care concerns but other concerns as well.

What these examples show me is that outrage is not only affective, but it is also a form of communication. This communication draws upon previous imagery and ideas in order to disseminate an idea to a stereotyped audience. I've attempted to trace out via a few brief examples how aggregated moments become the basis of a perceived singular outrage moment. The claims of anger at the government, economic disparity, and inequity are claims made over time and through imagery. The same is true for specific trigger terms such as socialism or death panels. This does not mean that inequity does not exist or that socialism is perfect, but what it does suggest is how these terms (and thus many others) are layered, embedded images designed to program audience response. The complexity of the appropriation of previous meaning is the focus of the next chapter, which begins with a lion.

Notes

1. "Page Engagement," Meta, accessed August 12, 2022, https://www.facebook.com /business/help/.

2. "Build brand awareness online," Meta, Accessed August 12, 2022, https://www.face book.com/business/learn/.

Four

Digital Outragicity

In a July 2015 *Atlantic* essay, James Hamblin tells the story of Cecil the Lion, the Zimbabwe lion tagged by researchers for scientific study. Cecil was killed by Minnesota dentist Walter Palmer, who paid fifty thousand dollars for an African hunting safari. While safari hunting provides some African countries with tourist revenue used for national park maintenance, as well as being a means for animal population control, Cecil's death was treated as an anomaly and a crime. A lion had been killed by an American tourist, and its reportage went viral. Safari hunting has long been aggregated into either animal cruelty images, colonial images, or preservation images depending on who is arguing for or against the practice. Palmer responded to the outrage over the lion's killing with a written statement meant to excuse his acts: "I had no idea that the lion I took was a known, local favorite, was collared and part of a study until the end of the hunt. I relied on the expertise of my local professional guides to ensure a legal hunt" (Walsh). The statement and its claim of innocence did nothing to stem the tide of outrage. The *Washington Post, New York Times, Salon,* ABC News, and many other news outlets covered the story of the killed lion and drew attention to the killer's profession in their coverage. Twitter and Facebook hosted angry discussions over the animal's death. These emotional tweets were often accompanied by claims of brokenheartedness—or broken heart emojis. The lion's death was thus deeply personalized and iconized as much as any human's senseless death might be. PETA, People for the Ethical Treatment of Animals, not only personalized the lion's death, but called for Palmer's hanging: "Celebrities as different as Ricky Gervais and Newt Gingrich condemned the lion killing. Mia Farrow tweeted out the dentist's business address—only to delete it—and she faced a backlash after some online mistakenly believed she'd published Palmer's home address" ("PETA Calls"). "Justice for Cecil the Lion" is a Facebook page with over 133,000 likes. The Facebook group "Shame Lion Killer Dr. Walter Palmer and River Bluff Dental" (Palmer's practice) has over 12,000 members. Tweets, such as that in figure 4.1, proliferated. A paid tourist safari experience in Zimbabwe was named after the lion. A year after Cecil's death, Leonardo DiCaprio posted

Fig. 4.1. Typical Cecil tweet.

to his Facebook page a tribute to the lion. *TIME* magazine reposted anti-Palmer tweets from celebrities including Mia Farrow, Debra Messing and Sharon Osbourne, who equated Palmer with Satan (Plucinska). "You don't want to hear some of the things I want to do to that man," ninety-three-year-old actress Betty White told the Associated Press ("Betty White Condemns"). More than four years after the killing, the Yelp profile for Palmer's dental practice, despite being closed, continued to receive one-star ratings with comments describing him as a lion killer and a murderer.

"The fact that the lion had a name, Cecil, humanized him," Frida Ghitis wrote. "Thousands of heartbroken Cecil fans had never heard of him. And, in this era of lightning-fast communications, the outrage (deserved at any pointless, unjustified killing) spread quickly." In the case of Cecil the Lion, it seems, names matter. Cecil, as Ghitis suggests, feels like a gentle name. The lion's name was not Frank, Bob, John, or some other boring and easily forgettable name. It was Cecil. Welsh in origin, the name Cecil also conveys the stereotype of British politeness and gentility. Afternoon tea. A nice suit and bowler hat. A gentleman. An innocent being. Such might be the internalized profile the outrage was responding to.

It's hard to think of a more innocent name than Cecil. Had the lion's name been Satan or Derek, the international firestorm might have been attenuated. Had Palmer not had a past that included sexual harassment complaints and pleading guilty to lying to federal wildlife officials about killing a black bear, he might have been less hateable. He also might have been less hateable had he been a humble cobbler, or literally anything other than a wealthy dentist. But every element of this story fell into place in a way that sparked international outrage beyond any outrage storm this year. (Hamblin)

Hamblin's argument draws attention away from the actual killing of a lion in Africa and points to the other elements within the network that he believes drove audience response, from the names of the lion and the dentist, to the question of professionalism, to past actions recently brought to light.

Most animals living in safaris do not have names, but because Cecil possessed a name, the lion as a personalized figure helped spread sympathetic and warm feelings among those who read about his demise. Once we name an animal, the animal is rhetorically transformed into a space of potential identification. As Burke wrote, "The mere act of naming an object or situation decrees that it is to be singled out as such-and-such rather than as something other" (*Philosophy of Literary Form* 4). Dumbo is not just an elephant. Bambi is not just a deer. They are something else, some sort of technical image individuals rally around. After all, in December 2019, Aaron Raby paid thirty thousand dollars to kill an elephant in South Africa on a safari, and while there was some media coverage of the killing, the large-scale emotional, personalized identification and outrage that appeared over Cecil's death never materialized. No Facebook groups were formed. No celebrities called for his arrest or death. His work address was not published. The elephant Raby killed did not have a name. Names personalize. From celebrities to everyday users posting online about the lion named Cecil and the dentist who shot him, I identify an initial case study for examining outrage over social media in more detail than my previous brief examples allowed for. In this chapter, I begin with the issue of personalization and move on to broader issues relevant to the technical image and its spreadability within social media.

The killing of the lion, and the anger it evoked, provided Hamblin with a focal point for discussing how outrage spreads in social media. How does one isolated safari killing spread so quickly? Tracking responses to the lion killing, Hamblin surveys social media as a space of "one-upmanship" where one outrage, such as a protected lion's killing by a tourist hunter, triggers another outrage which, in turn, triggers another outrage, and so on until various aggregations of whatever it is an audience is angry about build upon one another into an overwhelming digital anger removed from the moment itself. Such a chain reaction builds off the power of weak ties, as not everybody in this network is aware of one another, but they are aware of the continuing rage spreading across their social spaces. In turn, they help share that rage. Thus, there is another level of personalization occurring than the one I previously mentioned regarding Cecil. When Betty White or Sharon Osbourne become angry, I, too, may be angry despite not knowing either celebrity personally. My declaration can function as proof that I, too, am moral (assuming I believe these two individuals are moral as well). For some, this process is called virtue signaling, the notion that one communicates morality by taking public stances. Morality, as well, serves as a technical image embedded with the celebrities or personalizations viewers identify with. Getting angry about Cecil's killing, in this case, would mean communicating one's morally superior feelings regarding wildlife and safari hunting.

James Bartholomew popularized the term virtue signaling in *The Spectator*, noting its global reach and ability to shape opinion. Bartholomew's critique is that virtue signaling is more about the individual who posts, likes, or comments than the act itself which triggered the response. Public critique, such as that directed toward a dentist on safari, is really about the person issuing the critique and their desire to appear virtuous. "It's noticeable how often virtue signaling consists of saying you hate things. It is camouflage. The emphasis on hate distracts from the fact you are really saying how good you are." To this observation he adds: "Anger and outrage disguise your boastfulness" (Bartholomew). Helen Lewis offers a similar position: "A lot of what happens on Facebook, as with Twitter, is 'virtue signaling'—showing off to your friends about how right on you are." Critiques of virtue signaling adopt this stance.

> Have you changed your Facebook avatar to support a cause? Did you take the ice bucket challenge? Have you ever offered your thoughts and prayers in the aftermath of a disaster? Do you express your beliefs through hashtags? There's actually a name for that: virtue signaling. (Peters)

Virtue and outrage, of course, go hand in hand. An image easily evokes both emotional stances based on how it depicts, in an assumed single spatial representation, some atrocity or problematic event. The reason I'm outraged is that I have a virtuous belief that has been challenged or violated. Personalizing a wild animal can greatly help facilitate this type of digital response when that wild animal is hunted and killed.

As I have outlined with technical images and Barthes's *-icity*, the referent for the outrage (in this case, the lion) is overcome by the viral outrage itself, which aggregates a variety of stereotypes and imagery into a non-referential object, often based on perceptions of virtue. Whether or not each individual sharing the story of Cecil knew its complete details, the mere sharing of the story and the sympathies that followed such sharing provided enough outrage regarding virtue that it was able to communicate outrage further. "The Internet launders outrage and returns it to us as validation, in the form of likes and stars and hearts," Hamblin argues about this process. Hamblin's point reflects what Tony Sampson criticizes as a contagion, a spreadable viral moment often subjected to larger political or social control. "There is an interaction between code and environment," Sampson writes (74). The overall environment surrounding Cecil's death—which I will explore in this chapter—establishes an interaction of reactions and responses that code outrage. "How does individual behavior aggregate to collective behavior?" Duncan Watts asks (24). The Cecil outrage poses a similar question of how one or two individuals angry over a lion's death can be aggregated into a collective anger.

This point regarding the aggregation of collective anger will carry over into other examples. Exposure to the news is one aspect. Exposure to another's anger is another aspect. The algorithms pushing anger over a lion's death to the front of one's Facebook feed, for instance, are not just computer code, but the social environment and cultural code one already participates in. Supporters of Cecil were not suddenly thrust into a new environment of news feeds and public reactions, but were part of this environment and were making meaning out of this environment, whether or not they were cognizant of it.

In an oral environment, one would spread one's anger at work, at home, or in a physical location by telling someone what occurred. On Facebook or Twitter, one shares, likes, retweets or hearts. These actions are viewed by more than one person at a time (and some of these actions can in turn be liked, retweeted, or hearted). Sampson argues that contagions, or viral moments, "are able to route around the collective consciousness and contaminate the consumer, mostly unawares" (76). An audience, in its spreading of outrage, may not be aware of an incident's origin moment or connection to other similar or connected moments. That audience, as well, may not realize its role within the chain of spreading a particular message either; that is, the audience, by posting or retweeting or hearting or simply commenting, spreads the outrage even as it thinks it is only recording a singular reaction. Betty White is angry? I may like that because I like Betty White. My like, in turn, is seen by my followers, and possibly their followers who may not admire Betty White as much as I do, but who appreciate her emphasis on an animal's right to live.

The environment—such as a social media platform, or outrage itself—drives the virality in question. Following Barthes's notion of *-icity*, I call this activity *outragicity*. Outragicity, like Barthes's concerns with an Italian advertisement, is the digital aggregation of a variety of items that produce the feeling or sentiment of outrage because of the aggregation created (and not necessarily because of what has occurred). Digital outragicity, which I focus as the result of the technical image's dominance, is the digital manifestation of outragicity. Outragicity is an -icity of anger. Whatever is aggregated into the moment to cause anger is outragicity. Lions. Dentists. Hunting. Names. Celebrities. Other people's rage. All of these items aggregate within a given response posted online and shared. Outragicity, like any other digital moment, depends on how anger spreads and who spreads it. These types of connections are important within social media.

Central to Hamblin's commentary, as I briefly mentioned, is the notion of ties. Ties connect us online. Ties spread information. Without ties, social media is not effective, and aggregation cannot spread. Drawing on the pre–social media research of Mark Granovetter, the concept of weak ties and strong ties has been used to describe how information spreads across social media platforms depending on the knowledge individuals may or may not have of one another. This work stresses the role of connectivity within social media and other situations that foster interaction. "The strength of a tie," Granovetter states, "is a combination of the amount of time, the emotional intensity, the intimacy (mutual confiding), and the reciprocal services which characterize the tie" (1,361). Emotion, affect, and connectivity play mutual roles in spreading ideas. If one is already concerned with animal rights or feels a connection to someone like Betty White, one will likely respond in a similar way to Cecil's killing. Or if one doesn't want animals to be killed, one posts one's anger regarding an animal's killing. Seeing such a post, I, too, don't want animals killed, so I repost . . . and so on and so on among those who share emotional concerns regarding animal welfare. Strong ties reflect the people one knows best: friends, family, and coworkers. Weak ties reflect people one knows informally or not at all. "Weak ties are more likely to link members of different small groups than are strong ones, which tend to be concentrated within particular groups" (Granovetter 1,376). This logic runs counter to intuition. Wouldn't my close friends be better for linking ideas? We have fewer close friends, though, than we have weak ties (people who are not our close friends).

Paul Adams, former Facebook head of global brand design, argues that the average person has "fewer than ten strong ties, and many have fewer than five" (60). Weak ties—which have been theorized to be approximately 150 people one can maintain some type of relationship with and then 150 people beyond (i.e., Dunbar's Number)—may be more likely to share encountered content because their viewpoints will diversify as their connections become distant from the source. "Weak ties," Adams argues, "are at the periphery of our social network, which means they are connected to more diverse sets of people than our strong ties, which are more central in our network. These diverse ties pass on more novel information, and so they can often know more than our strong ties do" (64). While an initial assumption about "friends" may cause us to believe that strong ties are the best source for spreading messages because they are closest to us, they are not. First of all, our strong ties may simply agree and not spread our ideas. More important, we have fewer strong ties than weak ties. And our weak ties have further ties which indirectly connect to us—as do their weak ties.

No better model appears than that found on social media platforms where one's weak ties—friends one barely knows, if at all—have their own set of weak ties who, in turn, have their own set of weak ties, and so on. Sharing, as a public act often viewable on Facebook and Twitter, allows a great deal of information to spread rapidly among this vast network of weak ties, each of whom can see and spread the original message. "The fewer indirect contacts one has the more encapsulated he will be in terms of knowledge of the world beyond his own friendship circle; thus, bridging weak ties (and the consequent indirect contacts are important in both ways" (Granovetter 1,371). The spreadability of the Cecil moment can be attributed to an actual injustice, but like many viral moments, it is more attributable to the power of weak ties personalizing a relationship with an animal or a celebrity, since many within this network of outrage did not know one another and had never seen the lion. We likely are not close friends with Betty White. These weak ties did not need to know the history of hunting in Africa, the dentist's backstory, or even that Cecil existed. They only needed to have information shared with them and, possibly, they needed to share it as well. "You're no longer sharing life experiences or creating memories with these weak ties," Julie Beck writes, "but as you live your separate lives, you're forever in each other's periphery." Weak ties are attracted to engagement. They fulfill a purpose of social media: to spread and share information that wouldn't have otherwise been seen. That engagement increases with each tie's connection to the next, often without regard to content. "Social networks," Nicholas Christakis and James Fowler write, "tend to magnify whatever they are seeded with" (31). I note this point even if it may contradict further issues regarding technical images, aggregation, and algorithms. While weak ties do not need to know the overall content of a message to spread it, they work in tandem with these other issues to spread outrage. They magnify ideas.

Weak ties do not care about representation or referents. Is one referring to an actual animal in Africa killed on safari when one spreads a hateful post about the dentist who killed Cecil, or is one referring to an ambiguous ideal? Has an association been made with an aggregated profile (the pure animal; the evil dentist)? Ties need not be concerned with actual representations (embedded imagery, as the technical image shows, is not a representation with a referent but a spreadable or projected ideal). They simply share. Their sharing can be based on the emotional sharing of another individual, or it can be based on the relevance of past imagery embedded in the current image accessed. If one comes across a headline or post about a lion killed by a dentist, one is more likely to share that information without really knowing if the lion or dentist even exist or whether the dentist legally or illegally shot the lion. Interconnected users become outraged outside of the assumed referent that may have driven the outrage in the first place. If the Internet "launders" as Hamblin claims, it does so not through its own agency (as if the Internet has agency) but through the repetition and sharing of a moment, idea, or image generated by ties. Repetition hides referentiality at times, or it makes those who spread a message "unaware," as Sampson declares, of what they are spreading in the first place. Was the dentist a bad man? Was the lion unfairly killed (whatever that may signify)? It doesn't matter. We share.

Henry Jenkins referred to the overall process of contagions as "spreadability," the "potential—both technical and cultural—for audiences to share content for their own purposes" (3). Spreadability offers an explanation of circulation online; it recognizes "the importance of the social connections among individuals, connections increasingly made visible (and amplified) by social media platforms" (6). Cecil the Lion spread. But, as Hamblin notes, in that spreading across users and platforms, was the lion as referent present or was it erased among all the sharing, replaced with an aggregated ideology or belief? Did it matter, therefore, whether the response was to a lion, or to anything at all? Were outraged users actually aware of what they were spreading and for what purposes beyond merely being upset? Did they see a lion as central to their sharing, or did they view an aggregation of various images and beliefs that they mistakenly believed represented the lion? Henry Jenkins describes the transfer of narrative over disparate platforms as "transmedia storytelling," a process where TV, film, video games, novels, and other media tell a story, but they do so in ways that require one to engage with all the media employed and not just one strand in order to fully complete the narrative. His example of the movie *The Matrix* argues that to fully understand the futuristic narrative of a dystopian society, viewers must watch the three movies, but they also must play the video games, read the comic books, and so on. The narrative is being played out across a variety of media.

We might read the spreadability of Cecil as a variation of transmedia storytelling, where a narrative—hunter kills lion—occurs not in the place it might be represented (the safari, one newspaper account, an oral retelling, a Facebook post, an angry tweet) but across a variety of social media platforms and individual accounts read as a singular narrative. Viral outrage, too, is a form of transmedia storytelling. Its spreadability occurs over platforms, over representations, over assumed representations, over past imagery, over sharing, and over time. Weak ties create this storytelling. As is often the case with the examples I explore, the narrative created must be read over various platforms and expressions, and even then, it is not necessarily a referential narrative. It is a spreadable one. The spreadability of Cecil is thus attributable more to weak ties than situational knowledge. Weak ties created Cecil as a focal point of outrage. I cannot track and trace every instance of weak ties spreading outrage, but I can work to identify why they may do so. The first challenge for what I am calling digital outragicity, then, is tracing how outrage spreads as media. I treat Cecil as an example of outrage as media (as I will other examples). There exists the real-life instance of a lion killed during a tourist safari. There also exists the ensuing outrage that helps spread further outrage via weak ties and the lion as technical image.

Consider, for a moment, the spreadability of Cecil over other temporal and spatial moments that, no doubt, also deserved such attention. In his analysis of digital outrage, Hamblin interprets the Cecil incident as an aggregation that causes one animal's killing to attract more attention than other timely events. After all, the most important moment of 2015 was not a lion's death. And there is no evidence that Cecil was the only lion to die that year at the hands of wealthy hunters on safari. While it is too easy to accuse angry social media users as hypocritical in their choice of what to be angry about (a lion, for instance, as opposed to half a million dead in the Syrian civil war), I prefer to focus on the issue of aggregation, weak ties, and attention instead of group focus or moral choice of outrage. Through its spreadability, Cecil is no longer a lion but a layered, networked image of various references. Cecil, like Barthes's example of an advertisement for Italian food, is replaced by aggregated Cecil. This aggregation includes: lions (popular representations), the lion's comforting name (Cecil suggests innocence), the profession of his killer (we all hate dentists), celebrities' anger (we like Betty White), and the killer's past (a record of other violations). All of these items juxtapose for readers so that this killing (and no other hunting death or concurrent global event) sparks outrage. Cecil and the dentist are technical images.

The reference point for the killing, as I continue to note, is not just the lion. Dentists, for example, convey a specific, negative meaning to many in American culture. These meanings become culturally embedded through a type of temporal transmedia storytelling where an image is repeated throughout various media (in this case, the dentist as narrative) and builds a specific connotation for viewers. In these media representations that build narrative, dentists are typically evil people who inflict pain. Think of Tim Conway's portrayal of Dr. Keifer on *The Carol Burnett Show*, a bumbling, incompetent dentist who injects himself by accident with Novocaine. Think of Steve Martin's sadist dentist character in *Little Shop of Horrors*. Or think of Laurence Olivier's Nazi character in *Marathon Man*, Dr. Christian Szell, torturing Dustin Hoffman's character, Babe, with a drill to the teeth. Even W. C. Fields' comedic prying of teeth in the 1932 film *The Dentist* portrayed the profession as one of pain and agony. When Jimmy Kimmel attacked Palmer during the monologue of his late night show, he shared an assumed profile of dentists and wealthy men in America that mirrors these representations of the profile we often call "awful dentist": "If you're some shithole dentist who wants a lion's head over the fireplace in his man cave so his douchebag buddies can gather around it and drink scotch and tell him how awesome he is, that's just vomitous" (Kimmel). Nobody likes to go to the dentist, much less a "shithole" dentist. A dentist represents drills, discomfort, a bizarre chair, extractions, tools scraping at one's teeth, pain, and suffering. In this well-circulated mythology, whereas doctors cure us, dentists hurt us. Palmer embodied these representations for viewers reading about his hunt. If he had been a priest or a school teacher, the response may have been different.

Then there is the image of the lion. Lions and other wildlife are killed almost every day in Africa and other countries, for sport, for fun, for food, for protection, and often for no reason at all. In countries like Tanzania, for instance, where Cecil was killed, lions are often hunted for their interference with livestock or for the danger they pose to humans. One *Slate* article estimates that 665 lions on average are killed in trophy hunts each year (Cronin). According to the International Union for the Conservation of Nature and its Resources, approximately six hundred lions are hunted each year by tourists ("Big Game Hunting"). Writing in the *New Yorker*, Kerry Howley observers some of the contradictions that arise when one animal's death generates so much focus while other animals' deaths go unnoticed. For her, Palmer is the real focus, not Cecil: "The lack of interest in the plight of Serengeti lions concurrent with ongoing pro-Cecil protests is hard to square, and suggests that an African animal only interests us for as long as we can focus on something or someone closer to home." Lions, as well, are not the only animals reportedly poached or trophy-hunted in Africa. According to Matt Petronzio, "Lions are only one part of the story. In 2013, poachers killed more than 300 elephants via cyanide poisoning in Hwange National Park, in what was the worst poaching massacre in southern Africa in 25 years. Two years earlier, nine elephants, five lions and two buffalo were poisoned in the same way. This is despite the several anti-poaching efforts the Zimbabwe Parks and Wildlife Management Authority highlights on its website." And according to one Reuters report, local Zimbabweans expressed confusion over the massive uproar created by Cecil's death: "'Are you saying that all this noise is about a dead lion? Lions are killed all the time in this country,' said Tryphina Kaseke, a used-clothes hawker on the streets of Harare. 'What is so special about this one?'" (Dzirutwe). Palmer, if we follow this trajectory, serves as the technical image more than Cecil does. If lions and other wildlife are typically hunted or killed in Africa, Palmer, the dentist, must also be attracting public outrage. No one is focusing on the other individuals who killed lions or what their professions are. Both Cecil and Palmer, however, are technical images. The role each plays in spreading outrage depends on how that image is read by audiences.

Just as the dentist image directs angry focus because of cultural connotations related to going to the dentist, so does a lion direct focus. For instance, alongside the various dentist images circulating in popular imaginaries, some of which I noted, we could list aggregated lion images spread via media that shape audience attention in sympathetic and positive ways: The *Lion King* movie (loveable lions), the *Wizard of Oz*'s Cowardly Lion (a canonical depiction of lion as gentle creature), *Born Free* (orphaned lion cubs raised by humans), canonical hunting images now read as offensive (Teddy Roosevelt standing over a dead African rhinoceros, rifle in hand), and other narratives internalized by a general public into an -icity of lion traits overturned by one specific animal's death. In this particular moment, an audience identifies Cecil's death with a number of factors, situates those factors together as a current reality, and responds with outrage. Cecil must be innocent. Palmer must be guilty. These lion representations we recognize as reality are innocent (no one can hate Simba). Because of the aggregation, such as the one Hamblin outlines, audience outrage in social media environments can be understood as not directly tied to one occurring moment but, instead, as a response to multiple items juxtaposed into one representation, moments real and imagined. These juxtapositions generate identification.

We might consider, then, the Cecil outrage as related to more general moments of aggregated identifications that revolve around social justice issues (such as animal rights, health care, and women's rights). Regarding social justice, and in particular the MeToo movement, for instance, Emily Winderman raises the issue of volume as a rhetorical response to such issues. One form of volume, she argues, is "the amplification and diminishment of affective intensity or sound and the aggregation and dispersion of bodies, interests, and collective energies" (329). The volume of anger expressed, Winderman argues, depends on "a matrix of power relationships" (330). In addition to power relations, this volume, as seen with the Cecil example, also depends on how identification is informed by aggregation. By identification, I mean associating one's self or beliefs with some type of representation, such as a lion, a celebrity, a moment, or a movement. Cecil is a moment of social dissatisfaction: protest over safaris and animal rights. With identification, another prominent space of aggregation where social media launders outrage and produces volume, is the digital projection of social protest.

My brief example of Occupy and Kalle Lasn introduced social protest as a projection of digital outrage. Winderman reminds us that social protest often involves aggregation: "A viral moment like #MeToo's aggregation is documentable in a volume of tweets, messages, images, and corporeal bodies. In other words, volume aggregation argues for the sheer enormity of an issue. An abundance of angry bodies in close digital or physical proximity represents taking up space" (338). Aggregation, as many Internet users know, is the assemblage into one space of often disparate items. Known best as the RSS feed, aggregation within the browser compiles into a single reader publication from a variety of sources. I also understand aggregation as a type of digital response internalized by individuals, in which readers place into one space (i.e., the technical image) multiple readings (e.g., politics, economics, popular culture, war, etc.). As with the Cecil example, with protest, individuals respond to and identify with wrongdoing as the protests move from physical to digital spaces, fostering digital outragicity along the way. In this movement, a number of activities, current and past, become aggregated into the present image (whatever has occurred or is being objected to). I identify with Cecil. Maybe I am Cecil. Maybe I am the same as one of the more public protesters. Maybe I am the same as my friends who protest. This aggregated identification—the lion and the values I associate with its murder—makes me angry within digital proximity.

I AM

Cecil is one example of this process of outrage identification. Identification occurs in numerous outrage spaces, many of which involve moments of injustice or even death. A few other moments aggregated into Cecil's moment might help in this rhetorical breakdown. These, too, are digital outragicity moments that depend on aggregation for identification to occur. The *Charlie Hebdo* massacre of January 2015, in which cartoonists at the satirical magazine were murdered by Islamic extremists, produced a moment of digital outragicity aggregated into a single identifiable sentence whose focus stresses the individual: *I am Charlie*. Those who were angry at the murders posted this simple sentence online, and thus, transformed themselves into the magazine and its victims, not just readers of the magazine (and many of them were not even that, just readers of the news of the murders). The "I am Charlie" proclamations circulated from the physicality of France to online spaces, as those upset over the murders showed solidarity with French grief over these senseless deaths. One could have said: I support Charlie, or I sympathize with Charlie, or these murders should never have occurred, or we need better gun control, or some other type of statement. "I am Charlie," however, suggests an aggregation of my values with those murdered. "I am" is a moment of aggregated identification. By saying "I am," one positions one's self within a larger, spreadable outrage that is accessible, joinable, and repeatable. The murder the following day of four Jewish shoppers in a French kosher supermarket (which was linked with the *Hebdo* killings) was also followed by similar statements of aggregated identity. The proclamation "I am Jewish" (Je Suis Juif) quickly circulated as a response to these deaths, a response aggregated from the *Hebdo* moment as well as from contemporary French anti-Semitism towards its large Jewish population. Declaring "I am Jewish" online and in physical spaces situated protesters within a broader cultural and political narrative of anti-Semitism in France, one with deep historical and contemporary connections. "I am," as an aggregated digital response, generates outrage at the level of identification. This is not too far different from the identification expressed over a lion's killing. One could easily have responded to Cecil's death with the declaration, "I am Cecil."

The "I am" meme is a well-circulated digital response that, too, is an aggregation of outrage; each "I am" aggregates a previous iteration of this phrase in order to make a contemporary declaration. Many protest statements utilize "I am" to aggregate beliefs, and in turn, "I am" spreads across platforms, travelling from one moment of identified outrage to a completely different moment, creating a transmedia experience of identification. Weak ties identify with "I am" and spread the message further. "I am" is a digital response to events, one tied to previous proclamations of identity spread by digital media. As with the *Charlie Hebdo* and kosher supermarket moments, "I am" allows individuals to overcome a sense of anonymity in a socially oriented realm and adopt a unified cultural position. We've seen this gesture previously in other media, such as the anticonsumerist film *Fight Club*. The narrative's focus initially is on anonymity. The faceless, nameless rebellion without a cause spreads quickly among weak ties (men who learn about the movement) who identify with its ambiguity and erasure of identity and join the cause. When Robert Paulson (Meatloaf) is killed in a raid, his anonymity suddenly is replaced by another level of identification, the group chant, "His name is Robert Paulson." The chant aggregates the nameless rebellion into a figure (much as animal preservation might aggregate trophy hunting into one lion). Through social identity, Paulson becomes the rebellion. In France, "I am" allowed everyday residents to become the victims. With Cecil, the visually absent "I am" allows critics to feel present in spirit and to identify as animal rights activists.

Similar to the ways I consider the repeated phrase "I am," Laurie Gries traces the Obama campaign's Hope poster. In her extensive study of circulation, Gries follows the initial Shepard Fairey poster through a variety of iterations, each used for distinct purposes: "Obama Hope has since manifested in many different versions in a variety of media, locations, and genres. Like Mona Lisa, it has also transformed many times over in terms of form and/or function, depending on what associations it enters into" (40). Tying this process to digital culture and algorithmic logics, Gries terms it "disclosure," "a means to shed light on not only a single image's divergent actualizations but also on the divergent meanings that propagate as material consequences of a single multiple image's varied relations" (49). "I am" is an image of identification. Its meanings diverge to temporal or situational moments depending on how or where it is disclosed. With Obama Hope, divergent meanings transform the poster into critique, satire, or further identification, depending on how the poster becomes appropriated and with whom the Obama image is replaced (such as with the images of Mitt Romney, Alfred E. Neuman, and John McCain). With "I am," the divergence focuses on separate moments of group identity, each drawing from a circulated statement whose meaning remains fairly intact. The object of "I am" is replaced each time with an iteration of outrage.

Digital and social media prompt much of this disclosure. In a given protest, "I am" aggregates a number of digital moments within this simple yet powerful phrase. Occupy Wall Street circulated "I am the 99 percent" in order to protest issues of economic power. "Yo Soy 132" aggregated the claim for Mexican Ibero-American University students angry over police brutality in the state of San Salvador Atenco. Trayvon Martin's murder was followed by an "I am" social media campaign featuring photographs of Black social media users wearing hoodies like Martin's, thus demonstrating that they, too, were Trayvon. "I am Liberian" attempted to shift an assumed, biased identification (Liberians equated with Ebola) from its stereotype of a backward African nation to a reality not captured in the public imaginary aggregations of Africans and disease outbreak. So, too, did the "I am Harvard" campaign which challenged aggregated assumptions about race and enrollment at the elite Ivy League school by clarifying Black students' legitimate presence on a campus often viewed as homogenously white. "I am ALS" is a movement to fight the deadly disease. In 2018, protesters outside New York City's office of US Immigration and Customs Enforcement held up signs stating, "I am a Child." In this case, protest identification was with immigrant children held in detention cages along the US southern border. When Donald Trump's administration declared the "Muslim ban" on individuals from specific Islamic countries, protesters held up "I am Muslim too" signs. Sexual assault survivors have held up signs during protests reading "I am" followed by the name of a woman who has been assaulted. Each declaration of "I am" triggers further declarations by those who identify with the given cause. Weak ties spread the aggregation. In these types of digital aggregations, anyone can identify with anyone.

While the "I am" movement of digital aggregation offers various levels of symbolic action or even (in Burkean terms) equipment for living, it also provides an example of the power of social media circulation as each campaign gains traction through digital media platforms where weak ties forge identifications. Why, however, is "I am" so dominant, so sticky, so spreadable? Why not "we are" or "they are" or some other form of generic identification? The repetition of "I am" across disparate issues demonstrates an effectiveness other forms of identification seemingly cannot provide. Its significant repetition demonstrates stickiness and virality. "I am," once visualized in a protest, is a technical image. Within its declaration are embedded previous declarations, whether the speaker/writer knows so or not. These declarations function as the generic "speaker" who persuades a given audience. The declarations have a type of agency. As Burke writes regarding identification: "A speaker persuades an audience by the use of stylistic identifications; his act of persuasion may be for the purpose of causing the audience to identify itself with the speaker's interests; and the speaker draws on identification of interests to establish rapport between himself and his audience" (*A Rhetoric of Motives* 46). In this case, "speaker" indicates the divergent "I am" statements. The statements speak. They act. They engage more than the speaker because of their embedded iterations. These statements establish an identification of various interests ranging from social justice to animal welfare.

The origins of "I am" might be traced to 1968, when Memphis sanitation workers wore sandwich boards proclaiming "I am a man" in order to protest their lack of civil rights and equal pay. "I am a man" presented an enthymemic declaration of identification; viewers needed to fill in the missing pieces of the enthymeme (or the other layered technical image components) as derived from the *Declaration of Independence*, "all men are created equal." Media (e.g., newspapers, television) captured the declaration and projected it outward to 1960s audiences (weak ties) where it gained stickiness and cultural awareness, and to some degree, sympathy. I will return to this point in a later discussion of the enthymeme and outrage. The aggregation of this moment (recognized or not by those who perform the gesture) into contemporary "I am" statements of identification around discrimination and inequity offers additional insight into the technical image—that is, into the moment the image becomes a computation, a processing of a variety of beliefs and ideas outside of the representation itself. "I am" does not emerge out of one murder or one misplaced assumption about race and higher education. "I am" is an aggregation of other "I am" cultural responses regardless of the meme's creator's knowledge of these previous responses, much as the Cecil moment is not about one lion but about other moments viewed within one image. The aggregation reflects what Flusser called "programming." "I am" has spread because within its expression are layers of previous, programmed (like a computer program) usages whose presence provides greater impact than other phrases might.

The influence of "I am" on contemporary public outrage is visible, as well, in the Black Lives Matter movement, which without using this phrase isolates other identification-based phrases and moments that have emerged from discrimination and death. These phrases are meant to elicit group-minded identification. By using the plural "lives," Black Lives Matter suggests a group position. Not one life, but many lives. This position is extended by those embedded phrases and statements that become associated with the movement as well. "I can't breathe," the utterance associated with Eric Garner, who was choked to death by police officers after his arrest for illegally selling cigarettes, translated into t-shirts (Derek Rose, LeBron James, Kobe Bryant, and other athletes wore such shirts before games) and placards stating, "We can't breathe." The "we" of "We can't breathe" suggests a group dynamic beyond the individual's death. If Eric Garner cannot breathe, neither can we. This phrase returned when George Floyd was killed by a Minnesota police officer who placed his knee on the back of Floyd's neck for almost nine minutes, suffocating him. Protests over Floyd's death often included signs and shirts with the phrase "I can't breathe." The phrase "Hands up, don't shoot," spoken by Michael Brown just before he was shot by police officers in Ferguson, Missouri, offers similar moments of identification. Protests and marchers distant from and unconnected to the killing utilized the phrase as an identification with what was perceived as an unlawful shooting. They held up their hands and repeated the phrase as if they were Michael Brown. Michael Brown held up his hands, so will we. All of these phrases relate back to "I am" even if the utterances are made by those who do not realize the connection.

All of these moments, as well, spread from weak tie to weak tie, aggregating each injustice into another injustice's technical image. To paraphrase McLuhan and much of the media ecology movement he contributed to, one does not have to be aware of media and their logics in order to be influenced. Aggregation operates at the level of digital media logic, and a particular identification aggregation allows for these various social media moments. The process can be identified in a mimetic repetition of "I am" statements that, digitally reproduced, become associated with social protest (as was the initial 1968 "I am a Man" enthymeme). Or these moments become aggregated into the other level of Barthes's analysis: the notion of -icity. Protesticity or Identificationicity owe their existence to aggregations of previous iterations.

In other words, I identify with those who oppose safari hunting; therefore, I am against Cecil's death. I identify with a murdered cartoonist; therefore, I am Charlie. Identificationicity functions as one level of -icity signified by the repetitive aggregation of "I am." Identificationicity funnels outrage into a group dynamic whether or not we are in the group. I don't have to know or even visualize Cecil or Charlie or Eric Garner or Michael Brown. I don't need a referent for -icity to occur. Outragicity is another level of this process: the feeling or sentiment of outrage over something outside of referentiality. These iterations of -icity are based on various levels of conscious and unconscious aggregations ("I am," a lion's death, a massacre, economic inequality, a wrongful killing, racial discrimination). A Facebook profile functions as a type of Identificationicity. Going online and calling for a dentist's death is a type of identificationicity. So is the changing of one's profile as identification with political causes such as marriage equality or even the *Hebdo* massacre.

Consider the 2013 and 2015 marriage equality profile changes on Facebook, officially called "Let's Celebrate Pride." In 2013, in response to public debates regarding marriage equality, users changed their profile pictures to display an equality sign, and in 2015 users set their profile pictures to rainbows. Both alterations allowed the platform's users to express identification with equal rights for those denied access to civil marriage. Users aggregated the issues relevant to marriage equality, including the rainbow symbol associated with LGBTQ culture as well as a belief in marriage equality, and expressed a sense of identification by temporarily changing their profile image to blend already held ideologies with the symbol of the rainbow. Changing one's Facebook profile—even temporarily—is the same as declaring "I am." My reasoning for changing my profile—or declaring that I am Charlie—can stem from both the aggregation of my beliefs and the "I am" marker, as well as the weak tie interactions I am engaging with online (when you identify, so do I). As I have argued, weak ties assist in spreading this identification. Weak ties, as well, are aggregations, collections of visible and invisible social media friends and followers whose behavior influences us (and whom we, via our digital moments, influence). Weak tie aggregation is called social proof. We can also, then, consider the role of social proof in outrage's ability to spread.

SOCIAL PROOF

Social proof is the process in which individuals appropriate or copy others' behaviors in order to either maintain identification with the group or to avoid being categorized as acting against the group's interests. "The principle states," Robert Cialdini writes, "that we determine what is correct by finding out what other people think is correct" (110). He adds, "Apparently the principle of social proof works best when the proof is provided by the actions of many other people" (113). This process can be applicable to branding and consumption (I see others drink a soda; I want to drink that soda, too, so I share a picture of me drinking the soda; someone else sees me drinking the soda, and the process repeats), but it also affects political belief and the projection of that belief onto others. When I view celebrities denouncing the Cecil killing, for instance, I, too, may want to voice outrage so that my social media friends recognize me as sympathetic to just causes and not as indifferent or even supportive of someone like Palmer. This desire reflects social proof. I am copying behavior in order to identify. Social proof and virtue signaling can be related; one might advocate a public moral position based on how others do similarly and to project one's own morality. Jonah Berger writes, "We assume that if other people are doing something, it must be a good idea. They probably know something we don't"

(128). If other people I know support marriage equality, I should probably be supporting marriage equality, too. And if people I don't know support marriage equality and change their Facebook profiles, I probably should, too, so that I am not viewed as opposing this political gesture or as being on the incorrect side of an important issue. If other people are afraid of death panels supported by a health care proposal, I should probably be, too. After all, either the group is correct, or I am weary of being viewed as opposing the group. Cialdini describes this aspect of social proof as one based on affinity. "There is another important working condition: similarity. The principle of social proof operates most powerfully when we are observing the behavior of people just like us" (133).

Influence, too, spreads among social ties even if it is not changing a political reality. Writing in the *Washington Post*, Caitlin Dewy asked of the marriage equality profile change, "One big question remains: Does changing your profile picture ever *actually* transform anything?" Cultural change, she concedes, often does not occur when profiles are altered. Court decisions and public behavior are unaffected by profile changes. Declaring "I am" or succumbing to social proof, on the other hand, may never intend to change cultural norms. Instead, the overall purpose of declaring "I am" or changing a profile for one's Facebook friends is to reinforce one's group affinity. Changing our profiles or expressing likeminded anger extends a positive relationship with a given group and confirms our affinity with the group. Social media demands affinity, or it cannot function. Social media does not need to be prescriptive ("buy this," "believe this") when it offers affinity as a persuasive tactic. In fact, affinity is often more persuasive than prescriptive discourse. Caitlin Dewey draws attention to affinity and profile picture changes: "Profile pictures, arguably, are a very particular and effective type of message. They don't dictate how you should or must behave, as laws and PSAs typically do; instead, they simply tell you how your peers are behaving. In other words, they support marriage equality; why don't you?"

As persuasion, social proof is often more effective than directly telling someone what to believe or do because its social influence depends on users filling in the gaps of ethos (if you are correct to do X, I want to be correct too). Social proof is enthymemic. The Cecil/Palmer details I brought up earlier are not present in the headline regarding the lion's death. They are details I and others fill in depending on our past exposure to these details. Paul Adams does not view social proof as a conscious act dependent on awareness: "Not all social proof is conscious. As much research shows, we are also subconsciously influenced by the actions of others. We often change our behavior based on what people are doing around us, but don't realize that we're being influenced" (86). Without awareness, some may follow others' behavior because of how they subconsciously fill in the gaps (somewhere in my subconscious I may be thinking of the *Lion King*, for instance, or images of evil dentists). Social proof can function in openly persuasive ways, such as encouraging platform users to change their profile. It also occurs, however, through posts and likes, which offer suggestions for behavior change based on various assumptions. Many of those who were angry at Cecil the Lion's death also were responding to the barrage of anger that preceded theirs. In that shared, spreadable anger is identification. After all, if Betty White hates the dentist, why would I not also express my hatred for the dentist? I don't necessarily want to be Betty White, but I likely want to be on Betty White's side or, at least, the side my network of friends embrace, and they seem to indicate a preference for Betty White because they fill in details of Betty White's image that suggest her to be a friendly, sympathetic, and admirable public figure. To be on her side, however, I need to make sure that the group has taken the appropriate stand for me to replicate (thus, social proof). Bogdan State and Lada Adamic's research on the 2013 Facebook equality sign profile change demonstrated that "Most individuals need to observe several of their friends taking the action before social proof is sufficient to justify deciding to engage in the action themselves. This could be the result of effort (downloading the photo, and then re-uploading it takes several steps relative to a single click reshare), but also uncertainty about the meaning, importance and popularity of the initiative" (1,748).

I include this discussion regarding social proof because it speaks to the power of ties, aggregation, embedded imagery and identification that I have been tracing as central for generating digital outragicity. "I am" is a form of social proof. It mimics previous iterations in order to persuade by resemblance, and those who adapt it do so consciously or subconsciously because of its previous social justice iterations that encourage affinity. When uncertain about meaning, we can turn to social proof for confirmation that an act is just or wrong. When we do so, we also can engage with assumptions regarding what may be embedded in a given circulated image. Cialdini indicates that this gesture is problematic because it can be based on inaccuracy:

> There are two types of situations in which incorrect data cause the principle of social proof to give us poor counsel. The first occurs when the social evidence has been purposely falsified. Invariable these situations are manufactured by exploiters intent on creating the *impression*—reality be damned—that a multitude is performing the way the exploiters want us to perform. (149)
>
> [. . .] When we are uncertain, we are willing to place an enormous amount of trust in the collective knowledge of the crowd. Second quite frequently, the crowd is mistaken because its members are not acting on the basis of any superior information but are reacting, themselves, to the principle of social proof. (153)

An impression, often posed as immediacy, spreads via social proof (the need for affinity or to identify with others) and not always because of accuracy. This point is vital toward understanding digital outrage and the roles of aggregation and technical images. Most of my following examples will focus more on the imagery circulated than the ties spreading that imagery. Ties are essential, of course, to this process, but I want to begin to explore the overall power of technical images as circulated and embedded moments beyond the sharing enacted by ties. My examples will also focus on immediate impressions that are not entirely accurate because of how the technical images I describe rely on a variety of information, falsified or not. The question of how imagery is programmed is connected to Cialdini's point regarding "manufactured" impressions. As I noted in this chapter, the Cecil example is one type of technical image related to protest. In the next chapter, I provide a more detailed example of social protest and the technical image, one involving a well-circulated photograph of a campus police officer pepper-spraying students.

Five

Photographic Outrage

On November 18, 2011, during the early days of the Occupy movement, University of California Davis students gathered on the campus to protest a tuition hike and align themselves with Occupy. This was not the first such occurrence. Two years earlier, students at the University of California at Berkeley had expressed similar anger over tuition hikes and took over a campus building in protest. A description of that earlier event, published in "After the Fall, Communiqués from California," described the conflict as one between students and police, not students and university policy: "To turn the campus into a militarized warzone was the choice of the administration and the police; but it was also an implicit taunt, a challenge from which students and workers refused to back down, making it obvious that they would not allow the occupiers to be spirited away to jail in handcuffs without a potentially explosive confrontation." The Berkeley protest focused on emotionally charged issues that would be present at the Davis event and become mainstay beliefs within the Occupy movement. A lack of jobs for graduates. Insufficient educational preparation. Debt. These items aggregated into the protest in question.

These items, as I noted in an earlier chapter, are the aggregated basis of a great deal of social protest, from *Network* to Rush Limbaugh. As noted in "After the Fall," "The crisis of the university remains connected to a much larger crisis of employment and, in turn, a crisis of capitalism that permits of no viable solution. In other words, the jobs for which the university ostensibly prepares its students no longer exist, even as they are asked to pony up more and more money for a devalued diploma." Protest depends greatly on commonplaces and stereotypes. In a physical moment of anger, the stereotypes might be expressed via such commonplaces as "battle" or "explosive confrontation." Or, in order to generate believers in the cause who can identify with the issue, they might be expressed as other circulated commonplaces such as "financial exploitation" or "inequity." Calling these terms stereotypes does not mean that they do not reflect a reality. It simply means that, as aggregated profiles of a term or idea, they are easy fallback gestures for generating protest or for aggregating dissent. The Davis moment was no different from the Berkeley one. It followed a similar protest at the Berkeley campus on November 9. At that protest, police officers in riot gear had beaten back gathered students who chanted, "the whole world is watching" ("Occupy Cal"). During the Davis protest, Lieutenant John Pike pepper-sprayed kneeling protesters who were blocking a walkway. The digital photograph of this incident is the focus of this chapter. Physical anger, in this case, yielded to digital outrage because of a photograph.

At the heart of digital outragicity is the question regarding how one reads a given moment, image, event, headline, or text. How do we read such items? What is the methodology for doing so in the digital age? When we read digitally, are we reading a singular or an embedded representation? John Delicath and Kevin Deluca offer the term "image event" as one possible response to such questions. An image event, as it is disseminated by mass media, they argue, consists of fragments: "We suggest that image events are an argumentative form characterized by fragmentation. Image events communicate not arguments, but argumentative fragments in the form of unstated propositions, indirect and incomplete claims, visual refutation, and implied alternatives" (322). Readers of the image, in turn, construct meaning out of these fragments. The image event is enthymemic. It asks readers to fill in the gaps among the fragmented pieces they are exposed to as they attempt to read a coherent or argumentative message. The image event also prompts my interest in the John Pike photograph. Is this image a fragment among other fragments? Is this an image of police brutality, as one narrative will declare, or is it a fragment among other possible narratives?

Reading has long been a rhetorical practice; rhetorical analysis reveals the discursive features found in various texts and speeches that are, in general, necessary for conveying meaning. At times, rhetorical scholarship has relied upon interpretation or hermeneutics to "read" imagery or texts. As Michael Leff argues, "We might say that all interpretative work involves participation in a rhetorical exchange, and every rhetorical exchange involves some interpretative work" (99). Through critical reading, an image, moment, text, or event, some scholarship dictates, means something different than its initial representation. We decode in order to discover what that meaning might be. In addition to identifying rhetorical features of a text, decoding representations opens up awareness to other issues, problems, concepts, and concerns not initially obvious to the reader of a text or image. So far, I have not interpreted digital outrage as much as traced out some factors that contribute to outrage, notably the question of technical images and aggregation, and the role social media plays in outrage's circulation. One might consider these digital concepts to be related to the overall notion of digital rhetoric. Digital rhetoric considers traditional rhetorical concerns from a digital perspective (as generic as that definition may be). This may or may not include interpretation. "A theory of digital rhetoric that recognizes how the traditional rhetoric of persuasion is being transformed in digital spaces," James Zappen offers, opens up new questions for rhetorical theory in general (324). Social media, one might assume, belongs within such a query. Outrage, too, should belong since it dominates so much of social media discourse, but both are often absent outside of metacritique. By directing some attention to the digital rhetoric and public readings of circulated imagery, this chapter raises another issue relevant to social media and outrage: *the digital reading* of a well-circulated protest image. To explore that reading, I first turn to some additional methodological insight not often utilized when addressing digital outrage.

Following my earlier discussion of identity, outrage, and Occupy, this chapter explores a particular Occupy-centric image. How does rhetorical theory approach understanding textual and visual meaning online? Is there a way to read a digital image that complements what I've explored via the technical image? Typically, as with other scholarly pursuits, rhetorical theory works to uncover knowledge and cultural meaning via analysis. "The most complicated relationship between the photographic image and public opinion occurs because images communicate social knowledge," Robert Hariman and John Lucaites write in their study of iconic photography (10). Social knowledge, though, is itself complex and often yields to a generalized notion of "understanding" what something means, or what Sid Dobrin calls in a different context "the will to stability" dominant in rhetoric and composition studies (77). Hariman and Lucaites also argue that "Iconic photographs influence public opinion because, like all photojournalistic images, they are storehouses of the classifications, economics, wisdom, and gestural artistry that make up social interaction. Icons draw on this knowledge to create a web of social connections that lead to and from the historical event and provide multiple paths for both identification and criticism" (10). The John Pike photograph is, I argue, iconic. A police confrontation on a California university campus could, therefore, allow for a critical reading of social protest and digital imagery when captured in a photograph. As this chapter will argue, such a reading can reveal social connections (via the technical image) unless we apply only critique to that reading. As Brad Vivian writes, "Images evince virtual (or non-representational) functions by literally producing visual realities, including the modes of perception, visual practices, viewing subjects and forms of affect that comprise them" ("In the Regard" 479). The goal, then, of reading a photograph such as the one I begin with does not have to be rhetorical criticism. The goal may be to consider the realities Vivian foregrounds. Indeed, this is a point Flusser made about technical images in general.

Social media and circulated visual moments often attract critique as a primary reaction. Viewers read an assumed rhetoric of the image and offer criticism or critique in response. Cecil's killing resulted in immediate critique. John Pike's photograph, as we will see, did as well. I am trying to work through images and outrage differently. When I explored the killing of Cecil the Lion and the immediate outrage that followed, I focused not on an interpretative moment but rather a circulated one that repeated past imagery (a dentist is evil; a lion is gentle and loving). The public voices concerned with the lion's death focused on the interpretative: that is, when I hear that a safari lion was killed, I conclude that an evil man did the killing. From that, critics can generalize to other interpretive moments folded into issues related to hunting, the continuation of colonial practices in Africa, or the arrogance of the West—what we might call social knowledge. Often in rhetorical or media criticism, hermeneutics focus on textual interpretation (what does this digital artifact mean?) in order to reveal what has been hidden from immediate perception (for example, a lion's death might reveal larger issues regarding colonialism).

For instance, Shiva Vaidhyanathan and Alex Halavais treat Google and related search engines as texts they have decoded and interpreted, so that what appears natural (a search engine most of us use on a daily basis to find both banal and serious information) is, in fact, shown to reveal a greater meaning (a body of control that prevents search or allows it to occur). When Vaidhyanathan warns of Google's impending hegemony (as he later does with Facebook), he repeats a traditional form of critique: Whereas we thought X was innocent, it is really coded. Such is Johanna Drucker's claim when she argues, "So naturalized are the Google maps and bar charts generated from spread sheets that they pass as unquestioned representations of 'what is'" (Drucker). Naturalization has long been the enemy of hermeneutics. The job of hermeneutics is to show that nothing is natural. Everything is a construction. A lion is not simply killed. A police officer pepper-spraying kneeling students is not natural. Or is it? The outrage I will explore, despite a more common methodology of revealing, suggests otherwise.

This method of showing "what is," popularized by canonical texts such as Stuart Hall's "Encoding, Decoding," reveals covered histories that "natural" representations hide. Long before digital rhetoric, James Berlin championed such an approach to teaching and scholarship, writing that "all experience is situated within signifying practices and that learning to understand personal and social experience involves acts of discourse production and interpretation, the two acting reciprocally in reading and writing codes" (139). Thus, with digital work, such as an image, one might show coded meanings in various digital texts so that experience is better understood. Why do people become outraged online? Criticism uncovers myths (in the Barthesian sense) as they are located in the digital experience by turning to computer topics. Facebook is a way to connect people. Google will never be evil. These, the logic claims, are myths we must take apart. We take apart the myth by interpreting it (which is counter to what Barthes calls for). But does interpretation block our ability to examine a well-circulated photograph and determine what, as depicted in the photograph, took place? What did John Pike do and why do we believe he did it? Can his image be interpreted so easily? What about the image as a technical image?

ALGORITHMIC READING

One way to read a digital image is to do so algorithmically. Algorithms, some critics contend, reveal what representation often hides. Johanna Drucker writes: "Nothing in intellectual life is self-evident or self-identical, nothing in cultural life is mere fact, and nothing in the phenomenal world gives rise to a record or representation except through constructed expressions." The online journal *Culture Machine*'s 2011 issue focuses on interpreting digital texts similarly. In one essay, David Perry summarizes the project accordingly, asking for a practice that "might be called the digital 'folding' of reality, whereby one is able to approach culture in a radically new way" (n.p.). In this folding of a supposed reality (whereas one deconstructs a given myth), issues of representation and mediation mean the scanning of documents and the interpretation of those documents in digital environments, what Matthew Kirschenbaum identifies as projects such as the Text Encoding Initiative, the Shakespeare Quartos Archive, and the Preserving Virtual Worlds Project (56). In some cases, this scanning identifies intertextual or generic patterns across representations, such as a period, an author's work, or a literary movement (as in Perry's example of the data mining of Gertrude Stein's *The Making of Americans*), in order to better understand an author's repetition of words or stylistic choices.[1] As Katherine Hayles writes, "Once patterns can be discerned, the work of interpretation can begin" (51). Pattern formation indicates algorithmic presence.

Stephen Ramsey, whose algorithmic criticism searches for a hermeneutics verified through data mining rather than induced through speculation, embraces such an approach as a quintessential critical endeavor. Ramsey argues for tools that identify interpretative patterns. "Tools that can adjudicate the hermeneutical parameters of human reading experiences—tools that can tell you whether an interpretation is permissible—stretch considerably beyond the most ambitious fantasies of artificial intelligence" (10). Ramsey is concerned that algorithms are viewed with distrust, treated as "mere amusements" that are "unrelated to the practices of conventional critical reading" (38). By mining texts with computer algorithms, Ramsey advocates, critique can identify patterns not initially visible. In this case, data is not embedded, as it is with technical images, but instead resides on the surface where professional critics can utilize software to extract meaning that the naked eye (or mind) cannot. Pattern is more useful than layering. Perry writes that "pattern and narrative are useful analytic terms that enable us to see the way in which the computational turn is changing the nature of knowledge in the university and, with it, the kind of computational subject that the university is beginning to produce" (14). Patterns, identified in data mining algorithm operations, can reveal historical precedent or tradition. But what types of tradition?

The computational subject produced by text and data mining allows Ramsey to offer up algorithmic criticisms, such as the claim that Sinclair Lewis has a stronger "vocabulary richness" than William Faulkner (71–72) or that a character who is an authorial insertion of Virginia Woolf is the only character in the novel to speak of "England" (12). Software makes these points visible, though why they need to be visible is debatable. The computational subject produced by text and data mining also allows scholars like historian Dan Cohen the ability to "search for new interpretations" via computer-generated patterns that represent unknown phenomena. Cohen describes one graphic visualization of a data-mined Victorian literary period: "The frequency chart of books with the word 'revolution' in the title, for example, shows spikes where it should, around the French Revolution and the revolutions of 1848. (Keen-eyed observers will also note spikes for a minor, failed revolt in England in 1817 and the successful 1830 revolution in France.)"[2] Algorithms drove these observations out of the surface where they were hidden in plain sight. The knowledge these algorithmic gestures make, however, is disciplinarily limited. Identifying how many times the word "revolution" was written over several decades does not necessarily reveal invisible belief or ideology. It reveals word choice.

Most of these examples of scholarship treat data mining or algorithmic query as activities meant to reimagine artistic interpretation and not as responses to public reception. For whatever reason, the interpretation of an artistic text should be reread and reconsidered as if there are always secrets hiding beneath well-circulated interpretations. Emphasizing this focus on hermeneutics of literary or historical works, Frederica Frabetti concludes her *Culture Machine* introductory essay by arguing not only for algorithms that do such work, but for a digital response to the political. "If academic labour must resist instrumentality in order to remain political, then the digital humanities become an ideal place for a persistent critique of all instrumental modes of thinking" (17). Interpretation, Frabetti tells us, serves as a response to not just the literary or historical, but also to the political, where instrumental thought dominates, whether in a campus protest or elsewhere. Interpretation is not, supposedly, instrumental even though it repeats an institutional (and thus, instrumental) practice found offline (in literary, rhetorical, or cultural analysis). Even as I disagree with this assessment of interpretation as not being instrumental reasoning, Frabetti's framing of the digital as a space for political thought—as opposed to only a cultural or textual data mining project—offers me a context for continuing my exploration of outrage. The political can be data mined. The instrumental readings of the political, however, may obfuscate why a political act angers. This fairly lengthy overview is presented to show affinity between digital readings and algorithmic readings and to offer another exploration of digital outrage. This attention, however, is limited in its ability to differentiate between the artistic text—the novel, for example—and the political, which I will discuss using a campus protest example. While a novel can be data mined for patterns using computer software capable of noting how many times a specific word was used or how many times a character wore a certain article of clothing, how can a political photograph that generates considerable outrage be data mined when it appears to show a singular event? How can that mining reveal some understanding regarding a public's reaction to the photograph? I want to data mine the photograph that caused outrage. I borrow the concepts of data mining and algorithmic pattern thinking, but I change the objective from interpretation to something I have not yet discovered.

A PHOTOGRAPH

When a November 18, 2011, photograph of John Pike pepper-spraying University of California Davis students engaged in an Occupy protest circulated across the Internet, interpretation generated a great deal of outrage. The Occupy movement, which I described in earlier chapters, has been photographed and reported on by various media outlets since its inception. Occupy relies on social media to spread its message. Occupy is also a digital moment because of how it is largely informed by a specific digital and media logic: advertising. *New Yorker* reporter Mattathias Schwartz traces the Occupy movement to the media logic of advertising, as I earlier noted, through how it is embodied in the work of Adbusters founder Kalle Lasn. Adbusters has earned recognition for appropriating the digital logic of advertising and, through such logic, altering photographs to critique consumer habits and expose myths (such as those related to fast food consumption or capital investment) as coded representations that need to be decoded so that consumers become more critical about their habits. Adbusters was built on the logic of outrage. Outrage at consumption. Outrage at capitalism. Outrage at advertising. Outrage at politics. As Lasn writes in *Cultural Jam*, "The reality presented to us by the media always has a spin on it. Ads stretch the truth, news bites give only part of the story, and White House press releases are carefully tailored to make the president look good. We are constantly being hyped, suckered and lied to" (24). Anger is the response to government lying. So is suggestion. To overcome these lies and coded realities, Lasn tells us, persuasion must take the form of suggestion; suggestion "corrupts" previously held beliefs and feelings and allows an outlet for pent-up outrage. "Once an emotion is corrupted," he writes, "it can never be uncorrupted" (46).

Prior to Lasn, Stewart Ewen outlined the history of advertising, to which Lasn's Adbusters belongs, as one of suggestion as well. By the 1920s, American businessmen, Ewen writes, quoting Earnest Calkins, "were fast becoming attuned to the psychological utility of images, with their ability to 'suggest' more than simply to 'show,' and their capacity to 'strike out in new and unknown worlds of imagination'" (xxx). Advertisers, under these terms, corrupt emotions, much as Lasn's group—the anti-advertiser—does by offering incomplete messages that suggest. Lasn calls the process of corrupting emotions "leverage points," the moments when one "sees the situation in a novel way" in order to reverse the coded message (131). Suggestion is meant to reverse a coded message. It persuades by demythologizing. It does so, of course, by tapping into the immediacy emotions need.

By suggesting corruption, police brutality, an incompetent president, or a social injustice through the use of expected commonplaces (much as an ad can sell "Italian" food), one can push the needed leverage points meant to evoke outrage. Adbusters and Occupy are not meant to relieve outrage but are designed to perpetuate it by playing off of these leverage points. Inequity, for instance, is a highly emotional concept. Suggesting its existence by holding up 99 percent placards, as I noted earlier, was meant to function as a leverage point in which individuals reversed the accepted, but coded, message of American equality by drawing attention to themselves as photographed evidence that American equality is a myth (a fantasy that "we live in an economically just society where working hard leads to financial success"). A reader of the held-up placard immediately interprets its meaning as injustice. Photographs, and visuality in general, are ideal spaces for evocation. We look at an image. We respond. We respond to whatever the image suggests. In that response, we claim interpretation. A series of images attesting to income inequality was highly powerful for what it suggested (the person's plight) not for what it detailed (the individual's overall story separate from the repetitive "I am the 99 percent" image). One could data mine the series of images that made up this chain of outrage, but one would likely find the leverage point over all other available patterns: inequity. Occupy does not make its message difficult to understand.

The specific photograph I refer to in this chapter, the emotion-driven photograph taken by an Associated Press photographer at the UC Davis rally, quickly caught the public's attention for both its sense of brutality (innocent protestors pepper-sprayed in the face for no reason) and its digital-influenced parody that later followed. The photograph was Photoshopped into a variety of images and disseminated over the Internet as a meme: Pike pepper-spraying Pink Floyd's Dark Side of the Moon logo, Pike pepper-spraying a George Seurat painting, Pike pepper-spraying Little Sparkle Pony, and so on. The image of pepper-spraying at a nonviolent demonstration acted upon a collective leverage point that associated Pike with a history of police oppression. Readers of the image attempted to reverse its coded message via its assumed, critical oppositions ("police do not protect against but rather enforce oppression").

Following Frabetti, a digital-styled reading of this photograph could prompt a non-instrumentalist reading of a problematic campus response to protest. But how could that occur? An image, unlike a novel, cannot be data mined with software to tell a visible or invisible story where a word or idea is repeated across texts or time periods. Indeed, the image was never treated to such algorithmic tactics. Its meaning was read like a headline; it obviously depicted what it showed. Its interpretation rested at face value; what exists in the image can be mined for meaning. From that obvious depiction, a viewer would expect to be angry since the suggestion is that the police are out of control (which, embedded with the later Black Lives Matter movement, resonates as a strong, repeated trope). Early reporting of the incident focused on a variety of suggestions, but one was of Pike's supposed demeanor. His demeanor drove some of the initial critique as it was data mined for its supposed reflection on his actions. Notice, for instance, the way Mary-Elizabeth Williams describes the incident in *Salon*: "The gung-ho Pike, it should be noted, was swiftly joined by several of his similarly pepper-spray-happy cohorts. But it was the image of him and his confident, casual, almost bored delivery of a torrent of orange that ignited outrage—and then, inevitably, parody." Pike is "gung-ho," "confident," "happy," "casual," even "bored." Such commonplaces transform Pike into an emotionless tool of the apparatus who doesn't care about the harm he causes (much as a dentist might not care about inflicting pain on a patient).

If this type of reading is data mining the photograph, it is not doing so based on the presented representation since none of these items exist in the image. Williams interprets from a suggestion. Williams is not alone in her reading. Nick Carbone, too, described the image as "casual." "Images of the cop casually pepper-spraying protesters have gone viral." Jack Stripling used the same term when he wrote about the incident: "Lt. John Pike, who became the face of the incident when video of him casually dousing students with pepper spray went viral, had no clearly defined role in the operations plan" ("Scathing"). Casual is one type of affective stance; it is an indifference to an occurring brutality. Casual against the backdrop of pepper-spraying can evoke outrage from an audience that expects Pike and his colleagues to care about the population they protect. James Fallows called the incident "affectless sadism." Allison Kilkenny described Pike as acting "nonchalantly." NPR also described Pike as a "Casually Pepper Spraying Cop" (Memmott).

These readings, as I present them, could reflect a data mining–inspired inquiry, but I think of them instead as a circulation of a commonplace applied to influence. Clearly, these are journalists and not rhetoricians writing. The readings perform a response, one likely based not on the image itself (How does Pike look casual? Can we see beneath his helmet? What are the stereotypical markers of being casual? What does this pattern reveal about police confronting protesters?) but instead on a previous perception regarding police brutality and indifference—a technical image. Still, the digital nature of the image encourages a more "mined" approach that gets at the various algorithms possibly within this image or what I just named as a previous perception. These responses demonstrate that it is useful to treat the Pike image as a technical image.

This photo offers a space to continue examining digital outragicity, but not because of the sense of moral outrage evoked as pressure is put on a leverage point regarding public protest. Instead, I want to consider the tropes or commonplaces or even stereotypes that solicit reaction. This photo also evokes outrage identified as "police brutality," or the suppression of "free speech and peaceful assembly," as one UC Davis assistant professor and protest participant blogged (Brown). Whether or not that activity occurred (and I am not arguing that it did not occur), these types of phrases are drawn upon in an aggregated manner. The phrases lead to suggestion because one *expects* these acts during a protest. The photograph, like all photographs taken in the name of a given political moment, suggests. When the photograph acts upon a leverage point such as the suggestion of police brutality, it suggests an act that may or may not have occurred. The photograph does not tell its audience what actually happened prior to and following the moment it was taken. The photograph does not even show what happened in the moment (we see pepper-spraying occurring, but we do not know who the pepper spray hits, how it hits, if it hits, who is hurt, why the spraying occurs, etc.). The photograph, instead, suggests what happened.

Suggestion demands audiences fill in the details on their own. Suggestion is enthymemic. It depends on assumed premises and a conclusion supplied by a reader/viewer. Unlike Lasn's argument for suggestion as a critical tool that demythologizes, the suggestion I encounter foregrounds a network of meanings not present in the image, meanings that do not necessarily critique nor defend Pike's actions until a given audience interprets them or data mines the image. The network of forces embedded in the photograph—which I will explain shortly—come together to generate meaning and enable this suggestion. Those forces are pronounced in digital environments where the photograph circulated and where response largely occurred.

Suggestion, as an enthymematic enterprise, is the focus of the response to this or any similar photograph (and has long been central to Lasn's work with Adbusters which suggests corporate evil through remixed imagery). As John Gage writes regarding the enthymeme, "How does what I *do* say to make my point dependent on my unstated assumption of what my audience already knows or thinks" (39). Audiences make assumptions based on what is not present in the representation as much as on what is present. A police officer pepper-sprays a crowd of kneeling protesters. We assume something awful has just occurred because of assumptions that quickly come to mind and that are likely based on terms that function as leverage points, or on our knowledge of similar past events. Our leverage points, as well, might be based on a well-circulated dichotomy of innocent student vs. oppressive police officer. This dichotomy is internalized so that we will in the blanks accordingly, as enthymemes require.

Jeffrey Walker writes, "The enthymeme is a strategic, kairotic, argumentational turn that exploits a cluster of emotively charged, value-laden oppositions made available (usually) by an exetastic buildup, in order to generate in its audience a passional identification with or adherence to a particular stance, and that (ideally) will strike the audience as an *abrupt* and decisive flash of insight" ("Body of Persuasion" 53). Such is the case with political photography in general, or what Lawrence Prelli calls "rhetorics of display," "situated resolutions of the dynamic between revealing and concealing" (2). Historically, many political photographs function as rhetorics of display. They reveal and conceal. Canonical examples which have generated outrage include the photograph of a child running from a napalm attack in Vietnam and one of a female soldier pointing her fingers at an Iraqi prisoner whose face is covered by a bag. The information of the image—the way the image is coded—quickly is reduced by an audience's networks of assumptions to a suggestion because of what the image reveals as well as what it conceals (abuse, war, torture, abuse of power, etc.). Often, the photograph is assumed to be natural and not coded (we assume, rightly or wrongly, the female soldier should be condemned despite not knowing what came before or after the image).

Cara Finnigan calls this assumption of naturalness regarding whatever is revealed or concealed "the naturalistic enthymeme." She draws attention to assumptions regarding photography. Focusing on early 1930s photography that claim documentary status, Finnigan calls the naturalistic enthymeme the assumption that photographs "are 'true' or 'real' until we are given reason to doubt them" (135). Photographs, Finnigan argues, "may be considered to be visual arguments insomuch as they embody the possibility of the naturalistic enthymeme. That is, regardless of what else a photograph communicates, at minimum it is continually making an argument about its own realism" (143). This realism, I add, is based on suggestion—what the image suggests as well as what the viewer suggests upon reading the image. The enthymemic meaning the image's suggestion provides derives from "a 'web' or network of emotively significant ideas and *liaisons* that may or may not appear as a structure of value-laden oppositions" ("Body of Persuasion" 55). The suggestion in the pepper spray photo, for most audiences, is brutality and oppression; this suggestion challenges more accepted commonplaces, like protection, associated with law enforcement. Our emotively significant liaison draws a distinction regarding what we assume should be (police protection) and what we believe we are seeing in opposition (police brutality).

Such is how the image is interpreted when it is received in a variety of digital moments: on websites, in video commentary, on blog posts, in Facebook status updates, and so on. This type of suggestion supplies a digital-styled approach, such as that associated with visual rhetoric, with means toward critiquing or interpreting. Once I see the image, in other words, I understand its visuality because I have immediately interpreted it based on whatever data I believe I have aggregated: previous emotional conceptions, looking at the image, seeing it critiqued on a blog, retweeting it as a meme, watching others condemn it online, seeing it remixed into parody, offering my own response. These social media-based experiences, as well, function as data mining activities since my interpretation is based on the various digital interactions I encounter: commentary, sharing, liking. With this data, I can then decode the image and inform an audience of what it represents. Prelli, though, does not endorse a complete decoding of an image in the name of hermeneutics since such interpretative readings do not reveal all meanings available: "To be sure we can argue about a visual display in its situated context, point out what it may conceal, and explore the political, cultural, and artistic implications of whatever our criticism reveal. At the same time, our efforts to disclose truths are complicated by the introduction of our own critical perspectives" (10). Our own critical perspectives—whatever Prelli means by that phrase—are based on how a reader fills in the gaps or missing premises the image supposedly offers. These critical perspectives are as emotional as they are supposedly logical, for they are what shape the image's reading upon initial exposure. "There is, to put it directly, no way to see that which is displayed as it really is, unencumbered by our own partial points of view" (10).

One such partial view within an audience's network might be that any police act in a demonstration indicates "brutality." In the age of the police shooting of Michael Brown, the chokehold of Eric Garner, the suffocation of George Floyd, and the mysterious "suicide" of Sandra Bland, public partial points of view within some communities can easily read an image like Pike's as brutality, and for good reason. Culture has embedded in the image other images not present. Even though these moments occur after Pike's incident, its relevance is not diminished in shaping readings of post-Pike images (and other acts precede them: Arthur McDuffie's beating to death by Miami police officers, and the better-known case of Rodney King, among many others). They are hardly the only incidents to occur in the last hundred years. The visual display of a police officer wounding others, thus, also evokes a sense of communal wounding by the suggestion, in the image, that people are being harmed, whether or not harm is actually occurring. We have too many incidents of people harmed by police officers, no matter how much good police offers do in protecting citizens. This continual wounding sparks public outrage.

Roland Barthes named such wounding within visual displays the punctum. The punctum is a suggestive moment of meaning; a detail in the image sparks a meaning outside of the image itself. Something sticks out. Something strikes the viewer from outside of the image. Like my previous examples, the punctum does not rely on referentiality in order to produce meaning. In *Camera Lucida*, Barthes writes about photography, "I wanted to explore it not as a question (a theme) but as a wound: I see, I feel, hence I notice, I observe, I think" (21). The wound—the detail in the photograph which is neither connotative nor denotative—functions as heuristic. It leads to noticing, observation, response, and thought that the image represented in the photograph does not allow for. The detail does not provide interpretation of the image. The detail—the emotional, affective response as meaning—wounds. It strikes. It causes a non-hermeneutic response informed by, to paraphrase Prelli, previous perspectives and encumberments.

In this response, the photograph alternates senses of time as the reader of the image moves from the time of the image (the representation presented to an audience in November 2011) to another time (an emotional moment associatively tied to the representation in some form which may occur in the past or, depending on when the image is read, in the future). Time, Barthes's second level of the punctum outside of the detail's wound, is explained as "*This will be* and *this has been*" (*Camera Lucida* 96). In imagery, Barthes explains, we identify the wounded response with the suggestion that something comes before and after the moment is captured. The meaning that wounds is not in the image's representation itself or even in the detail which stands out (often identified as the focus of Barthes's concept of the punctum), but in these two other temporal moments, moments not represented in the image. The pepper spray photograph brings together a present-time image (the police officer spraying the kneeling, arm-locked protesters) with a series of mostly past images (California student protests, police abuses, etc.) that are not present. The photograph, of course, is a technical image.

On one level, those non-present images are the moments that occurred before and just after the photograph was taken. In addition, some of those images have occurred previously, not during the protest itself but in a collective memory (a punctum) regarding protest, civil disobedience and social justice, in what I call a network. The network aggregates the association and connection of various agents that are outside of the image itself, but which are present in collective memory, so that enthymemic moments occur. This process resembles, to some extent, what Danielle DeVoss and Jim Ridolfo call rhetorical velocity, a complication of digital delivery. "In the inventive thinking of composing, rhetorical velocity is the strategic theorizing for how a text might be recomposed (and why it might be recomposed) by third parties." In this case, the "third party" is a series of images outside of the initial representation whose patterns wound. Those images can be cultural as well as photographic. Laurie Gries argues that within circulated imagery, there exist "divergent meanings that propagate as material consequences of a single multiple image's varied relations" (49). That may be true. The Pike parodies exemplify this point. An image may not be single at all. Instead, these "varied relations" can be cultural or collective patterns whose data "mining" (i.e., algorithmic logic) reveals why a particular image sparks anger.

These varied relations also function as networks, joining previous iterations of cultural moments into a larger body of meaning. To data mine the Pike image, one might have to go deep beneath these iterations in ways software may not account for. Among those images embedded in American collective memory regarding protest around which readers of the John Pike image might algorithmically form emotional perspectives, we can include the Civil Rights protests of the 1960s, innocent Black people at those protests being beaten and attacked by police with German shepherds, tear gassing at numerous protests over time, the political protests of 1968, and, of course, 1960s antiwar protests on university campuses. University of California, which hosted major protests on its Berkeley, Los Angeles, and Santa Barbara campuses in the 1960s, is part of that cultural network.

Are these varied relations visible to the average viewer of the image? Readers of the image do not need to be experts on Berkeley protests, for instance, in order to form a collective association between the pepper-spraying incident and Berkeley students being maced in 1967. Readers do not need to have historical reflection that allows them to recognize Norman Mailer's description of a 1960s student protester whose "eyes were still weak from the Mace squirted in them by police in Oakland" (76). Readers of the image do not have to be aware of the Berkeley Free Speech Movement of 1969, "where, in front of 3,000 students [student activist Mario Savio] advocated passive protest, student sit-ins, and a shutdown of the Berkeley campus. The 32-hour event eventually led to a confrontation between students and Berkeley police during which 800 arrests were made" (Tywoniak 23). Readers of the image do not need to be experts on temporal protests mirroring California activities such as 1967 police attacks on students protesting Dow Chemical campus recruiting at the University of Wisconsin in order to form a collective association with the pepper-spraying incident. Readers of the image do not have to be familiar with every word of a Berkeley handbill from a 1967 protest in order to network current discussions with this document, either. The handbill reads: "We who have occupied the streets of Berkeley for the last three nights, returning in the face of tear gas, clubbings, and arrests, feel that the causes and issues of our militance run deep"

("Why We Fight"). Nor do readers of the image need to have explicit knowledge of the battle for People's Park, an infamous moment in the history of the University of California at Berkeley when, in 1969, police opened fire on protestors who attempted to keep a community garden open and prevent the university from building dormitories in the space. Calling on the National Guard to stop the protest, then Governor Ronald Reagan stated, "If it takes a bloodbath, let's get it over with, no more appeasement." One man, James Rector, was shot and killed by police during the protest.

I argue that "readers do not need explicit knowledge" of any moment in this network in order to avoid the question of direct agency regarding technical images' efficacy. Technical images do not rely on such direct agency. A collective memory, such as one that might equate California universities with social protest, exists without an individual being able to recall dates and names because it is, as well, an algorithm drawing from these past moments. This memory produces imagery based on generalizations (California university students protest; student protesters deserve to be stopped) and stereotypes or profiles (police are brutal; protesters disrupt public order). This memory produces an imagery of profiles based on aggregated, circulated images. These images circulate within various networks (images embedded in other images) generate patterns, and form suggestions out of the pepper-spraying photograph. These suggestions may be found on websites, in video commentary, on blog posts, and in Facebook status updates, or their associations may be reinforced by such circulations on these spaces and elsewhere, in the present or in the past. Time unites the imagery. So does association. California acts as its own leverage point where the connotation of protest as an aggregation (not just Riverside, then, but all universities in the UC system) unites public response regardless of what has taken place.

I don't limit emotional perspectives to only these moments, but they are obvious cultural markers that might collect into an overall technical image for a particular audience. The concept "protest" generates links of emotional connection; California is an emotional focal point of American protest because of, among other things, the 1960s, whose symbolic value wounds in a collective manner so that a variety of moments are captured as one representation. That representation is a profile. That representation, in turn, offers a suggestion, much as a Facebook's or Cambridge Analytica's profile is meant to suggest consumption or political leanings. The suggestion networks the reader of the photograph in such a way that she believes she has interpreted and decoded its meaning: a police officer has brutally and unjustifiably attacked student protesters. Facebook has interpreted and decoded its user base similarly: this user will buy this product. That may be true. Or it may not. The immediacy of the response, though, cannot be fixed as interpretative. It is suggestive. In both disparate examples, it is suggestive. There exists an algorithm of suggestion at work.

Instead of considering the interpretative moment as having a digital importance, I focus on *the suggestion* as the digital issue worth exploration. I shift attention away from whether police brutality occurred or not and toward the notion of digital suggestion. Suggestion is a digital rhetoric interest even if not often presented as such. Texts suggest meaning when read, or algorithmically mined, over time. By data mining a corpus of works from the nineteenth century, for instance, a scholar arrives at a suggestion of meaning based on repetition of keywords or ideas. If "train" is evident in one hundred nineteenth-century texts, then the nineteenth century must have been about trains. This is a suggestion shaped from identified patterns. If a set base of social media users clicked on a specific political ad, they will vote for a specific politicians. This is a suggestion shaped from identified patterns. Suggestion is not an act of referentiality. It is an act of aggregation. Suggestion also acts as a remythologizing of interpretation. I believe in a meaning because of how a series of aggregated images within a singular image suggest. Suggestion offers an alternative approach to visual and digital texts. Suggestion, too, can be algorithmic.

OCCUPIED IMAGE

Consider, then, Occupy as not just a movement with political force but as an image, the movement as an image and an image of the movement. These two images suggest. They suggest a great deal. *TIME* magazine's editors might have thought as much when the magazine argued for The Protestor as its Person of the Year in 2011. The generic protester does not signify an individual or even a protest, but instead focuses attention on the suggestion of protest and protestors as they are aggregated into the image of something influential. The protestor is a suggested profile. The promise of revolution that the protests of 2011 suggested—such as those associated with the Arab Spring or Occupy—reflect a programmed ideology which either believes in change as good or believes that change is possible. Indeed, *TIME* frames 2011 protest as a continuation of legitimate and accepted means of dissent against illegitimate forces. This embedded image is that of the citizen who overturns the state: "When citizen multitudes took to the streets without weapons to declare themselves *opposed*, it was the very definition of news—vivid, important, often consequential. In the 1960s in America they marched for civil rights and against the Vietnam War; in the '70s, they rose up in Iran and Portugal; in the '80s, they spoke out against nuclear weapons in the U.S. and Europe, against Israeli occupation of the West Bank and Gaza, against communist tyranny in Tiananmen Square and Eastern Europe. Protest was the natural continuation of politics by other means" ("The Protester"). Protest is an image. It carries embedded within it a romanticized ideology (rising up equates justice and the good). It suggests a superior alternative (the results of the protest will lead to a more equitable situation or society). The details of each moment listed in *TIME*'s aggregation are absent since the overall technical image does not need such items. None of the listed protests are, of course, the same. Instead, these moments, all very different in scope and internal concern, are aggregated as one profiled image of protest. *TIME*'s coverage depends heavily on words and phrases like "extraordinary," "unlike any other year," and "unstoppable." Protest must be good. It is unique. Opposition framed as protest suggests the other side is wrong. Even without knowing, for instance, what the Arab Spring demonstrated for or how its manifestation might have differed from country to country (Tunisia and Syria, for instance, were not the same nor did they face the same consequences of protest), the protest wounds. It wounds because its details are outside of referentiality (i.e., the various conditions that may or may not give rise to a protest) and focus on the passage of time (this event equates previous protest events regardless of content). Protest's image is programmed accordingly.

As an image, we might consider Occupy also as a programmed moment that draws upon a network of associations that have been scripted into a discourse of critique and interpretation so that in place of a revelation of some concealment, suggestion occurs. That suggestion wounds, as Barthes describes the punctum's function over time, but only because of the programmed moment the image conveys via networked associations over time. Barthes writes: "I have found what Calvino calls 'the true total photograph,' it accomplishes the unheard-of identification of realty *('that-has-been')* with truth *('there-she-is!')*; it becomes at once evidential and exclamative; it bears the effigy to that crazy point where affect (love, compassion, grief, enthusiasm, desire) is a guarantee of Being" (*Camera Lucida* 113). Unlike Barthes's interest in time as a wound (this has happened; this has been), the particular wound connected to the Pike photograph is based on implicit and explicit associations made with a police officer pepper-spraying students, which then becomes evidential and exclamative.

Occupy itself is a programmed technical image dependent on these associations. The associations act as evidence. "Programs," Flusser tells us, "enhanced by the most diverse array of actions awaken sensations, feelings, suffering in us, so that we will allow them to stimulate us" (*Does Writing Have a Future?* 135). Suggestive imagery plays a role in the process. The John Pike image is accompanied by a great deal of suggestive imagery. Pepper spray. Police in riot gear. Signs and demands. Protests. The 99 percent versus the 1 percent. These non-human elements align with other non-human elements: inequity, unfair bonuses, foreclosure, student debt. Out of that alignment, public emotions flare much in the way they have done in previous protest moments.

Flusser frames his discussion of the technical image as one of "scripts," as in "scriptwriting," as well as scripted programming. "One who writes scripts is committed body and soul to the culture of images" (*Does Writing Have a Future?* 137). Without knowing each individual's case, as they are documented in Occupy protests or even in *TIME*'s overview, we still have a script that can easily follow these suggestive images. That script can follow any of the moments I draw attention to here as well as the overall, powerful image of the student protest. As I will discuss in a later chapter, the student protest in general, as well, conveys various aggregations which suggest a romantic yet justified image of justice. These aggregations, following Barthes, are time-based. Roderick Ferguson argues that contemporary student protest is a continuation of past protest imagery: "Our present-day troubles are not entirely different form the ones that previous students struggled over. Like everything 'new,' they have part of their genesis in 'bygone' battles" (4). Or as Gerard DeGroot writes, "Student protest is not an isolated phenomenon which occurs in diverse locations at distinct times. It is instead a culture, with all the attendant accoutrements: myths, martyrs, ritual, language, costume, and formalized behavior" (4).

Protest is an image, and it is one that repeats. Images have been important to Occupy since it, too, functions as an image. Within its initial image of a police officer pepper-spraying protesters are repeated images. In addition to the pepper-spraying, one sees a group of individuals in the background of the Pike image photographing the moment. Flashes are caught in action by the principal photographer of this image. There are different layers of imaging occurring, different technical images at play. "The goal of the political demonstration," Flusser writes, "is not to change the world but to be photographed" (*Into the Universe* 56). Protest imagery, such as the Pike photograph, echoes Haskell Wexler's 1969 *Medium Cool*'s opening—a reporter shows more interest in photographing a car accident than in securing help for the victims of the accident. This imagery echoes the later television show *Black Mirror* and particularly the episode "White Bear," in which people photograph a fleeing woman with their phones and do not offer to help her. The narrative of the pepper spray photograph is not police brutality as much as it is the suggestion of watching within the technical image.[3] *Medium Cool* emphasizes the suggestion of watching in its conclusion; as news reports broadcast crowds shouting "the whole world is watching," bystanders to another car accident photograph that accident, and the camera pans to Wexler filming the bystanders, and eventually, filming the viewer. "The whole world is watching" is an Occupy phrase as well.

Is the John Pike moment also an extended image of a film like *Medium Cool*? *Medium Cool* deals largely with the question of watching and recording within the image. The overall image of protest always has embedded within it watching. In the film's opening sequence, the main character, John Cassellis, is asked about being a cameraman. "You're not a machine," he is told. "Actually," he responds, "I'm an elongation of a tape recorder." Immediately following, a fellow journalist declares that "I've made films on all kinds of social problems and the big bombs were the ones where we went into detail and showed why something happened. Nobody wants to take the time. They'd rather see thirty seconds of someone getting their skull cracked." Rather than read these representations of media as a critique of the news industry (as in *Network*), I understand them as suggestions networked with my own suggestion of the Occupy photograph: thirty seconds of brutality, or a photograph of brutality, suggests that an audience (a supposed "we") is watching and seeing what occurred. Brutality is what an audience would "rather see" because this suggestion is already programmed into protest imagery. People *want* to see brutality, as the character declares. Want may mean desire, but it also may mean expectation. Programmability. Protest must be accompanied by brutality because that is what we are watching for and programmed for. The world is always watching. Flusser argues, "To every photograph there corresponds a clear and distinct element in the camera program. Every photograph thereby corresponds to a specific combination of elements in programs. Thanks to this bi-univocal relationship between universe and program, in which a photograph corresponds to every point in the program and a point in the program to every photograph, cameras are omniscient and omnipotent in the photographic universe" (*Towards a Philosophy* 68). Correspondence facilitates repetition. Repetition shapes a belief. "The photograph is capable of providing deep knowledge of social reality, both in its specific manifestations and as it is itself an unending process of repetition" (Hariman and Lucaites 32). Repetition programs, as does doxa.

In this network of programmed imagery, *Medium Cool*'s photography corresponds with the 1968 Democratic Convention in Chicago, where protesters chanted, "The whole world is watching" (the chant *Medium Cool* highlights). That suggestion networks any public protest that is photographed and telecast (and thus, watched), from contemporary protests against Wisconsin governor Scott Walker to various Occupy signage where the phrase "the whole world is watching" repeats.[4] As one Occupy Wall Street protester responded regarding his willingness to be arrested: "Of course I am. The whole world is watching" (Tharoor and Rawlings). The initial nodes of a network that include photographers in the background, *Medium Cool*, a chant, and 1968 suggest a type of watching, not a type of interpretative reading (i.e., "brutality" or the media manipulates). "The program does not signify the photograph, the photograph signifies the elements of the program (concepts)" (*Towards a Philosophy* 68). The image presents the network of these moments for viewing, which, in turn, suggest an event. By making that statement, I don't deny the pepper spray moment occurred or that the moment is problematic for its unneeded aggression or that brutality does not occur at peaceful protests. Instead, I'm more interested in the image's ability to interact with non-present images so that a network of meaning occurs, a network that has a largely emotional component or response to these actors, a network that is a heuristic, even if programmed, a network that is a digital moment.

In this chapter, I have identified two principal concepts relevant to digital outrage that are lacking in digital rhetoric scholarship regarding patterns and identification: programmability and suggestion. These two concepts stem from aggregated and circulated commonplaces that function as profiles built from repetitive imagery. In the case of Occupy and the John Pike photograph, we find the true and the false. Brutality and freedom. Police and protestor. A privileged 1 percent and a non-privileged 99 percent. These are the binaries of programmable critiques; they are the leverage points that prompt a belief in meaning based on suggestion. The problem is not that a suggestion occurs or that suggestion will solve the problems of interpretation, but rather that suggestion based on immediacy ignores how images aggregate and then circulate.

To return to Frabetti, who starts my thought process regarding the political, the emphasis on critique and value—how we read the image—should liberate us from the oppression associated with the image or what the image represents. The technical image, however, cannot be liberated, nor can it liberate us. All mythologies remain in circulation despite our best efforts to critique or understand them. Some scholarship promises liberation through patterns, data mining providing the means toward discovering textual patterns that, in turn, free meaning from its constrictions. But these patterns, too, are mythical. They circulate and build upon their circulations as embedded meanings within a variety of imagery. The myths of protest and police brutality do not vanish, lose influence, or even gain influence via interpretative acts. Instead, their influence depends on how, as technical images, they suggest a programmed value or meaning.

This point is vital as I move toward other examples in this book. Programmability depends, as well, on immediacy. The circulated meaning of the John Pike photograph is not based on representational knowledge of the network, but on immediate reaction influenced by cultural memory, as I earlier discussed in the chapter on affect. By networking various associations embedded in the image, I come to a meaning outside of the interpreted one, a meaning that may wound as well, but for different reasons, because I have refocused and remythologized the role of suggestion from critique to network. As legitimate as the critique of attacking protestors may be, then, it can also be problematic since immediacy is not the best means toward understanding or discovering meaning in a communicative and embedded moment. Immediacy—and the suggestions that result—often lead to programmed responses.

By now we should be familiar with the problem of suggestion. We might consider Richard Jewell, the unfairly accused Atlanta Olympics bomber, as one obvious situation when suggestion fails but is powerful as an agent of outrage.

Or we might consider the Swift Boat campaign against John Kerry in 2004 as a moment of suggestion among networked moments aggregated as a suggestion for those who opposed Kerry (patriotism, privilege, political campaign backers, the legacy of Vietnam). Or we might consider the photograph of a police officer pepper-spraying kneeling protesters. Suggestion does not promise critical thinking or interpretative revelation or data mining as it puts pressure on leverage points and communal wounds. Instead, it is the force of meaning that drives our—mistaken or not—understanding of the political (among other activities). A technical image, like that of the pepper spray incident, can only suggest. The suggestion, when treated not as a leverage point of persuasion but as *a moment* of networked digital production (as I do briefly here with the complicated example of watching), can reveal the network of actors that have formed its representation so that some other form of communication may occur (a further remythologizing). Suggestion, as the Occupy photograph exemplifies, is a digital rhetoric influencing public outrage. Whether its outcome is positive or negative, suggestion is a project that should be relevant for rhetoric (digital or not) for how it demonstrates networked activities within the image. Regarding outrage, then, we might consider the project of working with suggestion to further demonstrate networked activities instead of only offering interpretive responses. In the next chapter, I further this line of thinking by drawing attention to how algorithms—as ideological programmable scripts—drive a great deal of suggestion and outrage.

Notes

1. See also Google's Ngram Viewer (http://books.google.com/ngrams) for another example of this practice.

2. This overview does not intend to exclude previous scholarship in rhetoric and composition that deals with issues relevant to the digital humanities such as Craig Stroup's "The Lost Island of English studies: Globalization, Market Logic, and the Rhetorical Work of Department Web Sites" (*College English* 67, no. 6) or Mary Queen's "Transnational Feminist Rhetorics in a Digital World" (*College English* 70, no. 5). Instead, the overview takes a broader, umbrella like examination of research in English Studies overall, an examination that applies equally to rhetoric and composition as it does to other areas with English studies traditionally associated with the humanities or even the digital humanities.

3. For readers not familiar with the film, *Medium Cool* layers media moments so that actual news events such as the 1968 Democratic Convention and rise of the Black Panthers juxtapose with fictional news reporting in order to offer a "watching" of how the news is interpreted by general audiences. Its purpose is critique. In the technical image, that critique is remythologized as a suggestion.

4. See http://farm6.staticflickr.com/5297/5474562507_f9667f0363_m.jpg and http://farm7.static.flickr.com/6038/6218220972_da2001099c.jpg.

Six

Algorithmic Outrage

In the 1980s, a popular circulated rumor accused the conglomerate Procter & Gamble as being a sponsor of Satanism. Supposedly, a 1982 *Phil Donahue* episode featured the company's president admitting its support for the Church of Satan and that its logo expressed Satanic themes. Because of this rumor, Procter & Gamble was inundated with thousands of angry phone calls, demands for a boycott, and public denouncement. Consumers believed that the company supported Satanism, and the *Phil Donahue* episode presented proof. As the *Washington Post* reported in 1991, there existed "thousands of Americans who continue to boycott Procter & Gamble products, convinced, beyond any measure of logic, that the corporation's president is in league with the Devil. Currently, fliers are circulating in rural Maryland, among other places, listing the allegedly damnable P&G products" (Blumenfeld). The only catch to this viral instance was that the episode had never aired, and the company's president had made no such admission. Quickly, the *Phil Donahue* rumor spread to other TV talk shows where the company's president supposedly made similar statements about the logo, such as a March 1, 1999, appearance on the *Sally Jesse Raphael Show,* and generic references to appearances on the *Merv Griffin Show* and the *Jenny Jones Show,* where the confession was supposedly made as well. None of these moments occurred. In this pre-Internet moment of anger, outrage, and circulation, how did a rumor spread so easily and upset so many so quickly? How did a "fake news" story dominate before social media and before Trump?

While it is not entirely clear how the rumor began, we do know that specific actors helped aid its dissemination. First, there is the logo itself, a half-moon face with "666" supposedly embedded in its beard and surrounded by a symbolic thirteen stars. Then there are the thousands of mimeographed leaflets making the Satanism claim which were distributed anonymously throughout New York City in the early 1980s. Then there was Guy Sharpe, an Atlanta weatherman who often gave speeches to local civic groups; during such speeches, he shared the rumor with audiences who, we might assume, spread it as well to friends and associates. Amway distributors, going door to door in their sales districts, also shared the rumor to potential clients, supposedly as a way to curb competition by scaring Procter & Gamble customers. Finally, many church leaders shared the leaflets with their congregations, who, in turn, shared the information with other friends and families. One syndicated report on the rumor made similar observations in 1982: "One woman in Phoenix, Ariz., said that she heard about the supposed connection with Satanism at a fundamentalist Christian seminar. Others refer vaguely to television programs. Supermarket managers in at least three states have reported the rumor to Proctor & Gamble sales representatives" ("Proctor & Gamble Fighting"). What we witness, therefore, in this 1980s moment is the power of weak ties—connections with minimal to no knowledge of one another—to spread outrage even when the outrage lacks referent. All of these disparate actors located within a vast network of exchanges contributed to spreading a message without necessarily being aware of one another. Even more, we witness the power of a circulated image, whose meaning becomes embedded in other circulated meanings, and whose ability to spark emotional responses overrides any sense of truth or referentiality. Thus, there are two levels of weak ties in this viral moment: human actors sharing a rumor, and the imagery which further spreads other imagery as it becomes embedded in previous iterations of its (and other) messages.

Those who expressed outrage that their favorite producer of soap, diapers, and other household items was really in cahoots with Satan did so because they already held religious beliefs regarding popular culture's evils, Satanic symbols, Christian fanaticism, and the Devil. In this example of weak ties movement, we also witness an aggregation of such items into a rumor (itself an image), which, in turn, was read as novel because of how it aggregated these other beliefs without weak ties being aware of the aggregation. What we witness, in other words, is a pre–social media moment of algorithmic outrage. Belief in a supposed problem (Satan's influence) allowed ordinary individuals to aggregate disparate items into a widely spread rumor in order to deal with an imagined situation: Satanism. The rumor, and its various embedded actors, acted as an algorithm.

Algorithms are mathematical codes designed to solve problems. In *Introduction to Algorithms*, Thomas H. Cormen et al. write: "An algorithm is any well-defined computational procedure that takes some value, or set of values, as input and produces some value, or set of values as output. An algorithm is thus a sequence of computational steps that transform the input into the output" (5). An algorithm, Ed Finn writes, "is a recipe, an instruction set, a sequence of tasks to achieve a particular calculation or result" (17). These recipes or tasks are based on data sets and a computer code's ability to navigate the data and produce a result. An algorithm, Finn argues, "is a culture machine: it operates both within and beyond the reflexive barrier of effective computability, producing culture at a macro-social level at the same time as it produces culture objects, processes, and experiences" (34). Or as one study claims, "any single algorithm operates in the context of a larger system it cannot easily be abstracted from" (Reider et al. 63). Algorithms belong within larger cultural, ideological, and technical systems. Algorithms are calculations. "Algorithms need not be software," Tarleton Gillespie argues; "in the broadest sense, they are encoded procedures for transforming input data into a desired output, based on specified calculations" (167). In the case of public outrage, particularly as it is currently performed in digital platforms, algorithms are circulation and anger machines, calculating viewpoints and positions based on complex aggregations within larger systems or networks of interactions. The Proctor & Gamble episode may not be the first pre–social media algorithmic moment of circulated anger, but it is a prominent one and an important exigence for understanding current, digital algorithmic outrage.

Consider how an algorithm similar to the Protctor & Gamble one recently aggregated outrage regarding child sex trafficking. Child sex trafficking, like the belief in Satanic forces at play in major corporations, projects its own technical image which may include Pizzagate—the conspiracy theory that the Washington, DC, pizzeria, Comet Ping Pong, colluded with the Democratic party and Hilary Clinton to traffic children—or that celebrities such as Oprah Winfrey and Tom Hanks are trafficking children. Current anger over alleged, but nonexistent, child sex trafficking may be related to 1980s fears of Satanism, when daycares, and not just toilet paper manufactures, were the target of outrage over accusations of sexual abuse. These are but a few images that could help spread a contemporary image of child abuse.

On July 9, 2020, a Reddit post posed the idea that Wayfair, a company that sells furniture and home furnishings, was trafficking in children. Like the Proctor & Gamble example, a fake news story was quickly picked up by weak ties who spread the story across various media, Twitter being a dominant one in this case. On Reddit, a user began the discussion by posting a screenshot of expensive cabinets and asking, "Is it possible Wayfair involved in Human trafficking with their WFX Utility collection? Or are these just extremely overpriced cabinets (Note the names of the cabinets) this makes me sick to my stomach if it's true."[1] The cabinets had names like Neriah, Yaritza, Samiyah, and Alyvia, and were priced in the five-figure range, which seemed too high in price. The matching of suspiciously overpriced cabinets to supposedly missing children (if one ordered the cabinet, the theory proposed, one would receive a missing child inside) sparked over two thousand comments on the Reddit thread and a massive Twitter thread over ten thousand tweets long with respondents proclaiming Wayfair as a the centerpiece of a child sex trafficking ring. Posters pledged never to shop at Wayfair again. Others posted screenshots of Wayfair's website copy that claims to carry "a wide selection of baby & kids so you can choose from many different options" (which is altered from the original copy for a company called Three Posts' page inside of Wayfair's site, which reads, "a wide selection of products from Three Posts baby & kids so you can choose from many different options").[2] As each individual posted a confirmation of Wayfair's guilt—from a screenshot of a man arrested in a prostitution ring while wearing a Wayfair t-shirt, to an etymological breakdown of the company's name to mean "waif" (a homeless child) plus "fare" (the price charged to transport a person)—the outrage spread further from weak tie to weak tie. Just a handful of likes or retweets from each post allowed the supposed outrage to reach new people who, in turn, could retweet or like and often did. Generic concerns for innocent children, previous public claims of child abuse in the 1980s, the presence of QAnon—the anonymous Reddit user (or users) who claim Trump is uncovering a massive pedophile ring among other things—the Jeffery Epstein case (the socialite and financier accused of sexually abusing underage girls), and accusations against the Catholic church for child abuse, all likely play into the technical image of sex trafficking. These images reside within the algorithm that is positioned to solve a general concern regarding children's welfare. They are used for other purposes as well, as this chapter explores.

Algorithms, I contend, aggregate a variety of experiences into a currently circulated image, and, in turn, produce outrage out of an ideological calculation, or, as I've written earlier, Flusser's technical image. "Information is a synthesis of prior information," Flusser argued. "This holds true not only for the information that constitutes the world but also for man-made information" (*Into the Universe* 89). Algorithmic outrage is the aggregated outrage assembled within a given image, but which is not typically read by a given audience as a synthesis. Previous examples have demonstrated this point, but in this chapter I want to explore the concept further. When I write that algorithms aggregate experiences into an image, I don't mean the computer code itself. I mean the ideological algorithms which shape thought and response. When I situate aggregation alongside the concept of the algorithm, I do so because both belong within the same technical conversation.

In this chapter, I trace out two examples of what I call algorithmic outrage. My purpose is to draw attention to the ways technical images are often read as singular moments of expression, when, in fact, they are algorithmically driven. These algorithms are not computer code but ideological codes aggregating a variety of experiences—experiences understood over time and place and belief—into circulated photographs. These algorithms extend the notion of the database from information stored in a computer server to information stored collectively and ideologically. As Gillespie points out, "Algorithms are inert, meaningless machines until paired with databases on which to function" (169). I treat "database" as a generic term for information storage and not only as representative of a computer server. The database, as previous examples have shown, can be an aggregation of information within the imaginary or within the public sphere. The singular representations we treat as objects of outrage, as I've also shown, are built from such databases.

While the Proctor & Gamble examples I began this chapter with introduce the notion of predigital aggregations functioning as an algorithm, my examples in this chapter look extensively at two digital images. My two examples of images that generate algorithmic outrage are a widely circulated photograph of presidential advisor Kellyanne Conway sitting on an Oval Office sofa during a visit by some presidents of historically Black colleges and universities (HBCUs) and another widely circulated photograph of former San Francisco 49ers quarterback Colin Kaepernick kneeling during the national anthem. The reasons these images evoked outrage, I contend, does not stem from the representations themselves or their immediacy, but instead stems from representations algorithmically embedded in the images by their angry audiences. Following Bruno Latour, I trace these examples in order to better understand their embedded nature. By trace, I mean that I follow their connections over brief periods of time and presentation. As Latour writes, "If the social is a trace, then it can be *re*traced; if it's an assembly then it can be *re*assembled (*Reassembling* 128, emphasis Latour's). I trace and reassemble the repetitions and moments connected to each example. While my methodology may feel as if it is merely referencing or glossing over moments, it functions as a trace that I retrace in order to reassemble. By tracing some of these images' algorithmic constructions, I can pose them not as singular moments of anger, but instead as collected assemblies whose importance to a given audience does not stem from the moment in question, but rather a lengthy history of visual moments not initially obvious to the image's viewer.

POSING OUTRAGE

Digital work, according to Flusser, is ideological as much as it is technical. A Procter & Gamble controversy in the mid-1980s would, then, be a technical image, as those in panic would have read not just the logo as the source of their angst, but any previous ideas, experiences, and moments regarding Satan, Christianity, conspiracy, and other related items. The combination of these items taps into preconceived ideas regarding Satanism, and those preconceived ideas (all negative, obviously) would be based on other networked, ideological interactions experienced over time and place (such as fear of the Devil or the occult). Flusser referred to this process as the programmed image. Imagery, for Flusser, is programmed whether or not it is made on a computer. Imagery is programmed because our previous interactions determine our current readings. Tony Sampson, with a slightly different perspective, offers the following regarding user tendency to follow preconceived belief systems online: "The end user becomes, as such, a prisoner of techniques of capture derived from routinization and habituation and inflows of contagious suggestibility" (166). We often become so habituated to belief that the image we engage with confirms a programmed sensibility easy for users to share without thought. Flusser explains: "A programmatic orientation rests on the belief in the eternal return of the same, on the indifference of every action. Programs actually reinforce this belief continually. It is the orientation of post historical consciousness" (*Does Writing Have a Future?* 135).

How does one respond to a technical image, then, if it is programmed? Under these terms, imagery does not need to be read for hermeneutical breakdown (i.e., "what does it mean") but instead should be read for its layered composition. Those layers are, I argue, algorithmic because of their "effective procedure," as David Berlinski writes of algorithms (xvi). While it may feel as if immediate reception is based on interpretation (decoding a representation for its meaning), if we reconsider the effective procedure as a programmed one, we can rethink digital, political, and popular receptions of anger, whether regarding an imaginary Satanism controlling the diapers one buys, or more serious issues. The technical image provides an opportunity to think through algorithms and outrage and how both impact the production of meaning in the digital age.

Algorithms allow meaning to spread. The Proctor & Gamble example allows us to consider, for instance, the moment a political controversy goes viral and spreads widely. As with that example, we can consider the specific ways such controversies move from user to user, image to image, platform to platform, headline to headline. This digital process of circulation and persuasion resembles what Henry Jenkins termed "spreadability" and the Heath Brothers called "stickiness," or what Tony Sampson called "contagions," or what many in rhetorical studies refer to simply as circulation: the repetition and spread of an idea across people and platforms. The repetition of an image across various platforms or among various users results in an aggregation that often generates anger and outrage as each user spreading the image embeds—via comment, context, suggestion, tweet, like, sharing—additional imagery into the image. The embedded content acts as if it is placed to solve a problem: Why is this image so awful, or why does this image deserve an angry response? The embedding attempts to answer these questions. Embedding, however, is not necessarily an instrumental or conscious process since it does not always involve the clicking of a like or offering of a comment.

To begin, we can consider the specific and notable 2017 image which generated a considerable amount of attention: Trump advisor Kellyanne Conway sitting in the Oval Office, a group of sixty-four HBCU presidents in the background conversing with Trump, her shoes off, her legs tucked under her, her posture suggesting the casual or even the indifferent, looking at her cell phone. This image went viral. Its virality was not based on the Trump administration's hosting of HBCU presidents (which did not generate any complaints directed at Trump or the academics) but instead was based on outrage at Conway. Social media, in particular, aggregated the photograph into a chain of outrage that quickly spread across various networks. Those who saw the image became incensed. They saw insult and disrespect in Conway's posture. But what happened here? Did anything happen here? Is this a moment of disrespect, a "small error," as the *Washington Post* declared, or a "lack of decorum" as many other news sites, blogs, and posts claimed? What else was being read or inserted into the image?

"Kellyanne Conway puts her feet on an Oval Office couch and the internet loses it," *The Daily Show* (2017) posted to Facebook. "I have so many questions about this photo, but chief among them is why nobody is telling Kellyanne Conway to get her damn feet off the couch," *Chicago Tribune* columnist Rex Huppke tweeted (Bever). *Mother Jones* editor Clara Jeffery tweeted: "The more you look at this, the more you recognize Kellyanne's play: one who flaunts their indecorousness as ultimate signifier of privilege." "Trump's diss of historically black colleges," a *Baltimore Sun* headline declared. Writer Shaun King posted the image to his Facebook page and wrote, "I sincerely doubt that Kellyanne Conway would be on the couch, shoes off, on her knees, looking at her phone, if the room was full of white dignitaries or CEOs that she actually respected." Damn feet. Privilege. Diss. Respect. White women vs. Black men and women. These are keywords of anger with specific political connotations and histories which, when aggregated, combine to foster ideologies not necessarily present within the image itself. These words are read into the image; they are not necessarily there.

The image, as Roland Barthes, wrote, is one "without a code" ("The Rhetoric of the Image" 43). For Barthes, the image's code (what these keywords signify for these critics) comes from the viewer, not the image itself. Only without code, Barthes argued, can the image be understood.

> In the photograph—at least at the level of the literal message—the relationship of signifies to signifiers is not one of "transformation" but of "recording," and the absence of a code clearly reinforces the myth of photographic "naturalness": the scene *is there*, captured mechanically, not humanly.
>
> [. . .] It is thus at the level of this denoted message or message without code that the *real unreality* of the photograph can be fully understood: Its unreality is that of the *here-now*, for the photograph is never experienced as illusion, is in no way a *presence* (claims as to the magical character of the photographic image must be deflated); its reality that of the *having-been-*

there, for in every photograph there is the always stupefying evidence of this is how it was. ("The Rhetoric of the Image" 44)

The having-been-there. The image is read by its critics as if one *was there* and one gives the image code or, as I will continue to argue via the technical image, as if the image *has been there* already in other iterations shaping its current reading and giving it code. To call Conway privileged or engaged in a "diss" is to treat the image as natural and not as a text read and coded as having been there or as having been programmed. When we look at this image, what do we, in fact, see? Do we see what happened prior to the image? Do we see what occurred afterward? Do we see any conversations taking place? Do we see the White House guests angry or happy or indifferent? Do we indeed see a white woman dissing Black visitors because of her cultural privilege? Or do we see what we believe is suggested not only by the image itself, but by many other images, headlines, ideas, and beliefs that we bring to this image the moment we look at it?

The Conway image is a technical image. Within this image, viewers embed programmed cultural beliefs not actually in the physical representation of the presidential advisor. Notice once more the keywords used by critics of the photo: privilege, white privilege, comfortable, disrespect. These are highly circulated terms—particularly white privilege—used to emphasize a specific critique of American economic, racial, and social relationships. A woman sitting on a couch with her legs tucked underneath, for instance, signifies white privilege. But why? Data. Previously engaged cultural data—whether it indicates posturing or how one positions one's self—suggests some type of result based on an ideological algorithm put into play by a specific audience with already formulated negative beliefs regarding the Trump administration and the ways white, wealthy and successful women might behave toward minorities from a perceived, different segment of society. After all, the image does not show Conway dismissing the White House visitors. *A reading of the image* demonstrates that data aggregation. The problem of white privilege exists. The algorithmic reading attempts to solve that problem, if only in a small way, by aggregating this reading and raising attention to the issue. Thus, the Conway image is a data set, only that data might not be initially evident.

The generic projection of a white woman on the couch, for instance, might draw from previously circulated data such as the common stock photo featuring a gendered pose often used to sell couches, ceramics, photo services and other objects. Such advertisements, easily identified in a Google image search or in stereotypical advertising, typically feature a white woman reclining or resting on a couch, the service or object for sale secondary to her image. Her reclining, leisure body, instead, is the image's focus. Or with the woman's posture with a phone in hand, this visual might evoke another well-circulated variation of the

stock image of leisure where a white woman does not have responsibilities beyond talking on the phone. These photos are often described by the stock photo
companies as "Happy woman using smartphone" or "Beautiful young woman
relaxing on sofa." Or the image may evoke the historic pinup-style photograph
or drawing of a half-dressed woman (depending on the time period the image
is circulated within) poses on a couch with her legs exposed, or for more modern photography, her rear exposed and projected upward. These past images of
a woman on a couch depict women in either superficial or derogatory poses,
valued only for their ability to sell objects, services, or their bodies. In addition, the presence of a white woman against a backdrop of mostly Black men
can also belong within an aggregation of a particular part of American history
where this specific data set (white woman/black man) suggests sex, sexual assault, wrongful claims, injustice, and other imagery as problematic as the murder of Emmitt Till for whistling at a white woman or *To Kill a Mockingbird*'s
plot. If any of these images are aggregated into a viewer's cultural reading of the
Conway image—whether in a cognizant or implicit way—they are because an
ideological algorithm aggregated past imagery into her pose. Woman poses on
couch is viewed as scandalous, provocative, and possibly inappropriate. Conway
does not create that imagery on her own. A cultural algorithm does. "There is a
seductive quality," Ed Finn writes, "to algorithmic models of digital culture even
when they are only partially successful because they order the known universe"
(49). Algorithmic outrage orders a known universe of racism and Trump for a
specific audience reading this image.

Thus, I ask why Conway's photograph evoked outrage not because I agree
or disagree with the response to the photograph, but because I'm interested in
the roles algorithms play when we respond to, among other things, imagery.
"Images model the behavior, perception, and experience of all other function-
aries" (*Into the Universe* 74). A reader of the Conway image who immediately
feels outrage likely does so because she believes the image conveys more than a
white woman on a couch taking a picture while visitors meet the president; the
image conveys a number of embedded imagery a viewer brings to its circulation.
This includes the visual depiction of a woman posing I briefly trace above, but
also likely includes a current administration's insensitivity to educational issues
affecting Black Americans, a nation's historical lack of attention to educational
equality, and privileged white women's historical relationship to Black men, particularly in disrespectful poses or false accusations of assault. As Flusser argues,
"The demythologizing question shows how information in the world and information in general is generated: by synthesizing previous information" (*Into
the Universe* 88). But how does the photograph synthesize any or some of this
previous information I list and assume is embedded in this particular technical
image? How does all of this aggregate into one image?

Flusser saw the problem as ideological—we embed our own ideologies and beliefs into imagery based on past exposure. The composer or photograph does not create the image. Viewership as algorithmic activity does: "Human freedom no longer consists in being able to shape the world to one's own desires (apparatuses do this better) but to instruct (program) the apparatus as to the desired form and to stop (control) it when this form has been produce" (*Into the Universe* 73). In this sense, imagery functions, as well, as software. Ed Finn writes, "algorithms have encoded a particular kind of abstraction, *the abstraction of the desire for an answer*" (25, emphasis Finn's). Why is this administration racist, a viewer might ask? This image provides the answer. Or the desire for an answer is organized around basic questions such as: how did a typically insensitive president and his staff treat Black visitors? Or how would this president treat Black visitors if given the opportunity? Or another similar question could be posed. The algorithm, generated by so many previous interactions, supplies an answer.

ANTHEM OUTRAGE

We can consider, as well, the widely circulated image of former San Francisco 49ers quarterback Colin Kaepernick kneeling during the National Anthem at a 2016 game. No sports image in the last ten years has caused as much controversy as this one; Kaepernick is no longer in the NFL, and the league continues to struggle over players kneeling and public anger at protests, prior to and after the death of George Floyd. During a 2017 campaign rally for Senator Luther Strange in Alabama, Donald Trump helped demonize Kaepernick by yelling, "Get that son of a bitch off the field." What was Kaepernick protesting? According to some critics, though not according to Kaepernick, the military. "The question being asked," The *New York Times*' Billy Witz wrote of the kneeling, "was whether Kaepernick was disparaging the sacrifices made by the military." *Bleacher Report*'s Mike Freeman repeated what NFL front office executives were supposedly saying about Kaepernick and his supposedly antimilitary projection: "'I don't want him anywhere near my team,' one front office executive said. 'He's a traitor.'" Others argued that the kneeling signified a lack of love for country. The *Atlantic* titled one essay about the kneeling "No Country for Colin Kaepernick." "When Colin Kaepernick says that he won't stand for the national anthem," Ben Shapiro wrote in *National Review*, "perhaps he's not being a philosophical coward. Perhaps he's just speaking a leftist truth that Hillary Clinton and Barack Obama won't speak: To them, the American story isn't one of restoration of founding principles and allegiance to eternal truths, but an ever-changing moral rubric in which the only constant is the evil of the past." Jim Geraghty offers his take on Kaepernick: "By not standing, the quarterback is not saying *I'm angry at that cop, or that police force, or that prosecutor's decision*. He's saying, *I'm angry at all of America.* Make no mistake, Kaepernick indicts all of America over what troubles him." A quarterback kneeling during a football game's introduction, therefore, quickly became read as something beyond what the physical body demonstrated. Writers read into Kaepernick's technical image ideas not necessarily relevant to the act of kneeling.

As a technical image, the Colin Kaepernick image conveys a number of conflicting meanings depending on audience. The image's basic representational meaning, however, is as such: Kneeling in front of his teammates and a stadium of standing fans, Kaepernick looks off into the distance, as if he is being monitored from afar or aware of those standing around him. That is all we see. This is the image we read—a quarterback kneeling—until we read the other images algorithmically embedded within it which typically identify anti-American or antipatriotic sentiment centered on the anthem supposedly playing while he kneels. Kneeling, identified as an act of protest, during the national anthem equates, for critics, antimilitary or anti-American sentiment because of a variety of emptions embedded into the image of a song. "The Star-Spangled Banner," written by Francis Scott Key on September 14, 1814, was inspired by the British bombing of Fort McHenry in the Baltimore Harbor. It did not officially become the national anthem until 1931. When it became the anthem, the National Football League did not yet exist and the anthem was not being regularly sung at sporting events. If one were to trace a history of the national anthem, which is basically just a song written during a war, to NFL games, it would begin with the connection between athletics and patriotism forged during World War II as a marker of patriotism, and it would likely continue on until 2009 when players began to stand on the field during its performance.

The outrage directed at Kaepernick for not standing does not acknowledge these discrepancies, but instead, assumes their natural presence within the image as well as a few more additions. What, then, programs public outrage so that the anthem and one lone quarterback kneeling connect? There is no causal relationship between an 1814 song and professional football, yet as a technical image, the anthem evokes that connection, and as another technical image, Kaepernick's kneeling offers a counter technical image focused on a generic "anti" sentiment often associated with protest. To understand how each image is programed (following Flusser's term), one could reference the patriotism angle that many rely upon in order to denounce Kaepernick, and which circulates through social media memes as attacks on Kaepernick for being "antimilitary" or even anti-American. This anger occurs despite the fact that the military does not play in the NFL, Kaepernick did not mention the military as a reason for protesting, and the historical military connection to the anthem occurred in 1814, not 2016, and without sports at its origin. One could also reference growing American nationalism and the influence of Trump's Make America Great Again platform as aggregated into these technical images. All of these may, indeed, be part of the algorithm driving Kaepernick outrage. But I also note that within the kneeling image, we can identify other embedded images which program, as Flusser might argue, the outrage algorithm. These images, as Barthes argues, show how audiences deal "with a normal system whose signs are drawn from a cultural code" ("Rhetoric of the Image" 46).

One such image might be hair. In the photograph of Kaepernick kneeling, his hair is in cornrows, a hairstyle historically indicative of Black American heritage and disseminated in popular culture as a cultural marker by hip hop artists such as Coolio and Snoop Dogg. NBA star Latrell Spreewell, known for choking coach P. J. Carlesimo when employed by the Golden State Warriors, wore his hair in cornrows as well. So did Stevie Wonder, whose iconic cornrow image is captured on the cover of the *Talking Book* album. As I noted in an earlier chapter, Roland Barthes defined aggregated cultural imagery into one space by the term *-icity*; his neologism for the Italian-ness he noticed in an advertisement for Italian food. The aggregated placement of red and green colors as well as spaghetti, tomatoes, and onions algorithmically generated an output of an idea called Italian, not the various and heterogenous foods Italians actually eat. The cornrow, along with other images I will note, signifies a certain -icity of black culture for white audiences, such as the often-circulated image of the so-called bad boy. Cornrows do not equate bad behavior or a "bad boy," but as part of a larger icity or cultural profile of Black men, they can project that image to a specific audience who has internalized this image. This bad boy image, as Kareem Abdull Jabbar writes in *TIME*, brings with it conflicting meanings: "While high-priced cornrows on a white celebrity on the red carper at the Oscars is chic, those same cornrows on the little black girl in Watts, Los Angeles, are a symbol of her ghetto lifestyle. A white person looking black gets a fashion spread in a glossy magazine; a black person wearing the same thing gets pulled over by the police." Cornrows can threaten. Or as Ayana Byrd and Lori Tharps write, for Black Americans, "many have to hope that their choice of hairstyle—hair that was not unnaturally colored, spiked, or mohawked—would not offend or scare" (107). In the algorithm shaping Kaepernick as outrage, hair appears to both scare and offend. If an audience is programmed to view hair as indicative of an imaginary "ghetto lifestyle" as Abdull Jabbar suggests, that image will become embedded in an image of his kneeling, and it will help shape a negative response.

Kaepernick's decision to switch hairstyles to an afro, as well, becomes part of the outrage algorithm. The November 2017 "Man of the Year" issue of *GQ* magazine featured Kaepernick sans cornrows and instead embracing an afro. Like cornrows, the afro carries its own series of embedded imagery. Writing in *The Undefeated*, Ameer Hasan Loggins (2017) noted the various imagery he identified in Kaepernick's afro.

Kaepernick's Afro shined like a crown of black consciousness on the cover of *GQ* serving as a crucial component for framing his unspoken love for black aesthetic affirmation. But if one picks through the historical roots of his natural hair halo, they will find a legacy of powerful black women affiliated with the Black Panther Party.

[. . .] Colin's homage to the aesthetics of the Black Panther Party on the cover of *GQ* continued via his adorning a black turtleneck and a black jacket with a peaked lapel, symbolically connecting his image to the likes of Huey P. Newton, Bobby Seale and many others wearing the Black Panther Party uniform, presenting themselves as a unified group moving in solidarity in the fight against systemic oppression.

Loggins notes the specific cultural imagery embedded in the *GQ* cover. His afro. His choice of a turtleneck. His leather jacket. These are signifiers of Black activists such as Huey Long, who, as well, wore leather jackets and turtlenecks and often sported an afro. One can call this image an homage, but I prefer technical image since those opposing Kaepernick's kneeling read it as a threatening activism. The cultural meaning to this gesture, Nikki Brown argues, is indicative of minority rights. "Each strand is a symbol of our strength, uniqueness and layered history. And when any person or institution threaten our ability to wear them freely." Soraya Nadia McDonald adds to the conversation by reading Kaepernick's hairstyle changes as growth in his activism: "When Colin Kaepernick first began sitting and then later kneeled during the national anthem to protest police violence, the quarterback wore his hair cropped close to his head. As the spotlight on his activism grew, so too did his locks, first into a mass of short curls, then cornrows, then a bigger crown of still-defined curls and, finally, a billowing, uncontrolled, woolly, seemingly semi-sentient mass that doubled as a silent trigger of white fragility."

A significant amount of imagery has been collected into what appears to be a singular hair style. The afro, as 1960s popular culture demonstrates, conveys a number of problematic images for white football fans or even white non-fans that overpower basic imagery of sports: black power, revolution, black pride, and, of course, the Black Panther movement. Diana Ross, Angela Davis, Huey P. Newton and other cultural icons of the 1960s wore their hair as an afro, and that stylistic choice represents an uncomfortable politics for many who feel their cultural status threatened. The afro, is "a way to fight the status quo without saying a word," Princess Gabbara (2017) writes in *Ebony*. Soraya Nadia MacDonald writes, "In his quest to draw attention to the injustice of lethal state violence exacted on unarmed black people, Kaepernick has become something of a walking museum exhibition, carrying 70 years of history, politics, resistance and symbolism within a few inches of black keratin emerging from his head."

Kara Brown offers similar thoughts: "Our hair often *means something*. It means something because we have adapted to the insistence by white people that it mean something. For most who are not black, there is nothing inherently political about wearing your hair the way it grows out of your head. For black people, it can seem that any style we choose—be it locs or braids or wigs—is meant to send some sort of message to the world, whether we want it to or not." That message is read as either antithetical to so-called American values or in support of Black American rights. Hair (and clothes) send a message. Tom Wolfe summarized the overall aggregation of 1960s Black Power fighting the status quo in "Radical Chic" when he wrote of "the tight pants, the tight black turtlenecks, the leather coats, Cuban shades, Afros. But real Afros." Real afros. Real resistance. Real revolution. Or that is what a viewership may believe. Popular writer Ta-Nehisi Coates recalls his childhood as one of hair and these various aggregated images that affect viewership: "Dreadlocks and Nubian twists, Afros as wide as planets or low and tapered from the temple. They braided it, invested it with beads and yarn, pulled the whole of it back into a crown, or wrapped it in yards of African fabric. But in a rejection aimed at something greater than follicles and roots" (94). One might argue that the presence of hair in Kaepernick's kneeling also evokes the embedded image of rejection that Coates alludes to, and in turn, fosters an audience angry at being rejected or an audience who reads the image of protest as a rejection of white culture, America, or its institutions.

This anger, and possible feeling of rejection, extends from hair to Kaepernick's raised fist as it is also featured in additional Kaepernick imagery of him on the football field. In more than one circulated image, Kaepernick raises his fist at the conclusion of a game, helmet removed, as he walks off of the field. The image of the closed fist, as Richard Marback has written, materializes "visions of the agency of unassimilated difference" (77). Marback, who writes about the Joe Louis fist statue in Detroit, also argues that the fist is, "an icon of the protest and cultural turmoil and racial tensions of the last three decades, the fist figures forth spatial interactions embodied in claims to contested cultural and physical terrains on which memories of racial injustice and hopes for democratic citizenship are written" (78). A generic, mostly white audience feels uncomfortable when confronted with a programmed image of racial injustice since such imagery suggests complacency or culpability regarding this injustice. As with the projection of hair imagery, within Kaepernick's fist we can find other fists layered upon each other, each aggregating previous representations, each, in its own way, conveying the algorithmic, programmed image of protest against injustice. In popular culture, such visual demonstrations are notable in the canonical image of Black athletes Tommie Smith and John Carlos standing on the Olympic podium in 1968 Mexico City where their fists were raised in protest. Or the fist is recalled as the ubiquitous symbol of the 1960s Black Panther party.

Public Enemy's video for "Fight the Power" showcases the fist as does the Black Lives Matter movement, which features the fist in social media and on protest posters and placards. Even the Howard Stern radio show represents itself via the fist (a protest against terrestrial radio's restrictions). Historically, regardless of race, the fist represents protest and resistance. Early-1900s labor posters featured a fist projected outward with a tool (the power of labor) or a closed fist (the power of the union). Or Spanish Civil War propaganda posters showcased fists wrapped around Soviet rifles, raised fists celebrating libertad or elevated fists welcoming the coming of the Spanish dawn. In 1965, Frank Cieciorka designed one of the most recognized drawings of the closed fist from a wood cut he created for cheap prints to be utilized by The Black Panther Party. The fist is an object within an aggregated icity of protest, much of it identified as central, directly or indirectly, to Black American identity and cultural response to white oppression.

Why, then, would Kaepernick not raise a fist? Doing so programs a specific technical image meant to evoke a series of layered meanings that accentuate the act of kneeling. The fist, like the afro or cornrows, contributes to an algorithm whose function is to evoke outrage by tapping into the ways certain viewers confront Kaepernick's kneeling as an insult or as disrespect while possibly also interpreting the fist or hair as specific markers of a Black American cultural identity read as alien or in conflict with white representations and meanings. These markers traditionally represent conflict, resistance, liberation, or differentiation. These terms circulate throughout both white and Black American culture carrying different meanings. Those who identify with cultural markers aggregated these markers far differently, such as a flag or an anthem, and either recognize the algorithmic differentiation as representative of a continuing call for equality or find it confrontational. Fists are, no doubt, confrontational, but also can be representative of continuing cultural struggles. Writing in *Buzzfeed*, Niela Orr argues that "certain mottoes and slogans from the civil rights and Black Power movements have fallen out of fashion, but the raised fist remains a hugely popular visual signal of defiance and solidarity. The co-optation of the raised fist as a patriotic symbol, winking cultural reference, and even totem of irony show that it is just as much about how we perform protest in the twenty-first century as it is about communicating resistance." To raise a fist for the cover of *GQ*, then, is to set in motion a programmed algorithm of resistance. This programming affects viewership. This programming affects outrage as response. This programming draws upon the mythology of embedded meaning and association.

Barthes noted that "myths are made up of associations" (*Mythologies* 119). Barthes drew attention to specific cultural constructions of representations assumed to be natural. These associations, what Barthes did not note, function as computer algorithms within social networks. Barthes also called myth a "mathematical formula" (132) for how it deals with meaning; "it has taken all possible precautions against interpretation" (132). One might argue, then, that the Conway and Kaepernick images are not being interpreted when outrage follows their circulation, as much as we may want to believe that their impact is based on hermeneutics and an ability to navigate the complexity of a situation by "reading" an image's appearance on a desktop, in a social media feed, in a print publication, or elsewhere. The reading, instead, is a mathematical calculation (an algorithm) that extends programmed meaning. Indeed, many of the instances I trace suggest immediate, published interpretations of the photographs (outrage) and do not focus on the embedded layering I claim exists and drives response (formula). Social media prompts immediacy, but it also prevents tracings because of how quickly we assume meaning is singular.

Instead of singularity, these images, as I've tried to demonstrate, are working off of programmed scripts which "rob" meaning (as Barthes might say) of the image itself. After all, as Barthes writes, "myth is constituted by the loss of the historical quality of things; in it, things lose the memory that they were once made" (*Mythologies* 142). Neither Flusser nor Barthes argues that viewers of myths or technical images understand the programming that occurs within the layered imagery. And I do not argue that point either. My central thesis is that readers of such images are not, overall, aware of the complexity of imagery and thus they assume meaning as an immediate (or even affective), and not a layered, algorithmic experience. Neither Flusser or Barthes, as well, argue for interpretation as a tool for decoding the algorithm or this layering. Anger at Kaepernick could never account for the historical discrepancy of an 1814 song and an NFL game no matter how carefully we disentangle this perceived connection. Nor is interpretation the goal of either writer's project—Flusser resists such a response and Barthes dismisses interpretation as a method for countering myths (he advocates remythologizing the myth). I, too, do not argue for closer readings or more critique. Focusing on hair styles and raised fists is not an attempt to read the image closer. Instead, I draw attention to our own (not others') reactions to algorithmic outrage via these two examples, not so that we may overcome our own programmed assumptions and ideologies as they are embedded in circulated images, but, at the least, so that we may be aware of the beliefs we bring to images, or, even more so, we may begin to think about circulating our own algorithms of outrage on social networks. Does knowing about the fist or afro change a reader's reflection on the Kaepernick image? Likely not. But it can shift response to how the embedded imagery shapes public opinion. This gesture does not need to lead to social change, though it could.

The digital implications of this type of work involve a more comprehensive understanding of the complexity regarding the causes of digital outrage. The two examples I provide are meant to stand for the many moments of outrage we succumb to digitally. We can label an event as "fake news" or we can support digital outrage as a legitimate response to injustice, but neither reaction accounts for the question of the technical image. A technical image, as I've tried to show, is not a specific type of circulated image; the technical image constitutes all imagery engaged with digitally. Recognizing how technical images play off of our own ideologies is, at the least, one step toward the recognition of outrage's place within our own complex and user generated ideological algorithms. If that recognition occurs, we may not stop being outraged, but we may become more attuned to the why and how of our outrage.

Notes

1. "Is it possible Wayfair involved in Human trafficking. . . ," r/conspiracy, Reddit, July 9, 2020, https://www.reddit.com/r/conspiracy/comments/.

2. Three Posts Baby & Kids, Wayfair, https://www.wayfair.com/brand/bnd/.

Seven

Enthymemic Outrage

Attunement to outrage should be a skill recognized by rhetorical scholars. As rhetoricians, we teach how to construct meaning and, therefore, how to be attuned to nuances in meaning and its circulation. We could, theoretically, understand the nature of outrage as a particular production of meaning or media form and how individuals might produce outrage intentionally. My examples so far mostly have come from non-academic sources, imagery produced by and featuring non-academics. Central to these examples has been the concept of the enthymeme, a foundational rhetorical strategy used often in persuasion and argumentation. Scholars, in general, one would think, would have some knowledge of enthymemic based arguments and how they might work in various rhetorical situations, particularly those connected to outrage. That knowledge should be based not just in recognizing outside enthymemic usage, but how one may be relaying on enthymemes for conveying ideas on social media platforms. In this chapter, I devote more attention to the enthymeme, particularly for how it is used by scholars online—knowingly or not—in moments of outrage.

How are scholars attuned to outrage? Can they recognize their own attunements or manipulations of the algorithms that shape outrage? Do they simply utilize outrage as a medium for their own grievances or affective reactions to various public moments? Like Facebook or other entities I earlier drew attention to, do they circulate profiles of stereotypes as interpretive moments when such moments are not? Do they understand some of the questions of audience and embedded imagery I have been outlining up until now? In this chapter, I examine two specific moments of professorial outrage as means toward addressing these questions via the enthymeme. I do so because professorial outrage often gains attention in academic, popular, and political leaning publications, though for different reasons than those I will explore. There are, in fact, two levels of digital outrage occurring in the examples I offer: a professor's outrage at a political issue or moment and an audience's outrage at the professor for such expression. My focus is not necessarily on whether the professor or the audience is justified for such outrage or whether or not the professor's claims are valid or not, but instead I focus on the specific rhetorical gestures made by both sides of this shared anger.

On December 24, 2016, Drexel University professor of politics and global studies George Ciccariello-Maher tweeted "All I want for Christmas is white genocide." Ciccariello-Maher's tweet functioned as a response to what he believed was American right-wing discourse framing "whites" as an endangered ethnic group threatened by minority cultures. Since white culture is not a minority in America (particularly in terms of power), the tweet reflected frustration with the complaint of endangerment, particularly when other ethnic groups often feel threatened as minorities or experience very real threats to their existence. White genocide, thus, is a marker of these white supremacist groups and the discourse they circulate. The Anti-Defamation League (ADL), which tracks white supremacist and other racist discourse, defines "white genocide" accordingly: "'White Genocide' is a term coined by white supremacists for propaganda purposes as shorthand for one of the most deeply held modern white supremacist convictions: that the white race is 'dying' due to growing non-white populations and 'forced assimilation,' all of which are deliberately engineered and controlled by a Jewish conspiracy to destroy the white race" ("White Genocide"). Shortly after this tweet was posted, condemnations of Ciccariello-Maher surfaced in a variety of media outlets (as often occurs with professorial outrage online). These condemnations (as noted in fig. 7.1) may or may not have interpreted Ciccariello-Maher as building off of definitions such as the ADL's. Either way, they offer the immediacy of angry reactions within a mostly conservative base whose immediate response to online discourse attacking white people typically is outrage. Writing for *Breitbart*, Warner Todd Huston described Ciccariello-Maher's "praise for the 'massacre of whites.'" Thomas Lifson wrote in response to the tweet: "The Caucasians among the tender young minds exposed to Professor George Ciccariello-Maher at Drexel University are on notice that their teacher wants them exterminated because of their race. Not exactly a welcoming atmosphere." Arguing against his tweet, but not calling for his dismissal from the university, Theodore Kupfer wrote in the *National Review* that Ciccariello-Maher's rants reflected the fact that he is, "a privileged white man working in one of the most exclusive sectors of the nation's economy, a devotee of dialectical materialism who ignores material conditions when they are at odds with his ideology. He is, put simply, a hypocritic." One conservative website would eventually write of Ciccariello-Maher's overall tweets, "There's only so much crazy even the most liberal universities will put up with" (Alexander). Several Pennsylvania state senators wrote to Drexel's president and demanded Ciccariello-Maher be fired:

New Real Peer Review @RealPeerReview · Dec 25, 2016
George **Ciccariello-Maher** is an Associate Professor of Politics and
Global Studies and a Visiting Researcher @IISUNAM. Not a fan of
Whiteness

The Safest Space @TheSafestSpace · Dec 25, 2016
Replying to @datnofact
Someone is in the holiday spirit 😊

(HT @datnofact)

George Ciccariello ✓
@ciccmaher

All I Want for Christmas is White Genocide

10:48 PM · 24 Dec 16

87 RETWEETS **111** LIKES

💬 26   ↻ 184   ♡ 247   ⬆

Fig. 7.1. Twitter reaction to "white genocide" comment.

Professor Ciccariello-Maher once again used obviously inflammatory comments to promote his own shocking brand to the detriment of the reputation of Drexel.

We are confident that continuing to employ this hateful and disgusting man will do nothing but tarnish the Drexel name. We encourage you to terminate him as soon as possible. (Murphy)

Eventually, Drexel's president denounced the tweet as well. Ciccariello-Maher, however, attracted further attention with another tweet. After Stephen Paddock murdered fifty-nine people on October 1, 2017, at the Route 91 Harvest music festival in Las Vegas, Ciccariello-Maher received negative public responses for a tweet he wrote connecting Donald Trump and whiteness to the killings. "White people and men are told that they are entitled to everything. This is what happens when they don't get what they want," Ciccariello-Maher wrote. He additionally commented in a related tweet that the event, as well, was the result of white supremacists worried over an impending "white genocide": "It is the spinal column of Trumpism, and most extreme form is the white genocide myth. The narrative of white victimization has been gradually built over the past 40 years."[1] On October 2, Ciccariello-Maher followed these angry tweets with "It's the white supremacist patriarchy, stupid." The overall profile Ciccariello-Maher built through these tweets (and others) was an image of a white majority (or white supremacist majority) in fear of losing its majority status to others, and therefore, with acts such as what occurred in Las Vegas, projecting that fear in mass murder.

These tweets, as I write earlier in this book, draw associations between disparate acts as if both are identical (think Trump equals Hitler). A mass murder becomes associated with white people fearful of their own mythical genocide, an interpretation released prior to any knowledge regarding the murderer's background, history or political views. His profile was assumed. As Wajahat Ali writes, "What unites this version of the far right is a shared belief that white people are victims, threatened by a growing non-white demographic that threatens to render them powerless." Ciccariello-Maher is not alone in identifying an aggregated profile of white people as afraid of discrimination. A 2017 poll conducted by NPR, the Robert Wood Johnson Foundation, and the Harvard T. H. Chan School of Public Health determined that "A majority of whites say discrimination against them exists in America today" ("Majority of White Americans"). In this overall profile—traced here briefly over a few citations—the massacre in Las Vegas exemplifies the feeling of being threatened or discriminated against. Though there has not been any published material connecting Paddock to white supremacy (one report tied him to antigovernment conspiracy theories), Ciccariello-Maher constructed a profile of the murderer from these various circulated stereotypes (much as Facebook does to sell advertising) so that an algorithm might develop the desired profile: mass murderer equals white supremacist. His outrage reflects that algorithmic conclusion. Whether or not Paddock was a white supremacist is no longer relevant. The profile suggests he was.

Much like one of the first examples I began with—University of Tampa adjunct professor Kenneth Storey's justification for Hurricane Harvey's destruction of assumed Republicans in Texas—Ciccariello-Maher works from an assumed profile. All Texans are Republican Trump supporters is one profile. Mass murders are created by white supremacists is another profile. So are "icities," aggregations of assumed traits typically stereotypical in nature. Assumptions can be based on associations (Amazon asks if you would to buy a product based on an association with what you have previously purchased and what others have as well). Such associations can equate white supremacy with national tragedy or can locate other comparisons to associate with mass killings (mental illness). For example. one might draw an association between Ciccariello-Maher's tweet and University of Colorado professor Ward Churchill's essay written the day after 9/11, "On the Justice of Roosting Chickens," in which he called civilians killed during the Twin Towers attack "Little Eichmanns." Churchill, too, assumed a profile—workers in The World Trade Center working in a variety of businesses and organizations equate the characteristics associated with Adolph Eichmann whose Nazi machine murdered 6 million Jews. The World Trade Center, the hub of financial activity, struck an associative chord for Churchill which highlighted bureaucracy and business as Nazi or Nazi-like (and thus, deserving of retribution). Both moments of professorial outrage following national tragedy assumed not just these profiles, but an audience sympathetic to specific ideas connecting guilt and complicities. Both comments, as well, circulated imagery that ran counter to other's impression of the events. Both also evoked outrage from general audiences whose own profiles of the killer or the victims differed dramatically. Churchill was eventually fired in 2007.

After another round of public condemnation for his association of the massacre with Trump and the topic of "white genocide," Drexel responded by placing Ciccariello-Maher on administrative leave. Ciccariello-Maher eventually resigned from Drexel, blaming white supremacists for the negative attention to his tweets and subsequent death threats he received. He also attributed his case to one of academic freedom. Writing on Facebook on December 28, 2017, he argued, "We are at war, and academia is a crucial front in that war. This is why the Right is targeting campuses with thinly veiled provocations disguised as free speech. My case and many others show just how cynical such appeals are, and how little the Right cares about academic freedom." This statement highlights another profile publicly connected to digital outrage when that outrage involves professors: academic freedom. Academic freedom, as I will argue in this chapter is, as much an aggregation of beliefs as the phrase white genocide is.

Academic freedom is a technical image relied upon in moments such as what Ciccariello-Maher experienced. Ciccariello-Maher is not the only academic whose tweets raise the question of academic freedom, prompt public backlash or lead to employment scrutiny. When posted by academics, angry tweets or Facebook status updates about politics, racial tension and discrimination, global events, sexual harassment and other topics demanding public debate often lead to a corresponding outrage: attacks on the professor posting online. One reason, as I briefly touched upon in an earlier chapter, is enthymemic. In this chapter, I use the Ciccariello-Maher moment as exigence for a broader examination of outrage, professorial tweets, and the rhetorical concept of the enthymeme. While I have focused on photography as image in previous chapters, in this chapter I treat the tweet as technical image and ideology as technical image, particularly the ideological concept of academic freedom. When I write of academic freedom, as Ciccariello-Maher does in his Facebook post, I write of it as both a concept and as a circulated technical image whose meaning depends on how it moves through time and usage.

The academic freedom image also links to another image, that of a body against academic freedom. Based on his own aggregated audience profile, Ciccariello-Maher points to a "war" waged by the "right." He is not alone in this gesture. Much of the vitriol directed against professors for expressing outrage online has been attributed to either a conservative body hostile to university discourse, as Ciccariello-Maher suggested, or even worse, a right-wing conspiracy to shut down academic speech in general. Such responses shouldn't appear out of place or unexpected. The profile we often associate with the academic or the academic's ability to speak out on a variety of topics includes the question of academic freedom and one's ability to be protected by it. When an academic "speaks," the profile, as it is internally formed within academia, associates freedom to speak as one wants. An academic's image may include other aggregated stereotypes within a publicly projected profile (bookish, out of touch, leftist), but within academia, the notion of academic freedom, too, is embedded in that profile. Academic writings about moments such as Ciccariello-Maher's outrage tweets, in turn, often attribute public discourse surrounding this issue to a crisis regarding free speech. Ciccariello-Maher becomes aggregated into other imagery of professors angry online, particularly for those who share leftist opinions or who have felt backlash for expressing anger at conservatives or their causes. One expects Ciccariello-Maher, in other words, to be the same as any other professor one objected to or supported in the past. This expectation, at least for those who support the outrage, becomes embedded in previous beliefs regarding negative response to tweets such as those Ciccariello-Maher posted. Over time, any negative reaction is interpreted not as offense to a tweet's content (which could be the case) but as one opposed to academic freedom. The distinction is relevant to the presence of a technical image. Ciccariello-Maher, thus, represents for many not a singular instance of public indignation at a professor's outrage, but a broader movement directed against academic speech in general. Ciccariello-Maher, this rhetorical framing posits, is one of many academic victims of right-wing abuse. Again, we witness programming. If that programming does occur, as I suggest it does, it is worth some unpacking for what the academic audience assumes or fills in, as enthymemes require.

Public writings on this issue demonstrate how the overall technical image of academic freedom becomes entangled within the outrage over a given tweet. After all, Ciccariello-Maher did not mention academic freedom in his tweets. The question of academic freedom violation is based on the response to this tweets and the profile of response as antiacademic. These responses work from a built-in profile that immediately associates the image of academic freedom with a professor's social media posts, whether the professor claims that image or not. As Chris Quintana and Brock Read write in the *Chronicle of Higher Education*, the actual tweet itself is not as important as the quick circulation of outrage over the tweet: "Review enough such cases of faculty polemic gone viral, and an archetype starts to emerge—an assembly line of outrage that collects professors' Facebook posts, opinion essays, and classroom comments and amplifies them until they have become national news." This circulation is profiled as right wing.

A series of internal aggregations assumes that vitriol at academic vitriol must be right wing. The best way to review that profile is to sample public writings about incidents such as Ciccariello-Maher's where response typically makes that claim. This sampling, or what I might call a brief tracing, is meant to demonstrate how the profile exists as a circulated aggregation and how that aggregation shapes belief.

Victor Ray, writing for InsideHigherEd.com, argues that "the political right has developed a coordinated network to systematically target the free speech of presumably left-wing professors" (Ray). In the same publication, Jessie Daniels views right-wing attacks on leftist professors as evidence "that colleges and universities need to do a much better job of protecting academic freedom in a digitally networked age." *Reason's* Robby Soave summarized Drexel's failure to support Ciccariello-Maher as one of academic freedom: "Drexel should not discourage a professor from expressing his mind on Twitter—if faculty members must worry that any stray thought can land them in hot water, then the university is failing to cultivate an environment of maximally free speech" ("Drexel"). Regarding these charged social media incidents and the reactions they generate, Christopher Newfield proclaims, "The right clearly feels threatened again today." Writing an op-ed in the *Washington Post* after being placed on leave by Drexel, Ciccariello-Maher agreed with these kinds of positions which focus on right-wing responses, arguing, "More and more, professors like me are being targeted by a coordinated right-wing campaign to undermine our academic freedom— one that relies on misrepresentation and sometimes outright lying, and often puts us and our students in danger." In *Counter Punch*, Mike King argued that not only was the response to the tweets antithetical to academic freedom, it was connected to white supremacists (the worst of all right-wing responses): "Whether Drexel administrators value the hurt feelings of white supremacist internet trolls more than free and critical thought, academic freedom and the future of one of their best professors, should have been an easy decision—one that required no public statements of deep concern and no questions about disciplinary action." There is, then, in the public response to the tweets a discursive profile regarding criticism of Ciccariello-Maher and right-wing movements. This profile stems from the overall conservative response to Ciccariello-Maher's tweets, including expected criticism from notable conservative outlets that have long profiled leftist professors as problematic or anti-American, including such sites as *Breitbart*, *The Blaze*, *Campus Reform*, *Professor Watch List*, and *Infowars*. In his op-ed, Ciccariello-Maher lists fellow academics whose social media posts also have attracted the wrath of conservative websites and news: Saida Grundy, Zandria Robinson, Tommy Curry, and Johnny Eric Williams. This list helps to build the profile as it offers further ethos to his cause by associating himself with other notable social justice voices. With so many incidents, the pattern suggests much of what Ciccariello-Maher proposes, or it at least insinuates focused attention on leftist-oriented professors who use social media to express outrage at a variety of events or political figures. The pattern suggests an image.

Rather than follow that line of thinking, however, I want to examine professorial outbursts differently and from a rhetorical, rather than political or conspiratorial, angle. The conspiratorial angle is itself a technical image, a calculated profile that reduces all outrage to one kind of figure—right wing or conservative (or an extreme variation such as white supremacist). Whether that figure exists or not is irrelevant to the type of examination I would like to do in this chapter. I don't deny that right-wing outlets attack leftist professors for what they say on social media, but I am more interested in the rhetorical construction of the responses than the immediate conclusion of conspiracy. I want to examine professorial outrage on social media and the responses that follow as a question of audience recognition and response, and not as one of organized conservative conspiracy or white supremacy.

I choose to focus on professorial posts because academics, one might assume, command a specific understanding of rhetoric (or at least, professional discourse) and interpretation (as I note in the previous chapter), as well as represent professionals who teach and, in theory, perform critical thinking when engaging with either contemporary or controversial issues. Critical thinking suggests a knowledge of rhetorical situations and the audiences one attempts to reach. Critical thinking, as well, assumes there exists an audience for a given speech or writing act. By offering this specific focus, I hope to bring attention to problems regarding professorial assumptions about audience, assumptions which misdirect academic attention away from the discourse itself in favor of other types of assumptions driven by enthymemes. Enthymemes rely on assumptions. The power of the enthymeme, particularly in online discourse, challenges academic responses to not just events, but academic response in general. Whereas I concluded the previous chapter with the notion that suggestion offers a digital approach to imagery, I continue that mode of thought by focusing on enthymemes in this chapter. Enthymemes depend on assumption, but also on suggestion.

In a given social media rhetorical situation what does professorial anger assume regarding audience and audience reception? When a professor makes an argument regarding white genocide or draws a connection between a mass shooting and the president, what assumptions does the professor make about his or her audience's contextual knowledge or even political sympathies? Does the professor assume the existence of an audience, does the professor assume audience agreement, or does the professor assume that the tweet in question serves as entryway or participation into a larger debate? Or does the professor simply assume agreement with the logic behind the tweet and that nothing needs to be assumed nor is it suggesting? Does the professor assume that the tweet or Face-book post will generate a rhetorical situation that can be academically debated or immediately agreed upon? When Ciccariello-Maher insists "It's the white su-premacist patriarchy, stupid" he must assume the presence of an audience who shares this aggregated profile regarding a segment of the population who either is part of the white supremacist patriarchy or who recognizes its existence. But why does he assume as such? And how does an audience assume such an entity might exist? How, in other words, is response imagined by the rhetor, and how does the rhetor trigger suggestions in that imagination?

There are likely examples drawn from, interactions which occurred, images circulated and believed in, and past responses to problematic events that lead a rhetor to believe an audience exists for the outrage, whether that assumed audi-ence is right or left oriented. Lloyd Bitzer canonically posed the rhetorical situa-tion as one of audience and response: "To say that rhetoric is situational means: (1) rhetorical discourse comes into existence as a response to situation, in the same sense that an answer comes into existence in response to a question or a solution in response to a problem; (2) a speech is given rhetorical significance by the situation, just as a unit of discourse is given significance as answer or as solu-tion by the question or problem" ("Rhetorical Situation" 5–6). For Bitzer, rhet-oric is situational because of how it functions in response to a given exigence. Response, in turn, participates in creating a reality. The ways we respond—in various forms of writing—shape the realities we believe in. "Rhetoric is a mode of altering reality," Bitzer argues, "by the creation of discourse which changes reality through the mediation of thought and action" ("Rhetorical Situation" 4). Bitzer's example of Kennedy's assassination focuses not on the killing of Ken-nedy but on the different types of responses the president's death evoked, and thus, whether in eulogy or reporting, the ways these responses created realities for different audiences, including more contemporary realities such as conspir-acies regarding the president's killing. A mass murder in Las Vegas provides an exigence for a university professor who understands the rhetorical situation as anger at Trump or at white supremacy. The Las Vegas killings create significance for Ciccariello-Maher and a supposedly imagined audience following him on Twitter. His tweet is a rhetorical situation, as much as a eulogy was for Kennedy.

In social media outbursts of anger, the exigence for professorial outbursts stems from a given problem (why did an individual mass murder people at-tending a country music performance in Las Vegas, for instance), and the tweet or post intends to form a new situation (white supremacy is to blame), but the response to these outbursts, as well, affects another rhetorical situation separate from the specific problem (why, for example, do professors take stances con-trary to majority opinion; are these stances violations of academic freedom). The question for rhetoric and social media is to distinguish between these two distinct rhetorical moments much as Bitzer distinguishes from Kennedy being assassinated and the responses to the assassination. These distinct rhetorical moments include a professorial moment of anger as response to a given event or moment and a public response to that response.

In this chapter, I approach this question via a discussion of the enthymeme in order to better understand these moments as more complex than a right-wing conspiracy or as coordinated political attacks. The enthymeme, I argue, offers rhetoric a way to better comprehend both the outburst and the response within digital contexts. The digital platforms where these outbursts occur are important because (as I've discussed in earlier chapters) digital audiences are not always obvious (who follows me? who follows who follows me?) and digital discourse spreads differently than print or oral exchange does. By focusing on enthymemes and the assumptions they must contain within their utterances, I am not endorsing nor denying the existence of troubling responses that often follow outbursts such as Ciccariello-Maher's: death threats, calls for rape, hate mail, or any other act of violence. These are other levels of response I leave aside for now. Nor am I commenting on the legality of response, as in the University of Illinois' decision to withdraw an offer of employment to Steven Salaita, a case I will later discuss. Instead, I am focusing on the assumptions implicit in many of the professorial moments of social media outrage that eventually earn public attention. I am focusing on the enthymeme as a rhetorical practice of digital assumption (and suggestion) and how that practice makes assumptions about audience and rhetorical delivery.

THE ENTHYMEME

Enthymemes have long been a focus of rhetorical studies. Walter Ong explains Peter Ramus' definition of the enthymeme as the origin of contemporary usage, "a syllogism which is 'imperfect' in the crude, *simpliste* sense that one of its premises is suppressed" (*Ramus* 187). This definition, though championed by Ramus, stems from Aristotle's brief note in *The Rhetoric* that the enthymeme is an "imperfect syllogism." That question of imperfection has led to a great deal of commentary and analysis on what an enthymeme actually is or how it should be defined or differentiated from the syllogism. Carol Poster traces the vast influence of Aristotle's statement, noting the many contradictory definitions of enthymemes among rhetoricians and teachers of rhetoric. Out of the many citations Poster offers, she cites Lloyd Bitzer's 1959 *Quarterly Journal of Speech* essay "Aristotle's Enthymeme Revisited" and Bitzer's focus that "the premises of the enthymeme be supplied by the audience" (qtd. Poster 5, Bitzer 405). Following a discussion of the traditional breakdown of major and minor premises, Bitzer also states, "The missing materials of rhetorical arguments are the premises which the audience brings with it, and supplied at the proper moment provided the orator is skillful" ("Aristotle" 407). Following Bitzer, I concentrate on the audience directed aspect of enthymemic discourse, and, in particular, the missing elements that audiences focus upon in order to draw conclusions.

For many scholars, enthymemes depend on assumptions regarding audience knowledge. "The structure of the enthymeme," John Gage writes, "derives its function from the relationship between a writer's intended conclusions and an audience's pre-existing assumptions" (39). In his pedagogical analysis of effective enthymemes, Gage draws attention to the assumptions "shared by or derived by the writer's audience" (40). "Essentially," James Raymond argues similarly, "enthymemes may be defined as assumptions used in public discourse" (144). Jeffrey Walker reintroduces the basic aspect of enthymemic thinking as the "tendency to emphasize the dialogic relation between writer and audience by requiring the writer to include the audience's thinking in the invention process" ("The Body of Persuasion" 46–47). Walker draws upon Axaximenes and not Aristotle, stating that in an enthymemic moment, "The audience is to feel not simply that the speaker's claims are true or probable, but that both speaker and claims are good and admirable, and the very opposite of what is false, bad, and detestable" ("The Body of Persuasion" 50). Enthymemes, therefore, carry an element of ethos with them, assuming that the audience will recognize that the speaker/writer and the content of the statement are valid and good. When a speaker/writer makes a public announcement about the president, a hurricane, or a racially charged issue, the speaker will assume his or her ethos is being read positively. "Professor" may add to that assumed ethos ("professor" contains its own various embedded imagery depending on the audience, from knowledgeable to radically out of tune with society). Online presence may as well. A tweet by a professor may indicate credibility ("professors must know what they are talking about; therefore, you will believe what I write"). Or it may not.

In his discussion of enthymemes, Walker deviates from the traditional emphasis on the syllogism and instead focuses on inference, "from probable assumptions granted by one's audience" ("The Body of Persuasion" 47). This non-Aristotelian enthymeme, Walker describes, "is a strategic, kairotic, argumentational turn that exploits a cluster of emotively charged—value-laden oppositions made available (usually) by an exetastic buildup in order to generate in its audience a passional identification with or adherence to a particular stance, and that (ideally) will strike the audience as an "abrupt" and decisive flash of insight" (The Body of Persuasion" 53). In such a stance, an audience, the speaker/writer assumes, will treat the rhetorical moment as insightful and based on ethos. The speaker/rhetor identifies the value laden point ("we all agree Trump is awful" or "Trump supports white supremacy") and builds up identification of that point with an assumed connection as insight ("the reason the Las Vegas massacre occurred was because of Trump who supports white supremacy"). A tweet or post, as a particularly compressed form of digital rhetorical expression, is posed as one such flash of insight in which limited characters focused on a passionate issue (race, the president, politics, global conflict) can produce audience identification based on assumptions. The tweet or post is an image. This image images an idea quickly to an assumed audience for followers or those who follow one's followers. To reach that audience, however, one assumes the audience in question exists and shares the tweet or post's passion. This point is key to how digital professorial outrage is responded to by an assumed audience. These outbursts, such as wishing for white genocide (whether as literal act or critique of white response to genocide or critique of white supremacists imaginary fear of their own genocide because of immigration or as satire), eventually *are not read* as insightful nor identified with by a specific and vocal audience. That audience, as I note, has often been profiled as right wing or extremist based on a variety of patterns that project the image of such an individual. In cases such as Ciccariello-Maher, that audience exists, but it seems that other audience responses eventually counter the speaker/writer's assumption regarding ethos, insight, and audience.

While Walker dismisses the term enthymeme as not relevant to rhetorical work and as too tied to Aristotle, I maintain the term as an essential feature of digital interactions across social media platforms. I add the word "assumed" to the overall definition of enthymeme that associates the term with audience. Assumed, continuing my interests in suggestion, plays a vital role regarding audience response. Assumed, a term present in many definitions of audience-based enthymemes, is not tied to the rhetorical gesture in a concrete way, but it should be, particularly when we discuss digital or social media interactions. As Casey Boyle argues, "the enthymeme, then, does not seduce audiences through logics of induction or deduction but, instead, transduces an incorporation." Through transduction, Boyle notes, "the audience who 'fills in' for 'missing' premises does so only according to their own capacities" (85). These capacities, I add, depend on assumptions. Emotionally charged statements, identification, the differentiation between what is good and what is bad, ethos, preexisting belief, acknowledgment of "other" forces working against one—these are rhetorical assumptions made when addressing an ambiguous and not always identifiable social media–based audience whose connections and networks make it both fluid and present during an interaction. "The object is always open to further invention as it becomes differently incorporated" (Boyle 86). The tweets I begin with here in this chapter pose as such objects. They ask for and assume identifications (either for or against academic freedom/for or against white supremacy) that may lead to further inventions (protest, support, more tweets, etc.). These tweets work from the power of enthymemic suggestion. "I am against Trump and white supremacy." "I am too." Assumptions about similar identifications occur. Invention occurs.

An audience must computate, as Flusser argued, a variety of positions, images, experiences, and knowledge into a singular image in order to draw a conclusion. Enthymemes depend on an audience maintaining some type of internal database in order to make an assumption, but Flusser's technical image assumes that all of us program various imagery into this database. While Flusser does not describe the technical image as enthymemic, he does indicate how audiences make assumptions based on how a given image is layered. "All technical images have the same basic character," Flusser wrote, "on close inspection, they all prove to be envisioned surfaces computed from particles" (*Into the Universe* 33). As I've written in earlier chapters, these "particles" consist of the various previously encountered images and ideas we bring to a reading of a present image. Flusser wrote: "At first glance, technical images appear to be surface. Observing takes more than just looking, which explains why we have insight into hardly any of the many things we see. Technical images seem to be surfaces as a result of our laziness about close observation" (*Into the Universe* 33).

While laziness seems to be a harsh criticism, we can extend Flusser's remarks to those who accept imagery for its immediacy. That immediacy could be the reaction to a national tragedy expressed in a tweet, but it can also be the reaction to the tweet. This immediacy is enthymemic for what the reader fills in based on her already established assumptions, stereotypes, and profiles. "I am a Man", as I noted earlier, demands a filling in of historic detail in order to understand the phrase's meaning and relevance to 1960s issues of race and labor. White genocide, too, demands users fill in details regarding the history of white dominance over non-white peoples in various parts of the world. But details based on what? Flusser's critique of those who he calls "lazy" also extends to how they are willing to follow programmed imagery even as they fill in such details. This runs counter to much enthymeme rhetorical scholarship which does not address programming. They, Flusser argues, are people who "unleashed processes into which they needed no deep insight" and "set events into motion that they cannot grasp, understand or conceive" (*Into the Universe* 35, 36). That is not a critique that Ciccariello-Maher or other professors I write about would accept. Still, I question the flash of insight or deep insight claimed by immediate associations of outrage.

This final point returns me to the issue of academic freedom, technical images, and outrage I have presented as joined in this chapter. Why does academic freedom return as a response to the response regarding professorial outrage? One answer might be in the idea of programmability and enthymemic assumptions. The layering of a history of concerns over academic freedom upon challenges to specific professors often leads to the charge of speech violations. That particular assumption, the violation, is programed by the technical image called academic freedom. All present images, for Flusser, are programmed images. The images are not natural but are composites of other images whose overlap programs an ideology, a bias, a position, a posture, a representation and so on. "I Am a Man" is a programmed image. It is not neutral because it depends on a layering of preceding imagery, such as what I previously outlined. Ciccariello-Maher's "white genocide," as well, is a programmed image dependent on previous understandings of genocide, critiques of "whiteness," and white complacency or involvement in discriminatory or oppressive practices. Flusser adds: "The signified of a technical image, whether it be a photograph of a house or a computer image of a virtual airplane, is something drawn from the inside toward the outside. . . . To decode a technical image is not to decode what it shows but to read how it is programmed" (*Into the Universe* 48). One public response to such declarations, and also an assumption based on enthymemic construction, is the invocation of academic speech.

ACADEMIC SPEECH

Academic freedom or academic speech, an important point of Ciccariello-Maher's defense of his tweets and the focus of much of the professorial rhetoric I will examine, is an enthymemic phrase. Academic freedom, as well, is a technical image. To say that the phrase is enthymemic and image-based is not to contradict one term for the other but to recognize the assumption/suggestive power of imagery, whether in text or in photograph. The utterance of this phrase makes several audience assumptions based on its technical image status. For instance, the claim for academic freedom is an argument that academic writing or speech should be protected as free speech in order to allow for the transmittal and circulation of controversial ideas or ideas that seem controversial for challenging the status quo (but which, in fact, may become the status quo at some point). Thus, any speech act or writing (digital or in print) delivered by an individual who holds an academic position should be protected as academic freedom in order to ensure academics the ability to pursue knowledge without fear of retribution from those who disagree. These are the most basic assumptions one fills in (the creation of a profile) when hearing the phrase "academic freedom." Such assumptions, as I will show in this chapter, stem from specific profiles built over the years regarding this issue.

Academic freedom is also an image within social media exchanges. In the case of Ciccariello-Maher, tweets by a professor about white genocide are assumed protected by academic freedom regardless of their reception or relation to actual academic work. To arrive at that final point, however, is to believe in either the preceding premises (all academic discourse is protected) or that the final point follows those premises (what was tweeted should be recognized as academic discourse). An audience who is persuaded that a call for white genocide is simultaneously protected as academic freedom is persuaded that the call is academic speech. The audience who thinks differently is not persuaded by the assumed premises and therefore becomes outraged and calls for a professor's dismissal in response. Both positions, however, arrive at their assumptions via a variety of previous interactions and beliefs that have generated a specific image called academic freedom. Based on these interactions, an assumption emerges regarding whether to accept the tweet as legitimate academic speech or to express anger at the tweet, or to regard the backlash at the tweet as uninformed or malicious. Academic speech depends greatly on how these previous premises are read and assumed to exist.

Academic freedom/speech is a highly persuasive term for professorial discourse. Enthymemes are often used for purposes of persuasion. I place the phrase academic speech/academic freedom in this tradition of using enthymemes to persuade, particularly regarding social issues. One assumption often made when hearing the phrase academic freedom is that it perpetually faces *restriction* or *constraint*. Historically, academic freedom has always faced such conflict. The 1915 Declaration of Principles on Academic Freedom and Academic Tenure, adopted at the AAUP annual meeting in Washington, DC, of that year, uses such language, emphasizing the threat of infringement: "The safeguarding of a proper measure of academic freedom in American universities requires both a clear understanding of the principles which bear upon the matter, and the adoption by the universities of such arrangements and regulations as may effectually prevent any infringement of that freedom and deprive of plausibility all charges of such infringement" (292). In 1943, the *Bulletin of the American Association of University Professors* reprinted the 1915 declaration as well as the 1925 American Council on Education's conference statement on academic freedom. This statement begins with the same concerns of infringement, using words like "restraint," "restriction," and "limitation" to stress the importance of free speech among professors, whether in the university or outside of it.

> a) A university or college may not place any restraint upon the teacher's freedom in investigation, unless restriction upon the amount of time devoted to it becomes necessary in order to prevent undue interference with teaching duties.
>
> b) A university or college may not impose any limitation upon the teacher's freedom in the exposition of his own subject in the classroom or in addresses and publications outside the college. ("Academic Freedom and Tenure" 76)

Over the years, the *Bulletin* has devoted considerable space to the subject. In 1954, Glenn R. Murrow wrote "a society that believes in orderly change, rather than revolution and violence—such a society cannot put restrictions upon inquiry in its universities and colleges without cutting the root, or circling the main stem, of all the varied and abundant growth of its free institutions" (533). In 2006 in the same publication, Geoffrey Stone repeated such warnings, updating them for contemporary politics: "The current challenge to academic freedom ranges across a broad spectrum, from the provisions of the Patriot Act and federal restrictions on the participation of foreign researchers in certain types of research to the possibility of new government constrains on universities with respect to teaching, research and the dissemination of scientific and scholarly findings" (17).

The *Bulletin*, of course, is not the only publication projecting a technical image called academic freedom. Many writers and publications make assumptions about the image called academic freedom and the profiles (i.e. the aggregations) of those who supposedly oppose it. "The risk of speaking out," Howard Zinn argues, "is always present in the academy, where jobs and prestige depend on the approval of administrators, businessmen-trustees, and politicians" (59). "Academic freedom is under attack," Philip Altbach begins a 2001 *Higher Education* essay (205). "Academic freedom," Laurence Cassidy writes, "defines itself as the principle that sets the university apart as an open market place where ideas may be reasonably discussed by reasonable people without fear of coercion, either external or internal" (7). "Any internal account of what goes on in the academic world must at the same time be a convincing rationale for maintaining the space defined by academic freedom," Louis Menand argues (4). "Academic freedom does and should tolerate even the outrageous and the bizarre in the interests of protecting legitimate, if often, controversial and unwelcome, speech," Robert O'Neil states (41). There is much layering to this image. Each image layered into the next makes assumptions about the subject and its assumed objectors.

Over time, these types of statements (and many more) become fused into a technical image. Academic freedom is not a singular idea but an embedded one whose power to persuade depends greatly on a reader filling in the missing gaps the phrase does not provide, but rather suggests: danger, restriction, constraint, free space, legitimate. The term circulates widely through texts and speeches, casual discourse, and currently, social media. Social protest often utilizes this phrase as a leverage point for emotional response. The question for rhetorical studies is whether the reader of an image can recognize these traits or not. Ciccariello-Maher may believe that yes, a reader can understand his implicit scattered traits and particles; the public outcry, on the other hand, did not. Audience is key to this question.

THE SOCIAL MEDIA AUDIENCE AS ENTHYMEMIC

The Ciccariello-Maher case occurred on Twitter (and my next example, as well, took place on the platform). Just as there are ties that connect various understandings of imagery such as academic freedom (what one reads, who one is colleagues with, who one converses with), social media is based on the question of ties, as I have noted. Within our social networks we have strong ties (who we know well such as our family, our friends, and our co-workers) and weak ties (who we barely know or not at all). As I noted in an earlier chapter, while we might assume that strong ties are an individual's most powerful connections in a given social media network and our most readily available audience, weak ties, in fact, are more powerful and more prevalent. Communication may take place more often among strong ties (paying attention to each other's updates or tweets on a regular basis), but for every 150 weak ties (Adams' number for the average member of a network), each one of those 150 has another 150 weak ties, and so on. Each set of weak ties can connect to what we say or share online. One will always have far more weak ties than strong ties. With every public like or share, this vast network is connected to us, as well; each sees our social media interactions or has our interactions shared with them. Strong ties are more likely to pass over controversial remarks or not share them with unsympathetic audiences. Weak ties—those 150 and then 150 beyond—may be more likely to share because their viewpoints will diversify. "Weak ties," Adam argues, "are at the periphery of our social network, which means they are connected to more diverse sets of people than our strong ties, which are more central in our network. These diverse ties pass on more novel information, and so they can often know more than our strong ties do" (64). In an audience driven rhetoric motivated by enthymemic exchange, how can one account for so many weak ties and their assumptions? One cannot.

My interests, therefore, are in extending the enthymeme (and its technical image counterpart) to an examination of what I call the *assumed enthymeme,* particularly for how it functions in social media spaces' vast networks of differing and unknown assumptions, and even more specifically, among academics in social media spaces. As with the Ciccariello-Maher case, in the last few years, there have been a plethora of controversial moments in which an academic posts a tweet or Facebook update that generates a considerable response. The initial post is typically angry, and the consequential responses, which typically spread out over weak ties and not just among right-wing conspiracists, are angry as well. In addition to assumptions regarding scattered traits and layered meanings, the immediate posting may be written with the assumption that only likeminded readers (strong ties) will encounter it, or that, at the least, an audience is limited to those who follow or who are friends. This impression ignores the weak ties extending outward who may differ in political viewpoint and technical image—thus the concern over a profile of right-wing respondents. Along with the technical image aspect of assumed enthymemes—the layered meanings within the image—is the question of connectivity and assumption.

Twitter often functions as a platform for projected anger as enthymemic expression. Twitter's basic unit of connectivity is the follow. Following provides exposure to other Twitter users' tweets. One may heart a tweet (signifying agreement) or retweet (sharing the tweet with one's own social network of close and weak ties and, as well, signifying agreement). Likes and retweets are assumptions of audience; I assume these acts signify connection or agreement. "On Twitter," Alice Marwick and danah boyd write in contrast, "there is a disconnect between followers and followed" (117). Marwick and boyd summarize their research via the observation that this disconnect stems from Twitter users neglecting audience: "They are uncomfortable labeling interlocutors and witnesses as an 'audience.' In bristling over the notion of audience, they are likely rejecting a popularly discussed act of 'personal branding' as running counter to what they value: authenticity. In other words, consciously speaking to an audience is perceived as inauthentic" (119). Twitter offers a "mode of expression," Dhiraj Murthy writes, "in that the unintended audience has an incongruous understanding of what the speaker may have actually intended" (780). Naaman, Boase, and Lai call tweets "social awareness streams," the networking of personal-public communication, brevity of content, and highly connected spaces (n.p.). Part of their quantitative study revealed that the "majority of [Twitter] users focus on the 'self'" (n.p.). Self-focus, in some situations, can lead writers to assume that audience belief is the same or likeminded because the self-tweets (or simply communicates) via its own technical images. Twitter users might assume that the tweets they project outward to their followers, and consequently, their followers' followers, are, without any question, persuasive on their own terms and not programmed computations, as Flusser might argue. Following boyd and Marwick's analysis, the projected technical image may not believe there exists an audience for a rhetorical situation, or at the least, there isn't an audience who disagrees. Ciccariello-Maher can only believe that those who object to his association between a mass murderer and the president are white supremacists because he focuses on the self (his own belief system). On Twitter, I express my beliefs, and whether there is or is not an audience, my expression is self-understood as persuasive because of what I am already persuaded by (or programmed). Audiences, of course, do exist, but the assumption of audience agreement often confuses public proclamations on social media and causes one to forget that point. The call for murder, as one very public case of Twitter self-expression demonstrates, reveals that confusion. From Ciccariello-Maher, I switch to another high-profile professorial example.

SALAITA

When then Virginia Tech professor Steven Salaita tweeted on June 19, 2014, "You may be too refined to say it, but I'm not: I wish all the fucking West Bank settlers would go missing," he was referencing the Hamas kidnapping and murder of three Israeli teenagers: Naftali Frankel, Gilad Shaar and Eyal Yifrach (@steve-salaita). Salaita's tweet, which would eventually be listed among other tweets as reason to not hire him at the University of Illinois, prompted considerable outcry both against Salaita's online commentary and in support of academic speech. Those who follow Ciccariello-Maher's and other like-minded thinkers' concerns believe a movement exists in higher education determined to squash controversial thought no matter its content. As much as it existed for Ciccariello-Maher, the technical image of academic freedom framed the Salaita case as well. The profile extended outward from white supremacists (not dominant in the Salaita case) to the university itself (often embedded in another technical image of corporate influence and neoliberalism) and an imagined Israeli monetary influence that overrides democratic decision making. "The Salaita case," Joan W. Scott concluded, "is also an example of the increasing calls for intervention by boards of trustees in the academic affairs of their universities." Joseph Massad called for a boycott "to deny the [University of Illinois] accreditation based on its suppression of academic freedom and its usurpation of faculty rights." In his own narrative, Salaita wrote in the *Chronicle of Higher Education* that his case illustrated the overall corporate mentality dominant within university culture and the desire of universities to control professorial speech. He also profiled the image of the professor as one who always challenges the status quo: "Whatever independence can be acquired in academe requires a fundamental distrust of authority, be it abstract or explicit. There never have been pure epochs of uncorrupted democracy, but increasing corporate control disturbs greater sectors of American life, particularly on campus. There has to be a better way to conduct the practices of education." The reaction, then, to the tweets is not the content of the tweets but the image of academic freedom and an assumption of its violation. But what did Salaita actually say, and how did its enthymemic gesture prompt outrage? Did he indeed represent the needed intellectual "distrust of authority" as his own imagined profile of academic life claims? Or did other technical imagery play into his case?

Salaita's tweet depends on specific enthymemic assumptions. Salaita's tweet, as well, assumes a few things about the readership who follows his self-expression. His assumed readership might think accordingly: 1. Readers believe Israel unjustly occupies the West Bank; 2. Israelis living in the West Bank do so illegally; and 3. The murder of Israelis who are in the West Bank is, therefore, justified because they are illegally present. There is, then, an enthymemic process at play. This was not the first time Salaita tweeted a call for Israelis to be murdered. Nor was it his only enthymemic tweet. On April 25, 2014, Salaita tweeted, "I think of all the pain Israelis have caused, their smugness, their greed, their violence, and yet I smile, because it's all only temporary" (@stevesalaita). Here, too, enthymemic assumptions occur regarding how an audience might accept such a statement: 1. Israelis are smug and violent and as Jews, are greedy; 2. Smugness and violence counter justifications for existence; and 3. Because Israel is smug and violent, it will soon no longer exist as other forces will rectify the situation. That final assumption, it seems, is a call to murder Israelis and destroy the country because of a prolific assumption regarding their character. As a call for murder (and dissemination of anti-Semitic tropes of Jewish arrogance and greed), Salaita's tweets, one might assume, would generate considerable outcry from academic and non-academic audiences. Calls for murder should generate outrage. Yet, most of the academic outrage directed at Salaita's tweets came from the returning technical image of academic freedom and not the murder call itself. I will address this point further after drawing attention to one other prominent Salaita tweet.

On July 19, 2014, Salaita tweeted "Zionists: transforming 'antisemitism' from something horrible into something honorable since 1948" (@stevesalaita). In this case, the enthymemic tweet depends on two premises for an audience to agree: 1. Anti-Semitism was previously bad; 2. Zionism, the Jewish nationalism formed in the nineteenth century and which led to the creation of Israel in 1948, is so egregious that it has created a current situation in which it is acceptable to be anti-Semitic; and 3. It is now acceptable to be anti-Semitic. This is a fairly broad reach, yet it did not raise concerns among other academics. If it, then, is acceptable to be anti-Semitic, one can tweet or say similarly anti-Semitic statements. We see those statements in other Salaita tweets such as the popular, repeated trope that Jews, once the victims of genocide, are now oppressors and have become Nazis or equivalent terrorist organizations which engage in ethnic cleansing such as ISIS. In making such claims, one works from associations and assumptions based on either semblance (though it's not clear what that semblance is) or the assumption of semblance ("I object to ISIS, I object to Israel, therefore, Israel is ISIS). Salaita has tweeted on numerous occasions this assumption of semblance regarding ISIS and other notorious entities. On August 2, 2014, he tweeted "#Israel is rounding up people and murdering them at point-blank range. The word 'genocide' is more germane the more news we hear" (@stevesalaita). On May 6, 2014, he tweeted, "#IsraeliIndependence-Equals sustenance of the European eugenic logic made famous by Hitler" (@

stevesalaita). On July 23, 2014, he tweeted, "#Israel and #ISIS are but two prongs of the same violent ethnonationalism" (@stevesalaita). One could make two different enthymemic assumptions based on these tweets. The first might follow accordingly: 1. It is now acceptable to be anti-Semitic; 2. One anti-Semitic statement often made is that Jews are Nazis or as bad as groups ethnically cleansing populated areas the way the Nazis did; and 3. I can now claim Jews are Nazis. A similar assumption might leave aside the claim that justifies anti-Semitic discourse and instead settles on something akin to: 1. Jews suffered under Nazi genocide; 2. Israel conducts genocide; and 3. Israel is today's Nazi Germany.

Assumptions do not need evidence for an audience to identify truth. Assumptions need semblance. Semblance depends on aggregations (like an Italian food advertisement). An enthymeme speaks to an *audience's assumptions* regarding what may or may not be true. An enthymeme speaks to an audience's -icity of a given situation, whether that is Italianicity (the assumption that Italians only eat pasta and decorate in green and red) or Israelicity (which, in this case, might be the assumption that Israel is evil). To equate Israel with Nazi Germany (much like the example of Trump and Hitler I offered earlier as affective), one does not need to prove that Israel is Nazi Germany (Israel, of course, has not conquered Europe, built a network of concentration camps, and murdered 6 million people). One needs only to suggest the image based on association, emotion, preconceived imagery, semblance, aggregated imagery, etc. These items program a profile that can be persuasive to an audience already convinced of the profile's accuracy.

At this point, one can read Salaita's tweets as directed toward perceived sympathetic political or anti-Israel audience assumptions. However, as with my previous example, another layer in this communicative stream occurs as one particular audience, mostly academic but sometimes journalistic, conveys its own enthymemic assumptions whose focus is not the anti-Israel sentiment but the nature of the speech itself. Response to Salaita follows closely the response to Ciccariello-Maher regarding the technical image of academic freedom. Public reaction in support of Salaita did not acknowledge any progressions of thought I outline above. Instead, those academics who supported Salaita built into the tweets not these premises (or some variation) but instead a completely different enthymemic conclusion based on the question of academic speech and its assumed enthymemic stance. Another level of assumption occurs: 1. A professor tweets about Israel (or any other subject); 2. Because the tweet was written by a professor, the tweet is academic speech; and 3. The tweet is therefore protected from retaliation of any sort (critical or professional employment). There are two levels of enthymemic assumption occurring: one regarding Israel and anti-Semitism and one regarding what an academic is allowed to say on social media without fear of retribution or critique. How these two assumptions are read and then circulated as response determines how the speaker is interpreted (his or her ethos) as well how the speaker interprets public reaction (response to the rhetorical situation).

The Salaita case allows for a return to the question of academic freedom as an enthymemic assumption. That academics would concentrate on the technical image of academic freedom and not the racism within Salaita's tweets is fairly predictable since academic freedom is central to professorial concerns and discourse (programming) and specific countries are typically peripheral (unless collected under specific profiles to object to). As a technical image, academic freedom projects any number of dominant images and beliefs among its professorial audience, which eventually translate into assumptions about professorial discourse in general. Many of these images and beliefs are based on previous actions by disparate universities to limit what professors can write about or say within the university, as well as the accompanying professorial fear that follows these actions.

Within the university, academic freedom is a dominant technical image. In addition to the previous layers I mention, part of this technical image may be based on post–World War II McCarthy influenced requirements that teachers sign pledges or loyalty oaths that they did not belong to the Communist Party or other "subversive" groups. Or this technical image may be partly based on The University of Chicago's 1967 Kalven report, often cited in academic freedom discussions. The report argued "By design and by effect, it is the institution which creates discontent with the existing social arrangements and proposes new ones. In brief, a good university, like Socrates, will be upsetting."[2] The university, the report continues, "arises out of respect for free inquiry and the obligation to cherish a diversity of viewpoints."

Within this image may also be the 1967 Supreme Court ruling in Keyishian vs. Board of Regents that the University of Buffalo could not force faculty to sign pledges that they had never been a member of the Communist Party nor could the university prohibit faculty from distributing materials or speech deemed "subversive." The AAUP's *1940 Statement on Principles of Academic Freedom and Tenure* outlined a number of points to protect teacher rights including its important first provision: "Teachers are entitled to full freedom in research and in the publication of the results, subject to the adequate performance of their other academic duties; but research for pecuniary return should be based upon an understanding with the authorities of the institution." But the document also contains the broader statement, likely folded into contemporary technical images professorial discourse identifies as authentic:

> College and university teachers are citizens, members of a learned profession, and officers of an educational institution. When they speak or write

as citizens, they should be free from institutional censorship or discipline, but their special position in the community imposes special obligations. As scholars and educational officers, they should remember that the public may judge their profession and their institution by their utterances. Hence they should at all times be accurate, should exercise appropriate restraint, should show respect for the opinions of others, and should make every effort to indicate that they are not speaking for the institution

In addition to his professorial status, Steven Salaita was a citizen as he tweeted anti-Semitic language to both his followers (strong ties) and his followers' followers (weak ties). These tweets could be folded into previous ideas regarding "upsetting" or "subversive" language one is allowed to make because one maintains the aggregated profile of professor working within another aggregated profile called academic freedom. If one has layered into a technical image of academic speech the image of the professor as citizen, then that part of the technical image may override other possible image inclusions such as being "accurate" or exercising "appropriate restraint," particularly as an audience (one's self or others who agree) is assumed among one's social media followers.

Among the many cases of professors losing or failing to gain tenure due to internal disagreement, institutional debate, publication controversy, contested classroom practice, or other issues, there emerge new layers that constitute the technical image called academic freedom or academic speech. All of these items aggregate into one image called academic freedom. Assumptions about the technical image are based on which items are drawn upon as premises. The University of Illinois' decision to withdraw an offer of employment to Salaita was read by supporters of Salaita as a challenge to academic freedom (Salaita is read as citizen and as professor) and was not read as a response to racist discourse or the call for murder. The two premises leading to each of the tweets, as I outline them, do not seem to influence the various critiques of academic speech violations or play a role in declaring an academic speech violation. Indeed, none of the supporters of Salaita address the implied premises of his tweets.

Instead of reading the content of the tweets and forming a response based on the tweets, Salaita's support read the technical image of academic speech and based its response on the already circulated fears of its erosion. This difference is important as it directs attention toward the kinds of assumptions audiences made and then circulated throughout various media—blogposts, newspaper interviews, or other social media responses. These assumptions are based on exposure to previously articulated issues regarding academic speech. "The summary dismissal of Professor Steven Salaita from a tenured faculty position at the University of Illinois is the single most brazen attack on freedom of speech in American universities in my lifetime," University of Chicago law professor

Brian Leiter argued in his opening remarks to a sponsored Salaita talk. Writing for the American Association of University Professors, Peter Kirstein summarizes much of the Salaita coverage and concludes with a claim about academic freedom, not the actual tweets Salaita wrote or the assumptions that they make: "In reporting the news, the media serve the common good. When revelations surface that students are being denied professors who are free to teach so that they are free to learn, education is protected." The *New York Times* covered the Salaita incident by reporting on academics who cancelled talks at The University of Illinois in protest. Each cancellation was based on a concern over academic freedom. As University of Minnesota History professor Allen Isaacman is quoted, "The University of Illinois's recent decision to disregard its prior commitment to appoint Professor Salaita confirms my fear of the administration's blatant disregard for academic freedom" (Dunn). "Don't Speak Out," David Perry's essay in the *Chronicle of Higher Education* was titled. Perry's conclusion regarding Salaita's case is not based on the enthymemic postings or what their assumptions might be, but the generic issue of academic speech which, for him, is layered with public response as improper (his calling out of "bloggers and local papers"): "We need to open pathways for more academics to speak out in public, not punish Salaita for doing so in ways that have provoked such strong feelings. But we can't ask scholars to embrace the risks of engagement in a system in which partisan bloggers and local papers can push timid administrators to fire, or in this case unhire, academics who leap into public debates." In *The Nation*, David Palumbo-Li called the Salaita affair McCarthyite and a "shock wave" sent throughout the university community. "A Six Figure Settlement on Campus Free Speech," an *Atlantic* headline read after the University of Illinois settled with Salaita, transforming the issue into one of paying off denied speech, and not the tweets themselves.

What we witness in these responses is an enthymemic response (academic speech) outside of the enthymemic assumptions the tweet initially made. One technical image trumps the other. Academic speech is a powerful and well-circulated enthymemic assumption within academic discourse. The shock at Salaita's predicament emerges from the vast social networked audience cognizant of the premises of an enthymemic academic speech declaration. The racist declarations of murder or anti-Semitism implicit in the tweet's premises, however, are not strong enough for this particular audience to override the academic speech technical image in favor of other types of technical images that might have been drawn from for meaning. These layered images might include those associated with anti-Semitism such as murdering Jews because of where they live (a history of pogroms in many countries, including the Middle East), associating Zionism with racism (the U.N. declaration in 1975) or the legacy of the 1967 Six Day War (and consequent delegitimatization of Israel conquering the

West Bank after Jordan's assault). This disconnect demonstrates how assumed speech is not "just is" when projected, among other places, online and in social media platforms where audiences can be imagined but not seen directly. Assumed speech is layered; it depends on previous interactions and engagements, whether the image is a protest against 1968 labor discrimination or a call to murder Israelis. But assumed speech also depends on the assumption of an audiences' existence, as well as that particular audience's likeminded technical images.

In this chapter, I have focused briefly on two cases of professorial outrage and the role of the assumed enthymeme within that outrage. Anger at a political moment, global conflict, territorial debate or similar issues lead to social media based rhetorical situations in which audiences are assumed to exist, but the premises of the tweets or updates, as well, are based on assumptions. "Few of us are called upon to address an audience," Gerald Hauser begins *Vernacular Voices*, "Most of our communication directed at persons or groups has some immediacy, and we know them in some way. We experience our transactions with them in concrete terms as addressed discourse: our own thoughts, our intended message, a specific audience to which we have adapted and that audience's perceived response" (5). The broader issue questions audience transactions as being based on assumptions, not concrete, addressed discourse. Assumptions regarding audience comprehension, agreement, or immediacy complicate how a rhetorical situation and the response it evokes are read across professional and personal communication. A tweet associating the president with a mass murder in Las Vegas may feel to its poster like a stance whose "flash of insight" (as Walker notes) will convince an assumed audience of truth or validity. But when that tweet is read as a different set of enthymemic premises than the poster appears to intend, any assumptions of immediacy prove irrelevant. Weak ties override strong ties (those possibly more likely to agree with the assumed insight) and bring to their reading of the tweet their own technical images— whether regarding mass shootings, presidential ethos, Las Vegas itself, professors as antigovernment leftists, or something else. Ciccariello-Maher, Salaita, and those who support each professor may believe that the negative response to their tweets was based on either right-wing or Zionist conspiracies, but a rhetorical answer to their falling out in academia demonstrates the complexity of audience response overall, the role technical images play in public response to public social media displays, and how enthymemic assumptions depend on which set of assumed premises might support the tweet or Facebook post's projection of meaning. Viewed this way, we are forced to consider our digital expression and our reading of digital expression far more closely than we currently do. In the next chapter, I offer another close examination of digital outrage, one that focuses on epideictic rhetoric.

Notes

1. While his account has been deleted, the tweet originally appeared at: https://twitter.com/ciccmaher/.

2. See http://www-news.uchicago.edu/releases/07/pdf/kalverpt.pdf.

Eight

Epideictic Outrage

Assumptions group together. Around certain technical images, such as academic freedom, they quickly settle into consensus as grouping. As with the previous examples, even when academic freedom does not exist within a tweet or post, its presence is still embedded in academic speech because of the larger technical image aggregated within. That image is an assumption (any controversy surrounding an academic tweet is assumed to involve academic freedom, whatever the content of the tweet may be). Around other issues, such as preconceived hatred for a country or a president, assumptions settle into another level of consensus. An assumption depends on agreement: this is what Italian food is, this is why privacy is sacred, this is why kneeling is anti-American, this is why Israel is evil, and so on. Assumptions also depend greatly on circulation; they must be spread from one believer to the next.

Consider the broader notion that the Internet leads to consensus. The "echo chamber" theory suggests that like-minded individuals join each other's social networks online and thus are receptive to only beliefs and opinions they already maintain. Online tools, the theory claims, such as the Facebook like button and Twitter's heart shaped like (once called "favorite") reinforce preestablished online behaviors of agreement. As I noted earlier, Facebook's Paul Adams calls this process social proof. "We copy other people's behavior," he writes, "especially people like us" (Adams 2012, 86). Social proof is the adjusting of online behavior based on a perceived group think, behavior, or shared communication (text or image). One adjusts to that group's position in order to confirm or publicly establish consensus with the group. Nicholas DiFonzo attributes social proof to the water cooler effect, the tendency to seek out like minded agreement. The water cooler effect often involves consensus-based response to political events: "When we hear a rumor denigrating someone in the opposing political party, we are far more likely to send it to friend—typically members of our own party— whom we think would enjoy hearing that rumor. Yet most people are far less likely to challenge false rumors about the opposing party, because that might be considered a social faux pas among their friends" (DiFonzo 2011). Water cooler effects often spin off journalistic accounts as they repeat across print and digital media: headlines, reports, images, or shared news. Cass Sunstein argues that because of echo chambers/water cooler effects, "the implication is that groups of like-minded people, engaged in discussion with one another, will end up thinking the same thing they thought before—but in more extreme form" (Sunstein 65). Echo champers can be based on groupings, such as Facebook groups or Twitter lists, where individuals gather to share beliefs or interests, not necessarily to argue with one another. For some writers, the water cooler effect is tied to social media: "The political conversations most Americans witness to-day usually involve Facebook comments, paid partisans yelling at each other on cable news, or televised primary debates that are promoted like pro wrestling matches. The American political class emerged from 2016 without much pause, running straight into the next election without taking a breath to ask if there might be a different way of doing business" (Hamby). This position attributes a current political climate as the result of social proof: watching pundits on TV or reading each other's thoughts on Facebook leads less to debate or critical thought and more to copycat beliefs. Copycat beliefs stem from affinity.

Affinity matters to social proof. Social proof allows for affinity to shape political opinion. Social proof functions as a digital marketing strategy (persuading people to promote products and services via likes even though they have no financial investment in the product). Amazon, Yelp, or other online reviews function as social proof, convincing other customers that products or services are worth purchasing because of previous positive experiences. "Groups for whatever you are into," Facebook's promotional video for its groups feature declares.[1] From the "Lady Bikers of California" to guys dancing on a rooftop, groups attract a variety of like-mindedness into one space. Like-mindedness supposedly encourages interaction via consensus (we get involved because we already like the same thing). "We tend not so much to have friends," Duncan Watts writes, "as we do groups of friends, each of which is like a little cluster based on share experience, location, or interests, joined to each other by the overlaps crated when individuals in one group also belong to other groups" (41). Up until this chapter, I have outlined how technical images and algorithms contribute to this grouping process, as well as how specific rhetorical gestures, such as the enthymeme, do as well. In this chapter, I introduce an additional rhetorical term, epideictic rhetoric, to further understand how consensus builds and spreads digital outrage. Epideictic outrage, this chapter argues, is also part of this larger network of outrage-based interactions I have been tracing.

Within this discussion of consensus, social media attracts the notion that online consensus is based on the assumption of shared values. To build communities of friends, followers, respondents, etc. one, it is sometimes assumed, must build among those who share similar values. "We're far more likely to text, email, and interact virtually with people who are physically close" Daniel Coyle states in an updated vision of the Allen Curve's thesis (72). The Allen Curve, proposed by MIT professor Thomas Allen, argues that the farther workspaces are apart, the more likely workers will not communicate with one another. Place individuals in proximity (i.e., in a physical space, move their desks near each other), and they will communicate more. Virtual proximity, though, can mean more than who is nearby (by desk or computer workstation) or who is in my contacts. It can also suggest ideological proximity. Ideological proximity depends on group think and affinity, as well the desire to follow circulated beliefs (social proof). Ideological proximity, as I will argue in this chapter, resembles what we often refer to in rhetorical studies as the epideictic.

Epideictic rhetoric suggests consensus. Take, for example, Facebook's option of changing a user profile image in order to project sympathy or solidarity with an issue. I have already noted the marriage equality option Facebook offered, but filters or profiles also have been changed by users to express solidarity with the 130 victims of French terror in 2015 (the French flag) or those killed in a Manchester, England Ariana Grande terror attack in 2017 (a picture of a heart with Manchester and the Union Jack flag within) and other events. Sharan Daniel defines epideictic rhetoric as contributing "substantially to the shared values that guide the conduct of public affairs by providing a forum in which a public participates in judging praiseworthy actions" (513). Traditionally, epideictic rhetoric has been interpreted as praise—in oratory, at funerals, at weddings, or at other celebratory or memorial events. Praise, too, evokes consensus—we engage in consensual positive emotions for someone or something. Laurent Pernot traces the origins of epideictic rhetoric to the notion of praise: "Aristotle joined praise and *epideixis* together, in order to create a new concept: encomium. Validating the development of praise in oratorical practice and in education, Aristotle gave it a name, a space, an aim: praise (and blame, its opposite) occupied a full third of the material on oratory" (5). Jeffrey Walker agrees, arguing that epideictic rhetoric was initially "identified with discourse delivered outside judicial and legislative forums, such as speeches performed at festivals and ceremonial or symposiastic occasions, and it was typically conceived as the discourse of praise and blame" (*Rhetoric and Poetics* 7). Shared values that praise, as these definitions claim, suggest consensus. Consensus allows for praise or blame because participants supposedly agree on the value of an image, event, or news item as it is publicly presented and shared, and they often do so via a belief in the agreed upon item's singular value or occurrence in the present.

Consensus and social media often comingle, and in doing so, they project a visual or textual based agreement on some form of shared value and perception. For some time, rhetorical studies has explored the meaning of consensus or shared values to rhetoric. Tom Farrell, for instance, based his notion of social knowledge on consensus. While not using the term epideictic, Farrell draws on

Aristotle in order to outline the ways a perceived common knowledge directs reception to events or beliefs. Farrell uses the phrase social knowledge in order to better clarify the kinds of common knowledge rhetorical acts depend upon. Farrell's social knowledge is described, as well, as a shared experience: "Social knowledge is a kind of general and symbolic relationship which acquires its rhetorical function when it is assumed to be shared by knowers in their unique capacity as audience" (Farrell 4). Social knowledge, Farrell writes, "depends upon an 'acquaintance with' (to use James' phrase) or a personal relationship to other actors in the comical world" (Farrell 5). These relationships build consensus so that participants in a given rhetorical moment can "endorse or condemn a person, action, or policy" (Farrell 6) or so that argument may culminate in the advocacy of choice and action (Farrell 7).

Social knowledge assumes a common belief in order for individuals to connect to one another. The Lady Bikers of California, according to Facebook, share a common belief (likely about motorcycles). Many of my examples in previous chapters, too, point to common beliefs, but these beliefs, as I also argue, are shaped by various forces and are not "natural" in their occurrence. Social knowledge is not an echo chamber, as the typical Internet critique professes, but it does assume consensus as a positive and worthwhile trait within rhetorical exchange, a trait to be shared or repeated via praise or blame. With Farrell's analysis, social knowledge appears to lead to some form of change or action. With many of the examples I explore, social knowledge may also lead to outrage. Digital outrage is directly related to consensus and affinity.

Social knowledge, Farrell argues, enables "isolated 'bits' of information to achieve meaning and significance. Rather cryptically put, social knowledge gives form to information" (Farrell 12). Lloyd Bitzer contributed to the discussion of social knowledge via his similar term, public knowledge. Bitzer argued that within public knowledge, "rhetors make claims, they often believe the claims to be true, and they seek to establish claims upon grounds thought to be true and unassailable" ("Rhetoric and Public Knowledge" 72). Public knowledge, Bitzer stated, emerges from an association with truth and the position delivering the truth. Public rhetoric (journalism, policy, citizen protest, tweets, published images, or public remarks) represents public knowledge as a consensual truth. "Journalists affirm that their task is to serve the public by conveying valuable information; elected officials are 'representatives' social critics, political speakers, ordinary citizens, service organizations-all from time to time, purport to represent the public. And all are thought to err or fail in duty if they present falsehood in the place of truth" ("Rhetoric and Public Knowledge" 73).

The determinant regarding truth or falsehood, Bitzer argued, can be located in the "public's tradition and experience" ("Rhetoric and Public Knowledge" 74) and the "contextual circumstances and consequences which generate it" ("Rhetoric and Public Knowledge" 78). How Bitzer imagines this process working, though, remains confusing. Bits of information as well as "contexts" and "consequences" suggest a body of previous information that is collected by a recipient in some manner and that, consequently, informs a contemporary knowledge base because of how it is shared. That base is often assumed to final- ize as consensus. With that consensus, whether repeated via a like button or the repetition of posts and updates or even the changing of an online profile picture to express sympathy and affinity, social media creates epideictic responses to specific political events.

In these responses, I contend, consensus becomes a problematic rhetorical response in digital media. That is, consensus is not necessarily a desired out- come of what has been called social knowledge or public knowledge. Consen- sus, as an epideictic rhetorical response, can mistake multiple representations of knowledge ("bits of information" or layered views) for a singular one, and thus, praise or blame can become problematic reactions since they, are in effect, based on circulated technical images. As Flusser noted, "The revolutionary re- construction of the current circuitry of technical images into a dialogical demo- cratic one presumes that a general consensus must exist in this respect" (*Into the Universe* 65).

In this chapter, I argue that epideictic responses are not based solely on the ambiguous terms social knowledge or public knowledge, as has been previously theorized, but on how these terms juxtapose with all of the concepts I have traced throughout this book. To explain water cooler effects or social knowledge sharing, I specifically continue with aggregation in order to build off of previ- ous discussions, but also to continue to show the complexity of digital outrage. The technical image updates Farrell and Bitzer by clarifying how echo chambers of agreement online are aggregations of bits, contexts, and consequences. The aggregation of these items, in turn, are epideictic because the knowledge they draw upon stems from the perception of shared beliefs and values. While the Internet may, indeed, be an echo chamber, that echo chamber, if it exists, is con- structed out of a history of assembled items consolidated within the perception of consensus or a shared image within selected groups. The exigence for this analysis stems from a concern over shared knowledge, social media, and the ease of consensus as well as a desire to understand how circulated images (which generate consensus) are not singular but are multiple in their construction. The technical image demonstrates aggregation as a rhetorical, and often epideictic, act. With social knowledge, agreed upon conclusions confirm previously held belief systems as consensus while also promoting policy. Jeffrey Walker argues this point, noting that epideictic rhetoric's foundational role "shapes and culti- vates the basic codes of value and beliefs by which a society or culture lives; it shapes the ideologies and imageries with which, and by which, the individual members of a community identify themselves." The epideictic also shapes what will "underlie and ultimately determine decision and debate in pragmatic forums" (*Rhetoric and Poetics* 9). These aggregations, therefore, can influence protest or public policy, or as I will explore via two examples, university racial politics and blame in Middle East conflict.

EPIDEICTIC VIEWS

Consider an example of this process. When the University of Missouri's system president Tim Wolfe resigned on November 9, 2015, he did so because of an inability to adequately respond to campus racism and the widely circulated critiques that he was insensitive to social justice issues and systemic discrimination. Much of the critiques dominated social media and brought national attention to the campus. "University of Missouri administrators seemed to stumble in response to viral-ready incidents," the *Los Angeles Times* reported, "and each stumble only made Wolfe a greater target" (Pearce). Public outrage over events attributed to him had exceeded to the point that Wolfe could no longer perform his duties. NBC reported on Wolfe's problematic presidency as one of neglect and indifference to racial discrimination: "The African-American students at the University of Missouri in Columbia were fed up. They were fed up with being ignored, dismissed, and disrespected: ignored by the president and administrators, dismissed by white students who remained silent amid discriminatory acts on campus and disrespected by racist students on a frequent basis" (Johnson). Jonathan Butler, a graduate student who began a well-publicized hunger strike in protest to Wolfe, wrote to the University of Missouri system Board of Curators that Wolfe's presence was detrimental to student success at the university: "[S]tudents are not able to achieve their full academic potential because of the inequalities and obstacles they face. In each of these scenarios, Mr. Wolfe had ample opportunity to create policies and reform that could shift the culture of Mizzou in a positive direction but in each scenario he failed to do so" (qtd. in Kovacs). Butler was not alone in his public critique. In response to a variety of events, on and off campus in Missouri, the Executive Cabinet of the Undergraduate Student Government penned an open letter to the University of Missouri System Curators expressing their anger. The 2014 killing of Michael Brown in Ferguson, Missouri, by a police officer was cited as exigence for the crisis. That killing, which also helped spark the Black Lives Matter movement, fostered affinity groups objecting to the University of Missouri leadership as semblance formed between campus and Missouri racial inequities. The letter partially read: "The academic careers of our students are suffering. The mental health of our campus is under constant attack. Our students are being ignored. We have asked the University to create spaces of healing and it failed to do so" ("Letter to the

UM System Curators). Even though Brown was killed in a town outside of St. Louis and not Columbia, where the university is located, his death drew a public association with racially charged events on the campus.

In 2014, for instance, students staged a "death in" on the campus' speaker circle in order to bring awareness to Brown's and other Black Americans' unjust deaths at the hands of white men. If Michael Brown's death was exigence for anger at Wolfe and the University of Missouri, so were other factors. During a Homecoming parade student demonstration in which Butler was present and protesters wore Black Lives Matter fist t-shirts, Wolfe's driver accidently hit a protester while trying to maneuver around the individual and other protestors. As the moment was reported: "On Oct. 10, a group of black students interrupted the Mizzou homecoming parade. Wearing T-shirts that read "1839 Was Built On My B(l)ack," referring to Mizzou's founding and slave labor, the students stopped right in front of the convertible that Wolfe was traveling in as he waved to parade watchers. The students took out a megaphone and one by one began speaking about incidents of systemic and anecdotal racism from the founding year 1839 through 2015" (Kingkade). Wolfe did not leave the car to deal with the situation.

That decision, too, contributed to the climate against him as the protesters perceived him as indifferent and unconcerned with their anger. Janet Saidi later wrote of the incident as a missed opportunity to defuse a tense situation: "Wolfe didn't realize he was staring in the face of history. One can only imagine that his entire life so far—with its diet of media images featuring black violence, black incarceration and segregation—had taught him that he was looking not at history but at a discipline problem." When students confronted Wolfe at a Kansas City fundraiser and asked him to define "systemic oppression," his response was: "System oppression is because you don't believe you have the equal opportunity for success." This answer provoked further outrage since it suggested that oppression was based on an individual's belief and not actual practice or institutional policy.[2] By focusing on a person's "belief," the statement also aggregated the other perceived moments of indifference into a single image of apathy towards Black outrage.

All of these events led to Wolf's resignation. Wolfe also resigned, I contend, because of an aggregation of a number of other items not entirely present in this brief narrative but that were aggregated into his presidency. In saying that, I argue that his presidency is not a singular projection or position held by one individual (as I do with previous examples), but instead it is an assemblage or aggregation of various "bits" of information, as Bitzer argues. This aggregation initially includes a number of temporally aligned images: several months of campus protest (caught on YouTube and shared over social media platforms), graduate student Jonathan Butler's eight day hunger strike (also shared digitally),

the systemic oppression comment spread via YouTube,[3] the Twitter announcement by thirty Black football players that they would stop playing until Wolfe
resigned, the threat of a faculty walkout, football coach Gary Pinkel's November
8, 2015, tweet expressing solidary with Jonathan Butler,[4] and a series of tweets
associated with the hashtag #concernedstudent1950. Concerned 1950 was a student group founded by Butler and named for the first-year Black students were
admitted to the University of Missouri. Concerned 1950 released a list of eight
demands which included Wolfe's resignation, the creation of a "comprehensive
racial awareness and inclusion curriculum," increased resources for mental
health and social justice, and an overall increase in the university's Black student
body.[5]

All of these events aggregated into both a technical image but also an affinity
group encouraged by acts of social proof (wanting to share the message regardless of one's personal connection to the events in question or even connection
to the university). In solidarity with Concerned Student 1950, several Black
players from the football team stated: "The athletes of color on the University
of Missouri football team truly believe 'Injustice Anywhere is a threat to Justice Everywhere.' We will no longer participate in any football related activities
until President Tim Wolfe resigns or is removed due to his negligence toward
marginalized students' experience. WE ARE UNITED!!!!!" (quoted in Nadkarni
and Nieves). The overall charges against Wolfe included insensitivity or lack of
action in these moments and also his and the university's response to several
campus racist incidents, which included the "n" word being directed at Missouri
Students Association President Payton Head, a swastika made of human feces
drawn in a residence hall, and the brushing of a student by the president's mo-
torcade during the homecoming parade. On Twitter, The Legion of Black Collegians joined in this affinity/social proof moment and shared a letter detailing
a racist incident in which "an intoxicated white male" talking on his cellphone
disrupted a performance rehearsal and refused to leave. When confronted, he
said "these [n-word] are getting aggressive with me."[6]

The charges themselves are initial images that become a part of the overall
Wolfe presidency technical image. Wolfe's presidency included many activities
and decisions (such as those associated with his administrative position in the
university), but these moments shaped another image of him shared over affinity
groups objecting to his presence on campus. Combined with the other images
which made up the time period leading up to and including Wolfe's resignation,
they project a technical image we can identify as the Mizzou presidency. The
initial image, then, of Wolfe's resignation can be defined as an aggregation of
contentious 2015 moments. That image, also initially constructed out of several
other images I list in the preceding paragraphs, drives a consensual response
among one part of the public, a response that repeatedly claimed the University

of Missouri was in crisis and its president must resign because of the preponderance of racism on campus. Whether or not daily events and interactions were constantly faced with such racism is debatable as is the notion that Wolfe approved of racist incidents which occurred. The projected and circulated image, though, made it clear that such was occurring, and the university president was to blame.

Many racist events connected to the university, however, began before Wolfe. In some reporting, the crisis was described as an assemblage or aggregation of other moments outside of this first set I trace. The *Economist* covered Wolf's resignation by reflecting on such other moments which likely influenced group opinion. The *Economist*'s aggregation, unlike the first set's temporality, is historical. It connects Wolfe to a history he is not physically part of, but emotionally and associatively became a part of when he became president. The aggregation notes: "Missouri was a slave state until 1865; its first public university was founded in 1839 by James Rollins, an owner of slaves. It first admitted black students only in 1950 (Yale's first black student graduated in 1857, Harvard's in 1870)" ("Of Slavery and Swastikas" 2015).

Gus T. Ridgel was the first Black student admitted to the University of Missouri even though the Supreme Court ruled in 1938, after Lloyd Gaines was denied admission to the university's law school, that it must admit Black students. Admissions was a major part of the Wolfe technical image. The university, even during the crisis, sponsored low Black student enrollments. Low enrollments, controlled by a variety of factors, as well, became associatively tied to the president.

Fox News bundled several other images together within the Missouri image, images which complement *The Economist* set and the one I begin with. Some of these incidents were not racially motivated, but nevertheless contributed to a consensual and shared atmosphere of anger at Wolfe. In this aggregation, the technical image's makeup is further expanded to include a variety of political moments in the university's more recent history. As *Fox News* reported: "The racial issues are just the latest controversy at the university in recent months, following the suspension of graduate students' health care subsidies and an end to university contracts with a Planned Parenthood clinic that performs abortions" ("University of Missouri President Resigns").

To the temporal, historical and political sets of images that constitute Wolfe, we can consider other images within the preliminary presidency image that could aggregate into outrage. As with earlier examples of digital outrage, these moments feed and build off of one another across new media. The *Chronicle of Higher Education* compliments and adds to *Fox News*' aggregation: "Concerns about race relations dominated national news coverage, but those issues were coupled with controversies over the slashing of health-care benefits for

Columbia graduate students—a decision that was later reversed—and the apparent forcing out of a relatively new dean at the School of Medicine" (Stripling). Anger at the racial issues on the Missouri campus may involve other reasons to be angry. Anger builds off of anger. Outrage, as I've written already, spreads outrage.

Beyond the publicly acknowledged consensus (racial history), other political images can be found in the Mizzou aggregation that are not necessarily obvious to protesters or critics, but should be considered as aggregations within the image: Missouri student Maxwell Little's 2015 petition to remove the Thomas Jefferson statute from campus because of its racist connotations, (Little) the killing of Michael Brown a year earlier in nearby Ferguson, Missouri, the 2013 St. Louis police killing of Cary Ball Jr. in a similar incident, the rise of the Black Lives Matter movement (and its accompanying hashtag of the same name), the killing of 1,134 Black Americans by police in 2015 (often under questionable means), the death of Sandra Bland after she was pulled over in Texas for not signaling a lane change, the 2010 University of Missouri cotton ball incident in which two white students dropped cotton balls over the lawn of the Black Culture Center, the low percentage of enrolled Black students at Missouri (around 7 percent of the student body), and other items.

In addition to directly related events to either Mizzou or the state of Missouri, there exist in this image associative imagery. If a student engages in a hunger strike, for instance, that image also may evoke more famous hunger strikes for social justice such as those associated with Mahatma Gandhi or Cesar Chavez and generate semblance and affinity. Hunger strikes incorporate other technical images into the present one. If cotton balls are thrown on a Black Student Union lawn, they will likely evoke the stereotypical association between Black people and cotton (based on slaves being forced to pick cotton, or racist popular culture representations such as the song "Dixie" and its wish to be in the land of cotton).

Outrage projected at the university's president, in this reading, is not based on a few current, isolated acts, but on a compiled and aggregated association of moments, images, texts, failures, associations, and related events. A user interacting with the president's image, then, is actually interacting with all these moments, yet that user is reading the presidency as one, singular image. In that singularity, the group finds a shared consensus (racism, discrimination) and projects it outward as if it is not layered and programmed, as Flusser would note. As figure 8.1 demonstrates, such a distinction between actual racist acts and the projection of an idea of racism (based on various prior imagery) is important because it situates the consensual nature of the moment as epideictic (social or public knowledge) as not the same as the moment under protest. There exist two visual moments in the Missouri example; one which protests racism and the

Travis Zimpfer @TravisZimpfer · Nov 9, 2015
"We Shall Overcome" being sung right now #ConcernedStudent1950 #WolfeGottaGo

○   ↻ 6   ♡ 2   ⬆

Fig. 8.1. Twitter reaction that aggregates 1960s Civil Rights into Wolfe protest.

culture of racism historically supported on a university campus and one which protests the image of that racism as it is aggregated within a circulated college president's image. The president may not be a part of a racist history, but his image—by default—is.

These circulated moments are conceptually visual (those who engage with the aggregations do so cognitively) and physically visual (images and texts circulate online, are viewed by weak and strong ties, are shared as consensual outrage); as such, they shape public opinion. They quickly become epideictic. As Ned O'Gorman notes in his definition of epideictic rhetoric as visual and not just as oral communication, "Rhetoric is for Aristotle an art that may shape opinion and direct the affections through the creation of images" (25) and "Aristotelian epideictic is a 'visual rhetoric'" (27). One might claim that the circulated images of Wolfe and the University of Missouri constituted a visual argument calling for removal or resignation. These images profess a visual truth for its consensual audience already prefigured to believe in the image's guilt. J. Anthony Blair, however, notes that the problem with a "visual argument" is that it can neither be true nor false. The technical image of Wolfe, thus, would not be the true or false image protesters claimed it was (or that many definitions of epideictic rhetoric depend upon), but simply an embedded image waiting for the protesters to make claims on its behalf as they already believe those claims exist. Blair writes: "For it to be possible for visual arguments to occur, it would have to be possible for visual images to be true or false—to have truth value. But a photograph or photographic collage or a piece of film or a series of visual images (as in a TV commercial), or a painting or a sculpture, are not 'true' or 'false.' The meaning conveyed is not propositional. Therefore such visual communications, however they work, cannot express arguments" (Blair 47).

If that is the case, then the argument would emerge out of either the en-thymemic assumptions an audience makes (filling in the gaps regarding the image called Missouri and even the image called American racism in order to arrive at a conclusion regarding the image called Wolfe's guilt) or the general agreement of an epideictic social knowledge (as in "Wolfe is guilty" regardless of any acts he actually committed because he represents the racism associated with the university). Or both. "Visual arguments," Blair writes, "are typically enthymemes—arguments with gaps left to be filled in by the participation of the audience" (52). These gaps can lead to affinity and consensus if enough people fill in the gaps similarly and then share, via social proof, the assumptions this filling makes.

In addition to the initial visual aggregations I draw attention to, we can turn to the aggregated hashtag for other instances. Hashtags are visual markers. Hashtags, i.e., the pound character, mark a social media space visually. To create associations among various, disparate users, the hashtag functions as a specified hyperlink across weak and strong ties. The hashtag, a digital marker of threaded discussion, visually indicates where conversations circulate similar points and beliefs. According to Andreas Bernard, the hashtag stems from two traditions: "The keyword as a unit for organizing documents, and as a characteristic ex-pression of a historical epoch or political agenda" (40). "The hashtag," Bernard writes, "is an index and a slogan at the same time" (42). Bernard draws attention to the political nature of hashtags in generating response. "The hashtag on Twit-ter or Instagram is always used to test its campaign potential" (46), he notes, and "The organization of statements and documents has turned the desire to 'trend' into a fundamental principle of communication technology" (47).

The November 2015 trending Facebook tag "University of Missouri" reveals how the University of Missouri technical image further directs visual affect via hashtags. Posts using this tag such as the *Los Angeles Times* ("the football team went on strike, adding pressure to the situation"),[7] the *Washington Post* ("The boycott is part of a student movement against the school administra-tion's response to a series of alleged racist incidents around campus."),[8] and other individuals ("For a college football team to refuse to play because of overt campus racism and to demand the resignation of a clueless president is un-precedented")[9] demonstrate an epideictic response focused on the perceived singularity of the University of Missouri as an image. As do Twitter responses aligned with the hashtag "Mizzou": "This is what happens when you organize and have a powerful message,"[10] "If the #Mizzou President didn't wanna be fired maybe he shoulda thought of that before White ppl invented Slavery!!"[11] "If you want to know what the REAL #FergusonEffect is look no further than #Miz-zou,"[12] and "#Mizzou players are winning something far more important than a game right now. It's called self dignity. I salute them. #BlackLivesMatter."[13] The hashtag "Wolfegottago," assembled cries of solidarity and anger. "Understanding the struggles of ALL your students should be a requirement for being a UM President. #Wolfegottago,"[14] "When YOU choose to stay SILENT and YOUR community is fighting systems that weren't made for them, you set the precedent. #WolfeGottaGo."[15] Affinity becomes promoted as social proof and allows these various hashtags to be picked up and spread.

Dustin Edwards and Heather Lang argue that examining hashtags alongside other forms of rhetorical exchange helps "unravel material complexities within the broader assemblages that animate [hashtag's] becoming" (118). Citing the subversion of #MyNYPD which was used to protest police brutality, Tracey Hayes argues that hashtags generate affinity spaces, or we might add, social knowledge gatherings that visualize communal agreement in public ways. "The protesters' participation, the hashtag's staying power, and the impact of the tweets all contributed to creating a different space, a space where a public and online discourse met as an affinity space" (131). There no doubt was a collected affinity space among the various hashtag users in the Missouri situation. Some of this affinity focused on the 1950 date and Jonathan Butler's hunger strike. Some of this affinity focused on the state and university's troubled, racist past.

Along with previously noted items, hashtags formed a circuitry whose assemblage led to a shared belief system's deliberative stance: Tim Wolfe must resign. These items also reflect various elements of the technical image as responses draw from consensual items not visible in the technical image, but which are embedded in the image (slavery, Jim Crow, Black Lives Matter, Ferguson). Comments and responses to Wolfe foreground these items as agreed upon images shaping a contemporary position and its blame. Aggregated consensus prompts the image's rhetorical power. Arguing that negative response to Wolfe is based on the projection onto the University of Missouri of these previous images is not to discount legitimate anger, existing and historical racism, or real discrimination but rather to recognize how the epideictic nature of the technical image can confuse a problem with the image of a problem. For Flusser, such distinctions are important, for without differentiating between the two (problem and image) we mistakenly focus on "images and human interests" as opposed to the "circuitry" or circulation of aggregated images. We accept, in other words, the message and the sending of the message as is without considering the aggregations that build the message's meaning. With Missouri, protestors search out human agents and "all evidence to the contrary, go on looking for manipulators and power brokers among the senders" (*Into the Universe* 69). Instead, Flusser would recommend looking first at how such images are believed in, how they build off previous incarnations, how they make previous images a part of the current moment. Knowing that "I am" builds off of "I am a Man" does not diminish Occupy,

Harvard students, or Paris mourners' social knowledge, but it does acknowledge epideictic aggregation.

By calling this aggregation epideictic, I am shifting focus away from the traditional definition of epideictic rhetoric as ceremonial. I am instead, focusing more on the future deliberative aspect of epideictic rhetoric, but with combined elements of embedment and the visual. As Brad Vivian argues, "epideictic organizes the terms of public remembrance in order to shape perceptions of shared values and commitments serviceable to future deliberative agendas" ("Neoliberal" 2). Those agendas, however, are not for purposes of praise, as the Missouri example shows, but also are for condemnation. The accumulation of supposedly consensual images (by association, history, memory, and affect) into one image prompts a deliberative act such as firing a president. That firing, in turn, is publicly promoted by many as a noble and virtuous act. By firing Wolfe's technical image (which I differentiate from Wolfe the human), one has supposedly fought racism and overcome the campus' obstacles to diversity. If that were the case, however, racism would no longer exist at the University of Missouri. Virtue, instead, prompts the feeling of justice resulting from the image's firing. "Aristotle also enhances the role of epideictic by assigning its practitioners the responsibility for telling the story of lived virtue," Gerald Hauser notes (Hauser 14). This narrative becomes a projected display. Wolfe's firing projects virtue as a display. "The epideictic speech does not seek to *tell* what a person did, but to *display* nobility at the level of praxis" [emphasis Hauser's] (Hauser 15). Hauser's attention to display also suggests a visual component of epideictic rhetoric. Hauser uses the same definition again when he writes that the epideictic "does not address a problematic situation requiring a decision. It displays honorable deeds and asks its audience to witness what appears before it" (Hauser 15). The tension between these definitions (deliberative/not requiring a decision) speaks to the difficulty of solving public problems via such gestures (inequity in the racial makeup of the student body; campus racism will remain after Wolfe) but also speaks to the simultaneous power of epideictic rhetoric to display the technical image of an assumed change (the president's dismissal). The image/display tension speaks to what Hauser calls "the communal ethos" (Hauser 16). That ethos is displayed, as well, in the numerous hashtags and Twitter discussions surrounding Wolfe. That ethos, as well, is displayed in the overall public response to Wolfe.

But that virtue—causing action, as Hauser claims—becomes problematic when we do not recognize the technical nature of displays, a point Flusser warns of. A display, in other words, is not just a display. A display is not just virtue. It is a set of layers. The ethos or virtue claimed by displaying the image is not a recognition, however, of the layers which form the aggregation in the first place. While there were critiques over insensitivity or delayed response to racism on the Mizzou campus, there did not exist evidence that Tim Wolfe was racist (there are no citations of Wolfe racism in the image) nor that he supported racist discourse or acts. His image, embedded in the larger image called Missouri or Mizzou, eventually is engaged as racist because of its aggregation with other, present racist images. Wolfe may have been insensitive or not aware of the campus' problematic history, but was he racist? Or is his technical image a display of racism? Debra Hawhee contends that "the very task of epideictic rhetoric is to rhetorically—through a host of images furnished by memory, by vivid comparisons, and projected into the future—produce magnitude . . . by calling up multiple images, and piling on excessive details" (Hawhee 149). Hawhee also argues that "the production of rhetorical vision, in other words, occurs on the part of the audience as a result of the 'bundle' of ideas contained in the image" (Hawhee 155). The bundle, in this case, is twofold: the projected image of virtue and ethos ("we fired the racist president") and the bundle of a history of images contained within either the University of Missouri or Tim Wolfe (the unrecognized layers). "Epideictic exhibits public morality," Hauser argues; "we learn it through *mimesis* of deeds unfathomable were they not publicly exhibited and validated" (Hauser 19). The question, at this point, is whether the replication reflects the unfathomable racism at stake, or the judgment itself. As with "I am" and the next example I explore, replication and repetition play significant roles in the process of translating outrage out of consensus and into affinity.

FLOODING THE IMAGE

Consider another example of a circulated technical image promoted as virtue, or what Hauser calls "public morality" and its overall aggregation from images, headlines, ideas, texts, and other items. In this example, I turn away from a university moment and focus on a web circulated headline and story regarding flooding in the "valley" of the Gaza Strip. While these two examples might appear disparate, their difference reflects the complexity and variance of technical images overall. This second example shifts attention slightly from the social media nature of the first example and shows how web images become technical through their repetition or what Walker calls the epideictic's enunciation of an "archival knowledge" as well as perceived "precedents and premises" (*Rhetoric and Poetics* 12). As was the case with my example of Steven Salaita, this example focuses on assumptions associated with Israel, a country which is often the target of digital outrage for various complex and ideological reasons. In this example, virtue and public morality are very much present and help spread a false headline. When one feels virtuous regarding a given issue, one feels more inclined to spread that issue via Twitter, Facebook, or even traditional journalist reporting. One spreads for consensus and affinity ("I have found a virtuous position and one should agree with me as well"). The epideictic requires a public declaration of virtuosity. The question for someone like Flusser or what I have been trying to trace out in this book is whether or not the virtuous is merely a repetition or programmed image.

On February 23, 2015, the *Daily Mail*, a major British newspaper, reported that Israel opened its southern dams and flooded the Gaza valley. Wadi Gaza, the area the journalistic reports focused on, is a small riverbed or stream, but because of its Arabic name, "Wadi" was interpreted to mean a valley (Wadi is Arabic for valley). The *Daily Mail*'s headline claimed that Israel flooded "the valley" and left hundreds of Palestinians homeless in the process. As with the University of Missouri example, this other 2015 moment relies upon a projection of a technical image (in this case, a country rather than a university president). Israel, more so than Missouri's flagship university, is a well-circulated technical image containing various meanings depending on either a sense of epidictic "virtue" (condemnation to achieve social justice) or enthymemic gap filling (premise 1, premise 2, it must be Israeli's fault). As Cary Nelson writes of this group think: "Those obsessed with the Jewish state, those who believe it is at the center of all the world's ills, do not entertain any doubts about their fixation" (20). Doubts are not entertained because the positions circulate as already accepted virtue. The example of dam flooding in Gaza speaks to this observation. A circulated headline about Israel already carries within the technical image called Israel negative feelings and a social knowledge based on condemnation.

The problem with the *Daily Mail*'s report is that there are no dams in Israel leading into Gaza, Gaza is not in a valley, and the act never occurred. Excessive rain, instead, caused the flooding. The report occurred seven months after Israel's 2014 summer war with Hamas in Gaza called Protective Edge. The fairly close temporal proximity of the two events—a war with Hamas in Gaza and Gaza flooding—in addition to consistent media reporting from Israel since, at least, 1967 regarding its never ending conflict with the Palestinians and the suffering of Gazans in general, aggregates in both the journalistic account (which is false) and in the reader's reception and response to that account (believed as true because of archived and previous image interactions). For those recipients of the report who were already angry over Protective Edge (and likely were angry over other events preceding and following the war such as Israel's occupation of the West Bank, response to the first and second Intifadas, or supposed cause of a Palestinian Nakba in 1948), the headline becomes aggregated into those other instances and images as well. The headline, too, becomes a technical image. The difference between this image and the University of Missouri/Tim Wolfe example is that, in this case, an event never occurred (racism does exist at the University of Missouri and can be traced throughout its history) and the image is also contained within a headline as much as within a shared photograph. The technical image, in both cases, projects a public meaning.

Fig. 8.2. *Daily Mail* headline; electric dispute aggregated into flooding lie.

Hundreds of Palestinians left homeless after Israel opens river dam and floods houses... hours before Jewish state's electric company cuts off power in West Bank cities

As with the Missouri example, the technical image circulates by way of digital participation, circuitry, or what Tony Sampson calls contagion effects. Contagions are cultural, ideological or economic repetitions, and as epideictic technical images, reflect Walker's comment that epideictic rhetoric is "designed to be memorable and repeatable" (*Rhetoric and Poetics* 11). For the University of Missouri image to resonate as a technical image, those elements that construct it have repeated numerous times over numerous media and have become memorable contagions that, in turn, repeat the University of Missouri/Tim Wolfe image as racist. Past events contribute to the repetition (retelling what has occurred) but so do ideological beliefs that become repeated until believed to be true and virtuous. Often captured in the discourse of memes or viruses, for Sampson, the contagion is not biological—as memes are often explained metaphorically—but social. Contagions construct cultural identity as repetitions become prevalent over social knowledge. The contagion, Sampson argues, involves "the microrelational forces of imitative encounters" (Sampson 19). For Sampson, imitation's agency is not with a person or figure (a university president or a country, for instance) but with the imitation itself, that which "makes the agent part of an assemblage of relationality" (Sampson 29). Outrage, too, is an agent, as I noted earlier in this book. Repetition and imitation allow outrage to spread and communicate itself. Sampson claims that repeated imitations operate not by "cognitive processing power" but by "the spontaneity of emotional responses to affective priming" (Sampson 42). Like Flusser's critique of the technical image, Sampson critiques the contagion for being superficial or what he deems the "cultivation of a blind love not directed at the intellect but operating through appeals to violent and conservative feelings that contaminate the thoughts and actions of an obedient, herd-like-crowd" (Sampson 81). In this case, the crowd already is anti-Israel.

Unlike Sampson, Flusser does not account for the affective dimensions of the technical image's repetition, noting that "once there is an image, everything is in the present and turns into an eternal repetition of the same" (*Into the Universe* 58). Sampson, however, is adamant regarding the affective dimensions of image repeatability. With imagery, Sampson argues that "contagions can be ignited by events imagined to be real by the crowd. This is perhaps how the ensuing image-event becomes a hallucinogenic phantasm that passes through the collective unconsciousness" (Sampson 82). Flusser does not argue that technical images enact the unconscious; instead, he argues that "the current interaction between image and human beings will lead to a loss of historical consciousness in those who receive the images" (*Into the Universe* 60). Flusser, like Sampson, is concerned with critical loss, but instead of attributing to repeatability an affective persuasion or psychological desire, he focuses on repetition's technical erasure of history and fixation on the present, as if the engaged image only reflects an occurring present. Flusser argues that "technical images translate historical events into infinitely repeatable projections" (*Into the Universe* 58) and "a consciousness appropriate to technical images operates outside history" (*Into the Universe,* 59). Even with an emphasis on the present, it is difficult to avoid the affective dimension of this process, as Sampson contends. Contagions, via their status as repetitions which create further repetitions, allow emotional responses to embed meaning in projected images regardless of the meaning's accuracy. Contagions promote the "rhetoric of belief and desire" (*Rhetoric and Poetics* 10). As a technical image, contagions are affective. With affect, as Sampson notes, the repetition overrides the message: "Once caught up in the everyday repetitions, routines, and mechanical habits of computer usage, a user can easily drift toward potential windows of opportunity, which, when opened, spread contagion without a guiding hand" (Sampson 187).

The opportunity to blame Israel via headline occurs often and via repetition posed as consensual, affective agreement. Regarding the Gaza headline, the *Daily Mail* was not the origin of the initial erroneous report, but rather was an affective repetition, a programming (adhering to the aggregated profile of evil Israel) that spread through spreading itself. The *Daily Mail* contained, in other words, other images within its image, images that had circulated in other moments and in other online spaces because of an affective anti-Israel stance already within the circulation. On February 22, Agence France Press posted a video to its website under the headline "Gaza village flooded as Israel opens dam gates," In the video, Gazans were cited for their claims that Israel opened dams. Agence France Press eventually retracted the video and webpage upon learning that no dams existed, but that retraction did not prevent the story's further circulation to the *Daily Mail* and elsewhere, sites where emotional responses to Israel typically flourish.

Al-Jazeera and *Maan* repeated the flooding story with emphasized agency attributed to Israel.[16] "Gazans flee floods *caused* by Israel's dam's opening," *Al-Jazeera's* February 23 headline proclaims. "Hundreds of Palestinians flee as Israel *opens* dams into Gaza Valley," *Maan* claims. The Canadian run website Global Research TV's headline from February 24 read: "Humanitarian Crisis: Israel's Open Dams *Flood* Gaza. Hundreds Evacuated." The website Antiwar.com published a February 22 headline "Hundreds Displaced as Israel *Opens* Dam, Flooding Gaza." Its reporter Jason Ditz wrote: "Hundreds of Palestinian civilians were displaced today when the Israeli military, with no prior warning, opened a dam and flooded out the Gaza Valley, destroying a number of homes and leaving many under nearly 10 feet of water." University of Michigan professor Juan Cole's popular blog *Informed Consent* repeated the claim via the February 23 headline "Hundreds of Palestinians flee as Israel *Opens* Dam into Gaza Valley." Cole later pulled the article, but left the *Maan* report as an excerpt, and by doing so, he continued to circulate the false report. I begin this tracing by noting the active verbs used in these headlines (which I italicize). By using active verbs, each headline builds off perceived outrage in order to further spread that outrage.

The 2015 headline, though, was not the first time a journalistic headline posed the dam lie. In 2012, Global Research TV posted the headline "Gaza Flooded After Israel Opens Dam Gates" and cited Iranian Press TV as its source ("Gaza Flooded"). A similar 2010 report was posted by the *Palestine Telegraph*,[17] where a story noted that "Many Palestinian houses were under water in Central Gaza after Israel opened a closed dam on Tuesday. Israeli authorities opened the 'Al-Wadi' dam without prior notice after heavy rainfall on the area." The claim was repeated, as well, in 2010 by the *Intifada Palestine* website. "Israeli officials opened the Al-Wadi dam east of Gaza" (Obeidallah). As noted, there is no Al-Wadi dam in Gaza. The weblog *Tabula Gaza* posted in 2010, "Israel Plays God: Floods Gaza Strip" (Rizk). The Middle East news website *Al Monitor* repeated the dam and flood claim in 2013 (Abou Jalal), as did *Middle East Monitor* in 2014, calling the dam the Wadi Sofa Dam ("Israel Opens Dam, Flooding"). "I do not want to stop here at the Israeli denial of the incident and how the Israeli media has refuted it," an anonymous writer noted in another 2014 *Middle East Monitor* story about the incident ("Israel Opens Dam Gates"). The Tehran based *Al Alam* news site also ran the same story, "Israel Opens Dam to Flood Gaza, Forcing Evacuations."[18] In 2013, the weblog *Zainaba's Lounge* wrote about the story "Israel opened dams east of Gaza drowning hope and the last vestiges of normal life" ("Drowning Gaza Deliberately"). The technical image of 2015 is based on a previous incarnation in 2010, 2012 and then in 2013. This image is a contagion,

Shehab Agency
@ShehabAgencyEn

#Israel opens intentionally the water dams east of #Gaza, which caused a significant destruction in the infrastructure, which already worn out because of the long Israeli siege. #GazaLives #EndGazaSiege #IsraelCrimes

0:11 | 15.7K views

6:30 AM · Jan 22, 2020 · TweetDeck

Fig. 8.3. Circulated repetition in 2020.

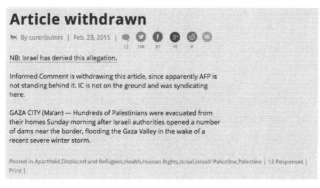

Article withdrawn

By contributors | Feb. 23, 2015 | 12   188   21   18   0

NB: Israel has denied this allegation.

Informed Comment is withdrawing this article, since apparently AFP is not standing behind it. IC is not on the ground and was syndicating here.

GAZA CITY (Ma'an) — Hundreds of Palestinians were evacuated from their homes Sunday morning after Israeli authorities opened a number of dams near the border, flooding the Gaza Valley in the wake of a recent severe winter storm.

Posted in Apartheid,Displaced and Refugees,Health,Human Rights,Israel,Israel/ Palestine,Palestine | 12 Responses | Print |

Fig. 8.4. Cole withdraws article but allows for further aggregations.

a programmed response to not rain but to an already agreed upon definition of a country. As Lazar Berman wrote in *The Times of Israel,* "Residents of Strip forced from homes after winter storm, and Jerusalem is blamed for opening invisible dams." On January 22, 2020, Shehab Agency, a Palestinian news agency, repeated the story with a tweet that notes "Israel opens intentionally the water dams east of Gaza, which caused a significant destruction in the infrastructure, which already worn out because of the long Israeli siege."[19] Same story. Same repetition. The area was suffering from torrential rains at the time.

One might think of the dam story as a modern variation of the blood libel tale. The blood libel's popularity and massive circulation throughout both

Europe and the Islamic world is based on an epideictic consensus-vision of Jews murdering non-Jewish children to use their blood to make matzah. These lies spread throughout communities the way a contagion spreads online, picked up by weak ties and assumed to be true from their immediacy. A lie, it nevertheless is believed to be true (virtuous reasoning) despite no evidence to support the claim. With the dam story, we see a similar effort to attribute such claims to an imaginary "murderous" Jewish body. The contagion aggregates other headlines into its repetition, thus building a technical image of words as well as of image, what Sampson calls "a counterpolitics of imitation that spreads not by way of love but similarly through sympathy" (Sampson 189). In that sympathy, we hear the shared values/consensus of epideictic rhetoric.

Sampson's reading of memetic culture requests "further questions about the kind of affective relations in which real and imaginary events become paradoxically blurred in the minds of network users" (Sampson 76). In the case of Israeli based headlines, one can research the role of the active verb (Israel *does something* to another entity, notably Palestinians)[20] and identify how this particular repetition can be aggregated into a current one regarding flooding. In these moments of circulation, a continued aggregation of the representation of Israel—its technical image—increases despite its basis in a lie, *even though that*

Fig. 8.5. Aggregating contagions. 61 likes. 74 shares.

Exposing Israel's Agenda
February 23 at 11:05am ·

Like Page

#Gaza Homes Flooded After #Israel Unbolts Dam Gates! #Palestine
http://falastinews.com/.../gaza-homes-flooded-after-israel-u.../

Gaza homes flooded after Israel unbolts dam gates
Share on Facebook Tweet on Twitter Share on Google Scores of Palestinian family homes east of blockaded Gaza were flooding after the Israeli occupation authorities (IOA) opened dam gates at dawn Sunday. The Palestinian Interior Ministry said in...
FALASTINEWS.COM

Like · Comment · Share

61 people like this.   Top Comments

74 shares

Fig. 8.6. Response
to erroneous
Vice story.

lie is posed as shared or public knowledge. Even when the inaccurate report is clarified or retracted, those who comment on the initial report continue to claim that Israel opened dams into Gaza (as figs. 8.5 and 8.6 attest), or associate the imaginary act with past imaginary or real acts, and the retracted claim remains in circulation in web cache or its repetition elsewhere. Such is the power of not only aggregation of previously held beliefs, as Flusser's concept of the technical image teaches, but also of an aggregated epideictic rhetoric based in shared beliefs. One reason aggregation affects digital response so greatly is because of the role of epideictic rhetoric. The events that preceded Tim Wolf's resignation occurred; those that precede and create the flooding story did not. Communal ethos, in both cases, allows for a visual water cooler effect among websites, social media postings, and eventual beliefs.

IMAGINARY EPIDEICTIC

To praise or to condemn depends on the imaginary, what Cynthia Miecznikowski Sheard calls "aesthetic modes of discourse" (769). One must paint a romantic or damning portrait of the subject in such a way as to tap into preconceived and often imagined beliefs. Donald Trump cannot just be a bad president; he must be, as I noted earlier in this book, Hitler. Gaza cannot be flooded by heavy rains and poor infrastructure unable to deal with serious weather; it must be attacked by Israel. The epideictic needs the imaginary: "By bringing together images of both the real—what is or at least appears to be—and the fictive or imaginary—what might be—epideictic discourse allows speaker and audience to envision possible, new, or at least different worlds" (Miecznikowski Sheard 770). In the case of the Gaza dam story, the real may be "a country whose existence I object to" and the imaginary may be "a story of maliciousness that confirms why that country should not exist." The repetition of the Gaza dam story, therefore, is told as an imaginary scenario that can focus outrage at Israel to such an extent as to increase negative feelings about the country. Repetition creates the semblance of knowledge. Juan Cole, of the University of Michigan, actively participates in this imaginary as do specific news agencies. "Information in epideictic, "Walter Beale writes, "is generally of a summary nature and has more the quality of re-iteration or reminder than of news" (238). Perelman and Olbrechts-Tyteca also comment similarly: "It is because epidictic discourse is intended to promote values on which there is agreement that one has an impression of misuse when in a speech of this kind someone takes up a position on a controversial question, turns the argument toward disputed values and introduces a discordant note on an occasion that is liable to promote communion" (53).

Some of this process reflects what Michael Carter calls "the rhetoric of display" (304). Carter defines two types of epideictic rhetoric, public and private. Public epideictic indicates the ceremonies, eulogies, and celebrations typically associated with epideictic rhetoric. Private epideictic is community or group based and may not have intrinsic value beyond its placement within the specific group other than ritual. Carter writes, "When we conceive of the rhetoric of display less in terms of the individual and more in terms of the community, less in terms of strutting and preening and more in terms of its ritual significance, the meaning of display changes in a very important way" (307). This change, I contend regarding digital outrage, is the imaginary. In both examples that I explore in this chapter, I have tried to show how embedded imagery prompts belief, whether in a university president, a country's ethos, or some other issue. "The program becomes independent of human intention" (*Into the Universe* 74). When Flusser attributed programming to the technical image, he also suggested the establishment of meaning prior to engagement. "Images will then always show the same thing," he claimed, "and people will always want to see the same thing" (*Into the Universe* 59). The assumption of consensus, as well, suggests repeatability. The implications, then, are that recipients of messages may come to those messages with preestablished beliefs (a university is racist, a country is guilty of transgression), but, also, that such recipients do so because of other images aggregated into the current one and repeated over digital spaces. As Damien Pfister writes, digital writing platforms, such as weblogs, extend the public sphere into a networked one "where opinion and information more easily cascade in networked environments" (59). What I have shown is how such a cascade occurs and problematizes social knowledge.

Dale Sullivan argues that epideictic's purpose is "the creation and maintenance of orthodox opinions within a culture or subculture" (117). Orthodoxy, in the case of the examples I present here, is troubling. Similar to Sullivan's position, Bernard Duffy argues that "epidictic oratory is uncontroversial" because factuality (accuracy) "matters little compared with the truth of the values they illuminate" (85). As with any act of consensus, though, the image of "the uncontroversial" allows for the projection of extremely controversial public voices which transform into an orthodoxy (unchallenged, accepted as "truth" of an illuminated value). The supposed uncontroversial statements—racism is bad; territory disputes need resolution—mask the other images embedded within, thus allowing shared knowledge or public knowledge to perform an uncontested projection, a projection which, counter to Duffy, is not accurate. Flusser was troubled by such projections, particularly for their supposed ethos or virtual values and the lack of recognition of other factors, such as programming. A Gaza headline is programmed via repetition. A university protest is programmed via a complex set of aggregated imagery. In this chapter, I have described two examples of such projections, drawing attention to how images proliferate because of their complex makeups. One can draw from these examples more significant consequences of epideictic rhetoric, its ability to transform consensus into water cooler discussion, or more seriously, falsehood, mob like behavior, or uncontested belief.

Notes

1. "Facebook Groups: Building Communities," YouTube, accessed August 12, 2022, https://www.youtube.com/.

2. "Tim Wolfe Systematic Oppression," YouTube, accessed August 12, 2022, https://www.youtube.com/.

3. Bomani Jones (@jomani_jones), "saw this last night. . . ," Twitter, November 7, 2015, https://twitter.com/bomani_jones/.

4. Gary Pinkel (@GaryPinkel), "The Mizzou Family stands as one. . . ," Twitter, November 8, 2015, https://twitter.com/GaryPinkel/.

5. DeRay Mckesson (@deray), "And here are the demands. . . ," Twitter, November 8, 2015, https://twitter.com/deray/.

6. University of Missouri Legion of Black Collegians (@MizzouLBC), "@__High Quality wrote a letter. . . ," October 5, 2015, https://twitter.com/MizzouLBC/.

7. *Los Angeles Times*, "The football team went on strike, adding pressure to the situation," Facebook, November 9, 2015, https://www.facebook.com/latimes/posts/.

8. *Washington Post*, "The boycott is part of a student movement. . . ," Facebook, November 7, 2015, https://www.facebook.com/washingtonpost/posts/.

9. Darrell Hucks, "Thanks for sharing. . . ," Teacher Education and the Black Community: A Special Issue of JNE (group), Facebook, November 9, 2015, https://www.facebook .com/groups/.

10. Wendy Spaulding (@SpauldingWendy), Twitter, November 9, 2015, https://twitter .com/SpauldingWendy/.

11. While the tweet has been deleted, it originally appeared at https://twitter.com/John RiversToo/.

12. Leslie Mac (@LeslieMac), Twitter, November 9, 2015, https://twitter.com/Leslie Mac/.

13. @Big6domino, Twitter, November 8, 2015, https://twitter.com/Big6domino/.

14. Kaley Johnson (@KaleyAJohnson), Twitter, November 7, 2015, https://twitter.com /KaleyAJohnson/.

15. @iamdwu, Twitter, November 8, 2015, https://twitter.com/iamdwu/.

16. Al-Jazeera later retracted the story, but its participation in the circulation of the fake story still exists.

17. The post has since been removed.

18. "Israel opens dams to flood Gaza, forcing evacuations," Alalam News Network, December 14, 2013, http://en.alalam.ir/news/1544505.

19. While the account has been suspended, the tweet originally appeared at: https:// twitter.com/ShehabAgencyEn/status/.

20. There are too many instances to cite, but see the notable CNN headline, "Deadly Attack on Jerusalem Mosque" from November 18, 2014. The "mosque" was a synagogue in which four Jewish worshippers were killed. http://honestreporting.com/. See also the Associated Press headline "Israeli Police Shoot Man in East Jerusalem" regarding a terrorist who ran a car into a crowd and killed an infant. Police, afterward, shot the terrorist. http://www.algemeiner.com/2014/10/23/.

Nine

The Discourse

An Outrage Conclusion

In February 2020, Wisconsin English teacher Travis Sarandos tweeted a response to right-wing radio talk show host Rush Limbaugh's admission he has cancer: "'Rush Limbaugh absolutely should have to suffer from cancer,' Sarandos wrote in the tweet. 'It's awesome that he's dying, and hopefully it is as quick as it is painful'" (Elassar). A fury of angry tweets followed, most questioning Sarandos' ability to teach in the public school system. Milwaukee High School of the Arts, Sarandos' employer, fired him, and Sarandos deleted his account.

Sarandos' tweet differs little from many of the brief examples I used to begin *The Rhetoric of Outrage*, or even some of the later examples I expand upon. The belief that one is speaking for a consensus ("Rush Limbaugh deserves cancer"), that this consensus is relatively uncontroversial ("we all hate Rush Limbaugh"), and that the consensus is based on aggregations (past Limbaugh commentary or his mocking of others' illness, such as Michael J. Fox's Parkinson's disease) all contribute to the desire to tweet about Limbaugh's cancer. Acts of aggregation, affect, enthymemic reasoning, communication, and epidictic assumptions are all working to produce this technical image. This rhetorical overlap leads to the digital posting of outrage as immediacy (no thought to what kinds of audiences might respond, how messages get shared among weak ties who may dissent, what else may be aggregated in the image one responds to). Sarandos' reaction, as well, belongs within a larger network of outrage, one likely associated with right-wing radio and television talk show hosts (Sean Hannity, Mark Levin, Ann Coulter), but also within the network of liberals and moderates angered by such discourse and elated when it appears hypocrisy is exposed (i.e., "the pundit who opposes universal health care now has cancer and will need health care; serves him right"). Sarandos wasn't the only person to post on Twitter a positive reaction to Limbaugh's announcement, but he was one of the few to earn attention and maybe the only one to lose his job over the tweet.

While I've stressed the term digital outragicity earlier in this book, Sarandos' reaction exemplifies what some have simply call digital discourse. If outrage dominates as much of online rhetorical exchange as I claim, then it is itself a form of commonplace discourse within the digital public sphere. Throughout *The Rhetoric of Outrage*, I have stressed this point by focusing on the rhetorical features of outrage as being more than basic anger. Outrage as a form of discourse is often directed at perceived moments of hypocrisy or injustice, as many of my examples demonstrate. A figure like Rush Limbaugh is a prime target, as he made a living fostering outrage on his radio show over positions, such as health care, that often run counter to the public interest. Other targets, as well, emerge quickly on social media platforms. These targets shape a specific type of discourse, one that is based on outrage. A tweet about Limbaugh deserving cancer is not an anomaly. It is digital discourse.

Writing for a non-academic audience in *The New Republic*, Nathaniel Friedman referred to the online outrage machine as the broader concept "The Discourse." The Discourse, Friedman wrote, is largely Twitter fueled. Friedman calls The Discourse a formula, a fairly predictable series of angry responses that often come on the heels of a moment, report, comment, other tweet, image, video, or whatever sparks immediate anger without critical thought. The Discourse, like Flusser's programmability, is easy to anticipate. If Rush Limbaugh says something stupid or experiences a life changing moment that might contradict his previous behavior (such as that related to health care) or that might encourage public retribution, we can expect fairly predictable responses on social media. Enough people are already angry at Limbaugh and the technical image of right-wing punditry he projects (and the same can be said if we flipped the political position or individual) that the response is programmed. Friedman argues: "The Discourse has little use for the affirmative, and good things fizzle out quickly. As long as it's (to take a partial, but broadly representative sample) shameful, offensive, idiotic, rude, humiliating, repulsive, violent, evil, inept, self-indulgent or self-satisfied, retrograde, or naïve, The Discourse can work with it. These judgments make no appeal to cohere as part of a larger moral or aesthetic framework. What matters is the identification of that bad thing. That's the spark" (Friedman).

Sarandos identified Rush Limbaugh as one such bad thing, likely representative of Republican positions regarding health care and their rejection of any form of universal care. Health care, after all, is highly affective. Sarandos also acted on impulse and immediacy based on his past hatred for offensive Limbaugh commentary; overall, such hatred is abundant. Sarandos' position is programmed. His position is programmed by a likely familiarity with Limbaugh, other right-wing talk show hosts, Republican rejection of Obamacare, and other issues. For Friedman, The Discourse has shifted us away from how we discuss current events and issues, particularly those that demand attention, and toward a never-ending series of poorly thought-out critiques and knee jerk reactions that are programmed. Being happy Limbaugh has cancer is not a critical analysis or observation (no matter how offensive Limbaugh's show can be). "The Discourse is inseparable from Twitter," Friedman writes. Twitter, as many commentators note, provides a space for these types of exchanges, those that are not thought out, to occur readily. Matt Taibbi follows this line of thinking when he argues that such programmable responses deviate public rhetoric from thought out ideas and commentary: "The leaders of this new movement are replacing traditional liberal beliefs about tolerance, free inquiry and even racial harmony with ideas so toxic and unattractive that they eschew debate, moving straight to shaming, threats and intimidation."

I begin this conclusion with Sarandos' tweet not because I think we should have an open, tolerant debate about Rush Limbaugh and his health, but because the Sarandos' tweet, for me, represents the observations Friedman and Taibbi make about social media in general. While I have used the phrase digital outragicity, Friedman and Taibbi settle for the generic term The Discourse. Other critics refer to these exchanges as "shit" or "shitstorming." "In our attempts to clean up the inherent messiness of social media," Matthew Sini argues, "lots of us are pointlessly flinging shit at each other." Byung-Chul Han calls this process the "shitstorm." "The shitstorm represents an authentic phenomenon of digital communication," Han writes (3). Han links outrage and discourse as elements within the shitstorm: "Outrage society is scandal society. It lacks bearing—reserve and posture. The fractiousness, hysteria, and intractability that characterize waves of outrage do not admit tactful or matter-of-fact communication; they bar dialogue and discourse" (7). Who promotes The Discourse or shitstorm or whatever term we want to use? Han calls this group "the digital swarm."

The digital swarm, like the notion of mob mentality, condenses group think into a supposed singular voice: "The digital swarm does not constitute a mass because no soul—no spirit—dwells within it. The soul gathers and unites In contrast, the digital swarm comprises isolated individuals" (10). The digital swarm, it seems, is a soulless network of individuals without a sense of community binding them to one another. Such a pessimistic view of how and why individuals respond in programmed ways, though, distracts from the ways individuals engage with circulated technical images, not because they are part of a soulless mass but because of many of the attributes (affinity, social proof, aggregation, etc.) I have been outlining. Images circulate as communal objects within communities such as those who yell "I'm mad as hell" out their windows. These communities build off of each other, not as soulless beings but as people caught within similar networks of meaning.

As I've tried to show in this book, writing on platforms such as Facebook or Twitter plays a vital role in spreading online outrage. Users, such as Sarandos, congregate within the platform to post their anger at every "offensive" moment they encounter. But outrage itself spreads outrage. Sarandos' outrage, or anybody else's, is not an isolated body collapsed within a larger digital mass. His outrage is part of this overall network. One person outraged at Limbaugh is likely not only the result of any Limbaugh declaration. One person's outrage at Limbaugh likely feeds other individuals' outrage and expression of that outrage because of other related factors including health care initiatives, talk radio, conservativism etc. Twitter, like other social media platforms, connects the weak and strong ties, allows for endless sharing, makes immediacy the most important thing one will ever experience, and showcases immediacy as a call to action (in words or in deeds). Shitstorm. The Discourse. Digital outragicity. These terms describe the feeding of outrage.

Outrage, as I've also tried to show, exists without social media, but it does so mostly alone, in one's privacy, away from spreading and influence. Despite pundit proclamations to the contrary, social media does not create outrage on its own and often not at all, and a digital swarm is not an agent spreading outrage. Outrage creates outrage because of how aggregation of imagery functions so that affective responses are communicated via the rhetorical gestures I have highlighted. I can be angry at Limbaugh or anybody else, or I can be a central figure in a shitstorm, but that anger is meaningless until it creates further publicly shared anger or a more widespread shitstorm which will continue to aggregate further. Such was the lesson of *Network*. Twitter and Facebook help outrage spread itself, but is either responsible for outrage? Or is the responsibility with the spreading, circulation, and the continuation of technical images as they aggregate various embedded moments and imagery? The Discourse, we might add to Friedman's insight, is itself outrage. It is outrage for the reasons I've outlined in previous chapters. The Discourse is another name for what I call digital outragicity. It simply lacks the theoretical reasonings I have explored.

Discourse has long meant the simpler definition of verbal or content exchange. But if we take Friedman's point seriously, it can also mean that typically contentious, online exchange reflects a capital D for discursive engagement. The capital D signifies the shift from a supposed public sphere willing to debate and discuss issues to one in which negativity commands our ability to communicate with one another. In this book, I have avoided blaming social media platforms for the rise and popularity of digital outrage as a dominant form of digital communication. While this blame gesture has traditionally been made by various critics, as if outrage never preceded digital media, it fails to address the complexity involved when we become digitally angry because of how we engage with technical images. Blaming a platform fails to address the rise of what Friedman calls The Discourse and I more simply call digital outrage or digital outragicity.

The Discourse does not negate or deny real social injustice when it occurs, nor does pointing out The Discourse suggest individuals such as Limbaugh do

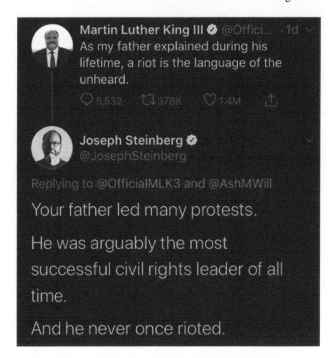

Martin Luther King III ✔ @Offici... ·1d ✔
As my father explained during his lifetime, a riot is the language of the unheard.

♡ 5,532   ↻ 378K   ♡ 1.4M   ⬆

Joseph Steinberg ✔
@JosephSteinberg

Replying to @OfficialMLK3 and @AshMWill

Your father led many protests.

He was arguably the most successful civil rights leader of all time.

And he never once rioted.

Fig. 9.1 Outrage at Martin Luther |King III.

not deserve criticism for hypocrisy. The Discourse, as I've noted via Flusser's work, often produces predictable (programmed) results regarding outrage. What Friedman calls The Discourse for a general audience reading *The New Republic*, I have called digital outrage. When "the identification of that bad thing" happens, one should expect The Discourse to assume its place within social media exchanges. When, during the upheaval that followed George Floyd's murder, Martin Luther King III tweeted his dad's famous words about rioting (shown in fig. 9.1), The Discourse stepped in to shame him or attempt to contradict his position.

This gesture regarding Martin Luther King Jr. and rioting was repeated across a number of exchanges by different individuals attempting to minimize the King quote, as if pointing out supposed discrepancy is either real (is it, indeed, a contradiction or is there more to the citation in question) or changes anything regarding rioting and social injustice (even if there were a discrepancy, how would that change a current situation?). Digital outrage does not choose a side or political position; it emerges at all moments of aggregated outrage, pointing out hypocrisy and contradiction, whether the focus is Limbaugh or King, two polar opposites.

Consider another example of The Discourse as outrage, the July 7, 2020, *Harper's* magazine posting "A Letter on Justice and Open Debate." This letter, signed by leading thinkers, artists, and academics, also occurred during the aftermath of Floyd's murder and the Black Lives Matter protests. Because of how its signees viewed difficult and often antagonistic online discussion after Floyd's death, the letter called for a rejection of The Discourse (without naming it as such) and requested open debate rather than the shutdown of dissent. The letter's attention appeared to be directed at digital discourse that is accusatory (or sometimes called "cancel culture"): "The forces of illiberalism are gaining strength throughout the world and have a powerful ally in Donald Trump, who represents a real threat to democracy. But resistance must not be allowed to harden into its own brand of dogma or coercion—which right-wing demagogues are already exploiting. The democratic inclusion we want can be achieved only if we speak out against the intolerant climate that has set in on all sides" ("A Letter"). Whether one agrees with the sentiment of the call or not, the Twitter response was vitriolic. This letter became "the one bad thing" that needed to be shut down. The magazine's call for openness resulted in a thread of anger and outrage. Responses called it the "weaponization of free speech," as well as "the whiniest passive voice." Critics of the letter alleged hypocritical positions held by some of the signees who were accused of various public shaming in the past (and, of course, some of the signees were labeled the pejorative "Zionist" though the letter has nothing to do with Zionism or Israel). The response was programmatic. If Rush Limbaugh is easy to call out for publicly drawing attention to his health issues, so, too, is it easy to identify in an open letter's signees previous behaviors or positions that supposedly run counter to the letter's call. Both Limbaugh and the signees are technical images, and as such, they aggregate enough material to always be contradictory. Friedman's concept assumes immediacy (it didn't take long for angry reaction to *Harper's* to occur) but unlike digital outragicity, it doesn't recognize aggregation even if such aggregation exists. The anger at *Harper's* is not just immediacy ("I am angry that someone who once dismissed trans individuals now calls for openness") but is also a collection of real or imagined past infractions that now become embedded in a person as image (the previous hypothetical parenthetical, for instance, refers to the author J. K. Rowling who was a signee). The only way outrage at the signatures can occur is if one aggregates into its signees actual and imagined prior activity, activity that may not even be connected to the content or intent of the letter.

The *Harper's* letter did not outline what, in particular, it was responding to: The Discourse? Shitstorming? Digital outrage in general? Something else? We might assume, though, that some of its focus was devoted to the events that followed the murder of George Floyd, and American culture's turn to projected sensitivity online. On May 25, 2020, George Floyd supposedly used a counterfeit $20 bill (knowingly or not) to make a purchase at a convenience store in Minneapolis. When police apprehended him, police officer Derek Chauvin arrested

Floyd by pressing his knee into the back of Floyd's neck and eventually suffocating him. Anger, outrage, and rioting understandably took place immediately. The image of George Floyd, as it circulated across social media, gathered many other images with it, including those indicative of past Black American deaths at the hands of the police, but also those images associated with related issues regarding racism within either the police force or society overall: civil rights, fair housing, fair employment opportunities, education, racism in general, and questions regarding white privilege. George Floyd's death, as well, occurred during the same time period that Louisville, Kentucky, resident Breonna Taylor was killed by police while sleeping in her bed and Brunswick, Georgia, resident Ahmaud Arbery was murdered by two white men who wrongly accused him of robbery. In addition to this temporal overlap, there exists in the public consciousness other notable cases worthy of outrage for their unjustified deaths (some of which I have already drawn attention to). Philando Castile, Sandra Bland, Michael Brown, Eric Gardner, and Jamal Clark are but a few of the recognizable names of Black Americans killed by or believed to be killed by police. Clark and Castile were killed by Minneapolis police officers too.

George Floyd became an immediate technical image that rocked the leverage point of digital outrage. George Floyd is a human, and he is a technical image. We see that technical image in Ibram X. Kendi's description of his research into racism. Within each racist act we encounter, the act functions as a technical image with other images embedded within it. For Kendi, there isn't a singular act of racism that we focus upon, such as one man's murder by police. There is, instead, an aggregation: "By the summer of 2012, I was finding and tagging every idea I could find from history. Racist ideas piled up before me like trash at a landfill. Tens of thousands of pages of Black people being trashed as natural or nurtured beasts devils, animals, rapists, slaves, criminals, kids, predators, brutes, idiots, prostitutes, cheats and dependents. More than five hundred years of toxic ideas on the Black body" (271). Ideas pile up into current imagery. Within the Floyd technical image are many historical instances of what Kendi describes as well as contemporary acts of police brutality, but particularly within this image is suffocation. Suffocation at the hands of the police is not limited to Floyd's death. Suffocation, too, is a technical image. Eric Garner famously uttered "I can't breathe" while being choked to death by New York Police officers. Manuel Ellis, who died in police custody on March 20, 2020, while being restrained, also uttered the phrase I can't breathe" before dying. In 2019, Javier Ambler uttered "I can't breathe" when apprehended and restrained by Austin, Texas police officers. In 2015, Jonathan Sanders complained that he could not breathe as a Jackson, Mississippi police officer put him in a chokehold.

I am concluding with this final image of a Black man's murder because of how all of the concepts explored in *The Rhetoric of Outrage* can be seen on display in reporting, response, and overall reaction. Injustice, as I have written in previous chapters, obviously sparks outrage. Death, however, is only one item within Floyd's circulated image. Within his image, other images regarding racial injustice were embedded by protesters and outraged individuals, as Kendi argues regarding his own research. Much of the reporting that followed nationwide riots focused not only on one individual's death, but the other social and political issues that had become embedded in Floyd's image. NPR's Scott Horsley focused on economic disparity in his reporting on Floyd: "A survey by the Federal Reserve last year found that even in good times, African Americans are less able to pay their monthly bills than whites or Latinos. And Blacks are also 40 percent less likely to own their homes than whites—depriving many African American families of an opportunity to build wealth." *Politico*'s survey of thinkers reflecting on George Floyd's death and the ensuing protests, on the other hand, begins with a historical nod toward previous social unrest: "In some ways, this wave seems familiar: It echoes what happened in Ferguson, in Baltimore, in Los Angeles and in every other city that has exploded in anger after a killing by police. The sweep of the current protests—in hundreds of cities across all 50 states, lasting more than a week so far—and the sense that a moment of national change might have arrived have drawn comparisons to other waves of social unrest dating at least to 1968" (*Politico*). These are items that quickly become embedded in the Floyd image because of perceived associations.

Floyd's image also includes the more ambiguous yet still powerful technical image of the "police officer," vilified for unjust murders of Black people, represented in widespread calls to "defund the police" and expressed in concerns over how police offers are represented in popular culture. Regarding the last point, The Discourse, for instance, quickly moved in a programmatic way to shut down police officer popular culture representations. It did so not to remove them from the larger police image which may or may not resemble the aggregation, but because the presence of a police officer image is believed to obviously cause offense. When I say "programmed," I follow Flusser's usage of the term. The public and circulated calls to change entertainment representations of police officers, for instance, have nothing to do with police brutality or how to prevent further police brutality but with a communal immediacy whose aggregation triggers the offensive police image much in the way Barthes noted an advertisement's aggregation triggers an image of Italian food.

Cops, the "reality" police show featuring footage of individuals being arrested as entertainment, for instance, was cancelled after airing for 31 years (though it was later rebooted). For 31 years it ran without much protest, but suddenly it was cancelled. Noah Rothman argued that the cancellation of cop shows, such as *Cops*, had little to do with morality: "The program effectively monetized what were, in many cases, the lowest moments of a person's life. Other critics of the program claimed that the show failed to depict police violence in ways that reflected their realities. Indeed, an average episode was dominated by the mundane day-to-day that is life in law enforcement. But this show wasn't canceled for any of these reasons. It was canceled in this moment *because* of this moment." Rothman called the rush to publicly denounce all police or to remove popular culture representations that are positive "a stampede." Other shows, too, were cancelled in response, such as *Live PD*. Lego paused marketing its police sets. Elsewhere, rumors spread that the cartoon *Paw Patrol* would be cancelled (it wasn't; the rumors were mocking the cancellations). Writing in the *New York Times*, Amanda Hess argued: "As the protests against racist police violence enter their third week, the charges are mounting against fictional cops, too. Even big-hearted cartoon police dogs—or maybe *especially* big-hearted cartoon police dogs—are on notice. The effort to publicize police brutality also means banishing the good-cop archetype, which reigns on both television and in viral videos of the protests themselves. "Paw Patrol" seems harmless enough, and that's the point: The movement rests on understanding that cops do plenty of harm." Satire took note as well, as in a *Hard Times* headline "Village People Kick Out Police Officer" (Crooks). If Friedman's assessment is correct, these brief examples would appear to exemplify The Discourse, a fairly programmed response to erase representation rather than discuss, challenge, or argue about it. Others have called this movement "cancel culture," but I return to an understanding that more accurately reflects an affective aggregation as outrage-based response.

I do not conclude with a man's murder to be callous. I choose this final example of digital outrage because of how it networks with other issues, many of which I've covered in this book. George Floyd. Black Lives Matter. Antiracism. Economics. Health Care. Education. Police. All of these images have appeared in the examples I explore. These kinds of issues surface, congregate, and aggregate around public response and criticism of Floyd's death as they have done with other circulated technical images. Because "speech" was a primary technical image in one of my previous examples, I find it necessary to focus on discourse in a similar fashion. Public responses, whether called The Discourse or digital outrage, often rely on a technical image not dissimilar form other speech related images, such as academic freedom: the rights of individuals to say or think as they like in public forums such as social media with the added element of immediate critique of projected singular imagery.

Writing in *The Chicago Tribune*, columnist John Kass treated the response to Floyd's killing as such a moment. Kass aggregates into the image of protests over Floyd's death a number of disparate items—kneeling, political TV discussion, Marxism—the way Sarah Palin once aggregated into health care reform the images of socialism and death panels.

What are you really seeing as Americans kneel, hands raised in secular prayer, repeating political creeds on the TV news? And that secular foot-washing?

You're witness to neo-Marxist appropriation of Christian symbolism, in the aftermath of the horrifying Minneapolis police killing of George Floyd.

This, too, is a programmed response: political protest, regardless of focus, must be Marxist, anti-Christian, or antipatriotic (as we saw with Kaepernick). The protests do not activate any of these images, but a particular audience embeds in Floyd these other images—much as other public responses I highlighted embedded health care or economic disparity into Floyd's image.

In the conservative publication *The Federalist*, John Daniel Davidson echoed this sentiment, transforming the protestors into revolutionaries attempting to overthrow the government and American way of life: "By rushing to profess their supposed guilt for racism, these people are admitting that they need publicly to affirm their allegiance to woke identity politics. This represents nothing less than the emergence of a new regime in American life. What is now a voluntary and seemingly spontaneous public affirmation of progressive ideology will in time become a requirement." For this imagined audience, the technical image of Floyd and the ensuing protest layers references to anti-Americanism but also to images associated with oppression such as generic censorship, the Cultural Revolution, Star Chambers and other centralized suppressions of opinion or belief. Protest or public response aggregates from a man's death into the prevention of speech.

Reason's Nick Gillespie's argument, for instance, examines the current political climate by juxtaposing traditional censorship concerns with the image of Maoist struggle sessions: "Twitter, YouTube, Facebook, Patreon, and other private services have been bouncing more and more people off their platforms for real and imagined crimes. The legacy media seems to spend more time conducting struggle sessions than reporting these days." Elsewhere on Twitter, #strugglesession serves as a circulated hashtag related to the notion of The Discourse. The hashtag, when applied to supposed moments, references 1960s Chinese reeducation camps and the Maoist cultural revolution as if certain political responses equate these two moments. This, again, is associative and affective, aggregated outrage. Struggle session is a term borrowed from Mao Zedong's China when individuals were publicly humiliated for supposed crimes and forced to confess in front of large crowds. The purpose was to instill fear in others through these public examples. A current, prominent example compared to a struggle session was the circulation on Twitter of a video of Minneapolis mayor Jacob Frey refusing to agree to a gathered crowd's demand to abolish the city's police. The crowd surrounding him and the speaker on a stage began shouting "Go home, traitor, go home," until he walked away in shame. In the *American Conservative* Rod Dreher called this moment McCarthyism of the left. Citing a number of examples, his exigence for this term was Marie Cisco's public Google spreadsheet whose purpose was to blacklist movie theaters that had not spoken out about Black Lives Matter. Even when they did speak out, they were often not removed from the spreadsheet. With this in mind, Dreher makes an association reminiscent of struggle session rhetoric: "It did not appear to be a coincidence that the following day, and into June, theaters began posting messages of solidarity with Black Lives Matter en masse, black theater artists said. The response was problematic because often the statements were perceived to have come from a place of shame and felt slapped together and hollow, Cisco said" (Gelt). Conservative writer Kevin Williamson calls such provocateurs the "American Association of Outrage Professionals." A public protest. A movie theater. A grocery store. An academic department. A mayor trying to calm a crowd. Such spaces can become outrage targets for not saying the supposed right thing or what another level of outrage aggregation has deemed the right thing. Apologize too late, the critique states, and one is now aggregated into complicity of injustice.

I don't list these moments because I agree or disagree with them. I list them in order to trace out some contemporary public outrage moments, particularly as they follow a man's senseless death, and what these moments and responses, indeed, look like to some critics. The Discourse, like other aspects of aggregation and the technical image I have drawn attention to throughout this book, relies on response. Social media does as well. We live in a cultural of endless response. With response, there will always be outrage. Something will anger us, and that something will trigger a need to write in response.

The Federalist, whose columnist I just briefly cited, runs an outrage link in its publication in order to keep track of what moments it feels demand attention for saying the wrong thing (its own right-wing version of The Discourse). Yet, one does not have to look only to right-wing publications to find response embedded with outrage either. Not long after Floyd's murder, Twitter and Instagram users demanding justice for Floyd's murder began their own internal debate over "the right thing" to say in response. One side, identified as the Black Out Tuesday movement, posted a black square with the hashtag #blackouttuesday almost 28 million times over a twenty-four-hour period on Instagram and Twitter. The posts were offered in solidarity with Black Lives Matter. In response, Black Lives Matter activists actively critiqued the square as clogging up the hashtag's feed, as too performative, and as preventing news and important information from being seen on the hashtag feed. Black Lives Matter leaders and supporters expressed anger at how the black squares were, in essence, shutting down social media (via blacked out post after post using the #BLM hashtag) at a time when the protest movement needed it most. As with social proof and virtue signaling, there was likely a desire to spread outrage by tapping into individuals' empathy and desire to be associated with the protest movement. Caroline Framke argued, "This rush to virtue-signal support without providing substantive aid is an all too familiar instinct on social media, where an issue can become a trend that people feel the need to address in some way, whether or not it makes sense or does any actual good." And Chelsey Sanchez added that #blackouttuesday was being understood, "as a form of virtue signaling, a pithy sign of solidarity that—without the accompaniment of material resources or support in the form of donations, information, protesting, or otherwise— renders the perhaps well-intentioned post moot." Yet, both sides felt that they were doing good for the same cause even while outrage occurred among like-minded protesters. This, too, I contend, exemplifies digital outragicity even if both sides agree on the need to digitally protest. Even in agreement there exists outrage. Even in agreement there exists programmable anger at either hypocrisy or injustice. What does this say about the ability to thwart or control outrage in general?

How does one conclude a discussion of outrage when outrage itself never seems to conclude? "It's hard to avoid constant triggering exposure to even most fleeting and superficial outrages of the day," Matt Lewis writes. "One side of the political aisle does something to outrage us. We can't avoid seeing it, nor can we avoid wrongly assuming that this is representative of the other 'tribe.' In some cases, outrageous behavior creates a backlash, whereby we are drawn closer to our side of the political aisle. In other cases, outrageous acts spark retaliation, thus igniting a whole new round of outrage and outrage backlash." Intellectuals yell at each other over a published letter requesting tolerance. A man's murder for supposedly passing a counterfeit bill leads to fears of a socialist takeover. Two sides agree on the need for social justice but get angry with each other regarding how to demonstrate for the cause. One does not need to look far to find outrage online. With all of the examples I share, with my attempts to theorize the "why" and "how" of digital outrage, I still make no claims to the end of digital outrage, digital outragicity, The Discourse, or any other term I've used as a synonym for this phenomenon. I have no arguments for how to overcome digital outrage and become a digital culture of acceptance, tolerance, debate, rational thought, or some other technical image posed as the utopian alternative to the cacophony of dissenting voices dominating online spaces. Without resorting to an outright pessimistic conclusion either, I note that digital outrage is not an avoidable feature of digital culture. It is a trait of digital culture. Much as we have been told that privacy violations are not a bug within Facebook, but a feature of the platform, so is outrage a feature of digital culture.

This feature returns me finally to health care. As I finished writing this book, COVID-19 had already claimed approximately one million American lives. The outrage over the pandemic—from the refusal to wear masks to recognizing scientific claims to social distancing to government financial support—spread along with the virus. *Politico* called this wave of anger "the outrage outbreak," continuing, "In this crisis, no one's totally certain what the next move should be. Public officials and business leaders risk being paralyzed by the pandemic's newest fear: becoming the target of a shame mob" (Heath and Rayasam). Shame mobs, I've noted, are part of digital outragicity and The Discourse. When Ohio state Senate candidate Melissa Ackinson was photographed, along with other protesters, screaming into the window of the Ohio statehouse, she was not the target of a shame mob, but appeared to be part of the mob itself, an aspiring politician contributing to a mob's demand's that the state not close businesses in order to protect its citizens' health during a pandemic. Her contorted face, mouth wide with a yell, and unheard shouting captured in the photograph symbolized the viral spread of anger at a government for either not doing enough to save lives or for doing too much. As with the John Pike image, this image contains much more than Ackinson. Health care is in this image. So is hypocrisy. So is antigovernment sentiment. So is any other item we might capture in this shared technical image of an individual running for a state representative job meant to care for citizens while simultaneously denouncing the state for its actions during a health crisis. What might be those additional elements embedded in the image?

I conclude with that open-ended question. The only thing I can ask of a readership is to consider when looking at an image, a tweet, a Facebook post, a headline, and so on: What might be those additional images embedded within what I am viewing and/or reading? Is this a singular image? How could it be so? What is this technical image that prompts me to be outraged, to become angry, and to eventually respond? I am sure that even with that information, or even with the later observation of that information, one will still be outraged. But, at the very least, one may have a better understanding of how social media made you angry.

Works Cited

"The 1915 Declaration of Principles on Academic Freedom and Academic Tenure." AAUP. org. Web.

Abou Jalal, Rasha. "Gaza Valley Faces Environmental Disaster." Al-Monitor. August 19, 2013. Web.

"Academic Freedom and Tenure." *Bulletin of the American Association of University Professors (1915-1955)* 28, no. 1 (1943): 75–81.

Adams, Paul. 2012. *Grouped: How Small Groups of Friends are the Key to Influence on the Social Web.* Berkeley, CA: New Riders.

"After the Fall, Communiqués from California." Libcom.org. 16 Feb. 2010. Web.

Ahmed, Sarah. *The Cultural Politics of Emotion.* Edinburgh: Edinburgh University Press, 2014.

———. *The Promise of Happiness.* Durham, NC: Duke University Press, 2010.

———. *Queer Phenomenology: Orientations, Objects, Others.* Durham, NC: Duke University Press, 2006.

Ali, Wajahat. "Deradicalizing White People." *New York Review of Books.* 16 August 2018. Web.

Altbach, Philip G. "Academic Freedom: International Realities and Challenges." *Higher Education* 41, no. 1/2, (2001): 205–19.

Alexander, Doyle. "Far-Left Professor Who Blamed Vegas Shootings on President Trump Just Got Slapped with Worst News Ever." *EnVolve.* n.d. Web.

"A Letter On Justice and Open Debate." *Harper's.* 7 July 2020. Web.

Anderson, Steve, and Tara McPhereson. "Engaging Digital Scholarship: Thoughts on Evaluating Multimedia Scholarship." *Profession* (2011): 136–51.

Anderson, Kurt. "The Protester." *TIME.*14 December 2011. Web.

Anderson, Virginia. "Rising Obamacare Premiums Anger Those Paying Full Price." *CNN.* 15 October 2016. Web.

Andrews, Lori. "Facebook is Using You." *New York Times.* 4 February 2012. Web.

Angwin, Julia, Surya Mattu, and Terry Parris, Jr. "Facebook Doesn't Tell Users Everything It Really Knows About Them." *ProPublica.* 27 December 2016. Web.

Banicki, Adam. "The Truth About Donald Trump Supporters: They're Mad as Hell and Not Going to Take it Anymore!" *Business Insider.* 25 August 2015. Web.

Barsade, Sigal. "Emotional Contagion and its Influence on Group Behavior." *Administrative Science Quarterly* 47, no. 4 (2002): 644–75.

Barthes, Roland. *Camera Lucida: Reflections on Photography.* Trans. Richard Howard. New York: Hill and Wang, 1981.

———. *Mythologies.* Trans. Annette Lavers. New York: Hill and Wang, 1972.

———. *Roland Barthes.* Trans. Richard Howard. Oakland: University of California Press, 1977.

Barthes, Roland. 1978. "The Photographic Message." *Image Music Text*. New York: Hill and Wang, 19–20.

Barthes, Roland. 1978. "The Rhetoric of the Image." *Image Music Text*. Trans. Stephen Heath. New York: Hill and Wang.

Berlant, Lauren. *Cruel Optimism*. Durham, NC: Duke University Press, 2011.

Berlin, James. *Rhetoric, Poetics, and Cultures*. West Lafayette, IN: Parlor Press, 2002.

"Betty White Condemns Cecil the Lion Killer: 'You Don't Want to Hear Some of the Things I Want to do to That Man'" *Hollywood Reporter*. 31 July 2015. Web.

Brown, Nathan. "Open Letter to Chancellor Linda P.B. Katehi." *UC Davis Bicycle Barricade*. 19 November 2011. Web.

Bartholomew, James. "The Awful Rise of 'Virtue Signalling.'" *Spectator*. 18 April 2015. Web.

Beck, Julie. "Facebook: Where Friendships Go to Never Quite Die." *Atlantic*. 4 Feb. 2018. Web.

Beale, Walter H. "Rhetorical Performative Discourse: A New Theory of Epideictic." *Philosophy and Rhetoric* 11, no. 4 (1978): 221–46.

Beck, Glenn. *Addicted to Outrage: How Thinking Like a Recovering Addict Can Heal the Country*. New York: Threshold Editions, 2018.

Bennett, William J. *The Death of Outrage: Bill Clinton and the Assault on American Ideals*. New York: The Free Press, 1998.

Berger, Jonah. *Contagious: Why Things Catch On*. New York: Simon and Schuster, 2013.

Berman, Lazar. "False 'Israel drowns Gaza' Claims Sweep Internet." *Times of Israel*. 25 February 2015. Web.

Bernard, Andreas. *Theory of the Hashtag*. Trans. Valentine A. Pakis. Medford, MA: Polity, 2019.

Berry, Jeffrey, and Sara Sobieraj. *The Outrage Industry: Public Opinion Media and the New Incivility*. New York: Oxford University Press, 2014.

Binyam, Maya. "Watching the Woke Olympics." *The Awl*. 5 April 2016. Web.

Bitzer, Lloyd. "Aristotle's Enthymeme Revisited." *Quarterly Journal of Speech* 45, no. 4 (1959): 399–409.

———. "Rhetoric and Public Knowledge." *Rhetoric, Philosophy, and Literature* (1978): 67–93.

———. "The Rhetorical Situation." *Philosophy & Rhetoric* 1, no. 1 (1968): 1–14.

Blair, J. Anthony. "The Rhetoric of Visual Arguments." In *Defining Visual Rhetorics*, edited by Charles A. Hill and Marguerite Helmers. New York: Routledge, 2004.

Bolstad, Erika. "What's the Secret Behind Palin's Ability to Draw a Crowd?" McClatchy dc.com. 2 November 2008. Web.

Booth, Wayne. *The Rhetoric of Rhetoric: The Quest for Effective Communication*. New York: Blackwell, 2004.

boyd, danah, and Alice Marwick. "I Tweet Honestly, I Tweet Passionately: Twitter Users, Context Collapse, and the Imagined Audience." *New Media and Society*. 13.1. July 7, 2010 (114–33).

Boyle, Casey. *Rhetoric as a Posthuman Practice*. Columbus: Ohio State University Press, 2018.

Brown, Kara. "Collen Kaepernick's Hair Sees Me." *Jezebel*. 17 October 2016. Web.

Brown, Nikki. "Why Colin Kaepernick's Glorious Afro is Significant." *Essence*. 4 September 2016. Web.

Burke, Kenneth. *A Rhetoric of Motives*. Oakland: University of California Press, 1969.

———. *Counter Statement*. Oakland: University of California Press, 1968.

———. *Language as Symbolic Action: Essays on Life, Literature, and Method*. Oakland: University of California Press, 1966.

———. The *Philosophy of Literary Form*. Oakland: University of California Press, 1974.

"Can I Play That?" *Saturday Night Live*. 9 March 2019.

Carbone, Nick. The Prevalence of Pepper Spray in Protests." *TIME*. 21 November 2011. Web.

Carpenter, Sade. "Blackface for Halloween? Don't Do It." *Chicago Tribune*. 29 October 2015. Web.

Carter, Michael. "Scholarship as Rhetoric of Display; Or, Why Is Everybody Saying All Those Terrible Things About Us?" *College English* 54, no. 3 (1992): 303–13.

Cassidy, Laurence L. "Creationism and Academic Freedom." *Academe* 68, no. 2 (1982): 7–9.

Cep, Casey. "The Perils and Possibilities of Anger." *New Yorker*. Web. 6 October 2018. Web.

Chandler, Adam. "A Six Figure Settlement on Campus Free Speech." *Atlantic*. 12 November 2015. Web.

Christakis, Nicholas A., and James H. Fowler. *Connected: The Surprising Power of Our Social Networks and How They Shape Our Lives*. New York: Little, Brown Spark, 2009.

Cialdini, Robert. *Influence: Science and Practice*, second edition. Glenview, IL: Scott, Foresman, 1988.

Ciccariello-Maher, George. "Conservatives are the Real Campus Thought Police Squashing Academic Freedom." *The Washington Post*. 10 October 2017. Web.

Cilliza, Chris. "Donald Trump's Craziest Day Ever on Twitter." *CNN*. 18 March 2019. Web.

Cohen, Dan. "Searching for the Victorians." *Dan Cohen's Digital Humanities Blog*. 10 October 2010. Web.

Confessore, Nicholas, Michael LaForgia, and Gabrielle J. X. Dance. "Facebook's Data Sharing: 5 Takeaways from Our Investigation." *New York Times*. 18 December 2018. Web.

Cormen, Thomas H., Charles E. Leiserson, Ronald L. Rivest, and Clifford Stein. *Introduction to Algorithms*. Cambridge, MA: MIT Press, 2009.

Coscarelli, Joe. "#BlackoutTuesday: A Music Industry Protest Becomes a Social Media Moment." *New York Times*. 2 June 2020. Web.

Cosman, Ben. "'Death Panels' Will Be Sarah Palin's Greatest Legacy." *Atlantic*. 30 May 2014. Web.

Coyle, Daniel. The Culture Code: *The Secrets of Highly Successful Groups*. New York: Bantam, 2018.

Crenshaw, Dan. "Dan Crenshaw: The Outrage Incentive is Dooming Our Politics." *Dallas News*. 22 July 2019. Web.

Cronin, Melissa. "Trophy Hunting is Surprisingly Popular, But That Could be About to Change. *Slate*. 29 July 2015. Web.

Crooks, Patrick. "Village People Kick Out Police Officer." *Hard Times*. 7 June 2020. Web.

Daniel, Sharan L. 2002. "Integrating Rhetoric and Journalism to Realize Publics." *Rhetoric and Public Affairs* 5, no. 3 (2002): 507–24.

Daniels, Jesse. "Protect Scholars Against Attacks from the Right." *Inside Higher Ed.* 26 June 2017. Web.

Davidson, Cathy. "21st Century Literacies: Syllabus, Calendar, Assignments." http://www.hastac.org/blogs/cathy-davidson/.

Davidson, Cathy, and David Theo Goldberg. "Manifesto for the Humanities in a Technological Era." *Chronicle of Higher Education.* 13 Feb. 2004. Web.

Davidson, John Daniel. "The Struggle Sessions are Here, and They are Not Going Away." *The Federalist.* 4 June 2020. Web.

Daum, Meghan. *The Problem with Everything: My Journey Through the New Culture Wars.* New York: Gallery, 2019.

Delicath, John W., and Kevin Michael Deluca. "Image Events, the Public Sphere, and Argumentative Practice: The Case of Radical Environmental Groups." *Argumentation* 17 (2003): 315–33.

Dennis, David. "I Shouldn't Have to Say This in 2013—Blackface Halloween Outfits Aren't Ok." *Guardian.* 30 October 2013. Web.

Dewey, Caitlin. "More than 26 Million People Have Changed Their Facebok Picture to a Rainbow Flag. Here's Why That Matters." *Washington Post.* 29 June 2015. Web.

DeGroot, Gerard J. *Student Protest: The Sixties and After.* London: Routledge, 1998.

DiFonzo, Nicholas. "The Echo-Chamber Effect." *New York Times.* 22 April 2011. Web.

Dionne, E.J. "Yes, We Should Be Outraged About Facebook." *Washington Post.* 21 March 2018. Web.

Ditz, Jason. "Hundreds Displaced as Israel Opens Dam, Flooding Gaza Villages." *Antiwar.com.* 22 Feb. 2015. Web.

Dobrin, Sidney I. *Postcomposition.* Carbondale: Southern Illinois University Press, 2011.

Donoghue, Frank. "Can the Humanities Survive the 21st Century?" *Chronicle of Higher Education.* September 2010

Doyle, Andrew. "Why I'm Anti-Woke." *Spiked.* 5 Feb. 2020 Web.

Dreher, Rod. "McCarthyites of the Left." *The American Conservative.* 11 June 2020. Web.

Dreyfuss, Emily. "Gillett's Ad Proves the Definition of a Good Man Has Changed." *Wired.* 16 Jan 2018. Web.

"Drowning Gaza Deliberately." *Zainab's Lounge.* 19 December 2013. Web.

Drucker, Johanna. "Humanities Approaches to Graphical Display." *Digital Humanities Quarterly* 5, no. 1 (2011).

Duffy, Bernard K. "The Platonic Functions of Epideictic Rhetoric." *Philosophy and Rhetoric* 16, no. 2 (1983): 79–93.

Dugan, Christina. "Controversial YouTuber Logan Paul Sparks Outrage After Saying He Will 'Go Gay' for 1 Month." *People.* 11 Jan 2019. Web

Duhigg, Charles. "The Real Roots of American Rage." *Atlantic.* January/February 2019. Web.

Dunn, Sydni. "University's Rescinding of Job Offer Prompts an Outcry." *New York Times.* 31 Aug 2014. Web.

Durham Peters, John. *The Marvelous Clouds: Toward a Philosophy of Elemental Media.* Chicago: University of Chicago Press, 2015.

Dzirutwe, MacDonald. "'What Lion?' Zimbabweans Ask, Amid Global Cecil Circus." *Reuters.com.* 30 July 2015. Web.

Edwards, Dustin, and Heather Lang. "Entanglements That Matter: A New Materialist Trace of #YesAllWomen." In *Circulation, Writing, and Rhetoric,* edited by Laurie E. Gries and Colling Gifford Brooke, 118–34. Logan: Utah State University Press, 2018.

Elassar, Alaa. "An English Teacher was Suspended After Tweeting That it is 'Awesome' Rush Limbaugh is Dying from Cancer." *CNN.* 7 Feb. 2020. Web.

Ewen, Stuart. *All Consuming Images: The Politics of Style in Contemporary Culture.* Basic Books: New York, 1999.

Fadel, Leila. "Cultural Appropriation, A Perennial Issue on Halloween." NPR. 29 October 2019. Web.

Fallows, James. "The Moral Power of an Image: UC Davis Reactions." *Atlantic.* 20 November 2011. Web.

Farrell, Thomas. "Knowledge, Consensus, and Rhetorical Theory." *Quarterly Journal of Speech* 1, no. 62 (1976): 1–14.

Ferguson, Roderick A. We Demand: *The University and Student Protests.* Oakland: University of California Press, 2017.

Finn, Ed. *What Algorithms Want: Imagination in the Age of Computing.* Cambridge, MA: MIT Press, 2017.

Finnigan, Cara. "The Naturalistic Enthymeme and Visual Argument: Photographic Representation in the 'Skull Controversy.'" *Argumentation and Advocacy* 37 (2000): 133–49.

Flusser, Vilém. *Does Writing Have a Future?* Trans. Nancy Ann Roth. Minneapolis: University of Minnesota Press, 2011.

———. *Into the Universe of Technical Images.* Trans. Nancy Ann Roth. Minneapolis: University of Minnesota Press, 2011.

———. *Towards a Philosophy of Photography.* London: Reaktion, 1983.

———. *Writings.* Trans. Erik Eisel. Minneapolis: University of Minnesota Press, 2002.

Frabetti, Frederica. "Rethinking the Digital Humanities in the Context of Originary Technicity." *The Digital Humanities Beyond Computing.* Spec. issue of *Culture Machine* 12 (2011): n.p.

Framke, Caroline. "Why Posting Black Boxes for #BlackoutTuesday, or Hashtags Without Action, Is Useless." *Vanity Fair.* 2 June 2020. Web.

Freeman, Joanne. "America Descends into the Politics of Rage." *Atlantic.* 22 October 2018. Web.

Friedman, Nathaniel. "Moments Without Truth: Making Sense of Online Discourse in the Age of Trump." *New Republic.* 21 October 2019. Web.

Frier, Sarah. "Facebook's Crisis Management Algorithm Runs on Outrage." *Bloomberg.* 14 March 2019. Web.

Gage, John. "Teaching the Enthymeme: Invention and Arrangement." *Rhetoric Review* 2, no. 1 (1983): 38–50

Garber, Megan. "The Art of Giving a Damn." *Atlantic.* 9 August 2019. Web.

"Gaza Flooded After Israel Opens Dam Gates." *Global Research TV*. 5 March 2012. http://tv.globalresearch.ca/.

Gelt, Jessica. "The Spreadsheet that Shook the Theater World: Marie Cisco's 'Not Speaking Out' list." *Los Angeles Times*. 9 June 2020. Web.

Ghitis, Frida. "How Outrage Over Cecil the Lion Killing Misses the Point." *CNN*. 3 August 2015. Web.

Gillespie, Nick. "Let's Stop Talking About Free Speech and Start Defending It." *Reason*. 18 June 2020 Web.

Gillespie, Tarleton. "The Relevance of Algorithms." In *Media Technologies: Essays on Communication, Materiality, and Society*, edited by Tarleton Gillespie, Pablo J. Boczkowski, and Kirsten A. Foot, 167–93. Cambridge, MA: MIT Press, 2014.

Gitelman, Lisa, and Virginia Jackson. "Introduction." In *Raw Data is an Oxymoron*, edited by Lisa Gitelman, 1–14. Cambridge, MA: MIT Press, 2013.

Glieberman, Own. "Why Kevin Hart Was the Wrong Choice to Host the Oscars." *Variety*. 6 December 2018. Web.

Gonyea, Don. "From the Start, Obama Struggled with Fallout from a Kind of Fake News." *NPR*. 10 Jan 2017. Web.

———. "Majority of White Americans Say They Believe Whites Face Discrimination." *NPR*. 24 October 2017. Web.

Granovetter, Mark. "The Strength of Weak Ties." *American Journal of Sociology* 78, no. 6 (1973): 1360–80.

Gries, Laurie E. *Still Life with Rhetoric: A New Materialist Approach for Visual Rhetorics*. Boulder: University Press of Colorado, 2015.

Halavais, Alexander. *Search Engine Society*. Malden, MA: Polity, 2009.

Hallinan, Blake, Jed R. Brubaker, and Casey Fiesler. "Unexpected Expectations: Public Reaction to the Facebook Emotional Contagion Study." *New Media & Society* 22, no. 6 (2020): 1076–94.

Hamblin, James. "My Outrage is Better Than Your outrage." *Atlantic*. 31 July 2015. Web.

Hamby, Peter. "'Intense Democracy': How Two Academic are Trying to Break the Outrage Cycle." *Vanity Fair*. 19 September 2019. Web.

Han, Byung-Chul. *In the Swarm: Digital Prospects*. Cambridge, MA: MIT Press, 2017.

Hariman, Robert, and John Louis Lucaites. *No Caption Needed: Iconic Photographs, Public Culture, and Liberal Democracy*. Chicago: University of Chicago Press, 2007.

Harpham, Geoffrey Galp. *The Humanities and the Dream of America*. Chicago: University of Chicago Press, 2011.

Harris, Adam. "America Can't Seem to Kick its Racist Costume Habit." *Atlantic*. 31 October 2018. Web.

"Harry and Louise on Clinton's Health Plan." *YouTube*. 15 July 2017. Web.

Hauer, Thomas. "Ontology of Technical Images." *Global Journal of Arts, Humanities and Social Sciences* 5, no. 2 (2017): 33–46.

Hauser, Gerard A. "Aristotle on Epideictic: The Formation of Public Morality." *Rhetoric Society Quarterly* 29, no. 1 (1999): 5–23.

———. *Vernacular Voices: The Rhetoric of Publics and Public Spheres*. Columbia: University of South Carolina Press, 1999.

Hawhee, Debra. "Looking into Aristotle's Eyes: Toward a Theory of Rhetorical Vision. *Advances in the History of Rhetoric* 14, no. 2 (2011): 139–65.

Hayles, Katherine N. "How We Think: Transforming Power and Digital Technologies." In *Understanding Digital Humanities,* edited by David M. Berry, 42–66. New York: Palgrave MacMillan, 2012.

Hendrickson, Mark. "President Obama's Marxist-Leninist Economics: Fact and Fiction." *Forbes.* 26 July 2012. Web.

Hess, Amanda. "Earning the 'Woke' Badge." *New York Times Magazine.* 19 April 2016. Web.

Hayes, Tracey J. "#MyNPD: Transforming Twitter into a Public Place for Protest." *Computers and Composition* 43 (2017): 118–34.

"Healthcare." *Tea Party Patriots.* n.d. Web.

Heath, Ryan, and Renuka Rayasam. "The Outrage Outbreak." *Politico.* 6 May 2020. Web.

Hess, Amanda. "The Protests Come for 'Paw Patrol.'" *New York Times.* 10 June 2020. Web.

Horsley, Scott. "From Jobs to Homeownership, Protests Put Spotlight on Racial Economic Divide." NPR. 1 June 2020. Web.

Howley, Kerry. "What We Mourned When We Mourned Cecil." *New Yorker.* 29 September 2015. Web.

Ingraham, Laura. *Power to the People.* Washington, DC: Regnery Publishing, 2007.

International Union or the Conservation of Nature and Its Resources. "Big Game Hunting in West Africa." IUCN.org. 2009. Web.

"Israel Opens Dam, Flooding Gaza Strip with Rainwater." *Middle East Monitor.* 10 Feb. 2014. Web.

"Israel Opens Dam Gates to Increase Suffering in Gaza." *Middle East Monitor.* 23 Jan 2014. Web.

"Is The Health Care Ire Part of A Larger Anger?" NPR. 15 August 2009. Web.

Jimmy Kimmel Live. 28 July 2015.

Johnson, Natalie. "'It's Time to Say Something': Mizzou Student Speaks on Campus Racism." *NBC.* 9 November 2015. Web.

Karppi, Tero. *Disconnect: Facebook's Affective Bonds.* Minneapolis: University of Minnesota Press: 2018.

Kass, John. "Politics as Religion After George Floyd. This Isn't an Orwellian Novel. This is Your Country." *Chicago Tribune.* 11 June 2020. Web.

Kirschenbaum, Matthew G. "What is Digital Humanities and What's It Doing in English Departments. *ADE Bulletin.* Number 150, 210 (1–7).

Kirstein, Peter N. "Steven Salaita, the Media, and the Struggle for Academic Freedom." *AAUP.* January–Februrary 2016. Web.

Kaur, Harmeet. "This is Why Blackface is Offensive.' *CNN.* 7 February 2019. Web.

Kaye, Randi. "Town Hall Anger Over Health Care Bill." *CNN.* 28 June 2017. Web.

Kendi, Ibram X. *How to be an Antiracist.* New York: One World, 2019.

Kilkenny, Allison. "Occupy Wall Street and the Importance of Creative Protest." *Nation.* 21 November 2011. Web.

King, Mike. "George Ciccariello-Maher vs. the White Power Alt-Right." *Counter Punch.* 28 December 2016. Web.

Kingkade, Tyler. "The Incident You Have to See to Understand. Why Students Wanted Mizzou's President To Go." *Huffington Post.* 12 November 2015. Web.

Konnikova, Maria. "How Headlines Change the Way We Think." *New Yorker.* 17 December 2014. Web.

Kovacs, Kasia. "Update: MU Student Embarks on Hunger Strike, Demands Wolf's Removal From Office." *Columbian Missourian.* 2 November 2015. Web.

Kramer, Adam D.I., Jamie E. Guillory, and Jefferey Hancock. "Experimental Evidence of Massive-Scale Emotional Contagion Through Social Networks." *PNAS.* 17 June 2014. Web.

Kupfer, Theodore. "No, George Ciccariello-Maher Doesn't Believe in Academic Freedom." *National Review.* 12 October 2017. Web.

Kurtz, Stanley. "IPAB, Obama, and Socialism." *National Review.* 18 April 2011. Web.

La, Sha. "North Korea Proves Your White Male Privilege Is Not Universal." *Huffington Post.* 19 June 2017. Web.

Lakoff, George, and Mark Johnson. *Metaphors We Live By.* Chicago: University of Chicago Press, 1980.

Lasn, Kalle. *Cultural Jam: How to Reverse America's Suicidal Consumer Binge- And Why We Must.* New York: HarperCollins, 1999.

Leff, Michael. "Hermeneutical Rhetoric." In *Rhetorics of Hermeneutics in Our Time,* edited by Walter Jost and Michael J. Hyde, 196–214. New Haven, CT: Yale University Press, 1997.

Leiter, Brian. "Salaita Appearance at U of Chicago Tonight." *Leiter Reports.* 7 October 2014. Web.

"Letter to the UM System Curators." *Missouri Students Association.* No date. Web.

Lewis, Helen. "The Echo Chamber of Social Media is Luring the left into Cosy Delusion and Dangerous Insularity." *New Statesman.* 22 July 2015. Web.

Lewis, Matt. "America's Outrage Machine is Spinning Us Into a Death Spiral." *Daily Beast.* 15 June 2019. Web.

Lifson, Thomas. "Professor tweets 'All I Want for Christmas is White Genocide.'" *American Thinker.* 25 December 2016. Web.

Limbaugh, Rush. "Dastardly Obamacare Plan Seeks Government Control of Life, Death." *Rushlimbaugh.com.* 21 July 2009. Web.

———. "The Shrinking American Economy Should Be the Only News." *Rushlimbaugh.com.* 25 June 2014.

Little, Maxwell. "Remove the Statue of Thomas Jefferson From Campus." change.org. January 1, 2022. https://www.change.org/.

Liu, Alan. "Digital Humanities and Academic Change." *English Language Notes* 47 (2009): 17–35.

Livni, Ephrat. "How Americans Can Break Their Outrage Addiction." *Quartz.* 21 July 2018. Web.

Lukas, Carrie. "The Truth Behind Obamacare's 'Death Panels.'" *US News and World Report.* 12 December 2012. Web.

McCullough, Kevin. "Obama as Hitler." *Townhall.com.* 1 March 2009. Web.

McDonald, Soraya Nadia. "Kaepernick's Afro and the Visual Shorthand of Radicalism." *The Undefeated.* 17 October 2018. Web.

McFarland, Michael. "Ethical Implications of Data Aggregation." *Markkula Center for Applied Ethics*. 1 June 2012. Web.

McGann, Jerome. "On Creating a Usable Future." *Profession* (2011): 182–95.

Magary, Drew. "How I Learned to Calm the F*#% Down in the Age of Trump." *GQ*. 21 September 2017. Web.

Mailer, Norman. *Armies of the Night: History as a Novel, the Novel as History*. New York: Plume, 1968.

Madrigal, Alexis. "Why I Feel Bad for the Pepper Spraying Policeman—Lt. John Pike." *Atlantic*. 20 November 2011. Web.

Markowicz, Karol. "Maybe It's Time for Everyone to Give Up on Social Media." *New York Post*. 11 March 2018. Web.

Massad, Joseph. "Academic Civility and Its Discontents." *The Electronic Intifada*. 9 October 2014. Web.

Massumi, Brian. *Parables of the Virtual: Movement, Affect, Sensation*. Durham, NC: Duke University Press, 2002.

Medium Cool. Dir. Wex Wexler. H&J, 1969. Film.

Memmott, Mark. "'Casually Pepper Spraying Cop' Meme Takes Off." NPR. 21 November 2011. Web.

Menand, Louis. "The Limits of Academic Freedom." In *The Future of Academic Freedom*, edited by Louis Menand, 3–20. Chicago: University of Chicago Press, 1998.

Miecznikowski Sheard, Cynthia. "The Public Value of Epideictic Rhetoric." *College English* 58, no. 7 (1996): 765–94.

Miller, Mike. "PETA Calls for Salter Palmer to be 'Hanged' for Killing Cecil the Lion." *The Washington Post*. 30 July 2015. Web.

Montanaro, Dominco. "Trump's 'Socialism' Attack on Democrats Has Its Roots in Cold War Fear." NPR. 12 February 2019. Web.

Morgan, Piers. "I'm so Sick of this War on masculinity and I'm not Alone—with Their Pathetic Man-Hating Ad, Gillette Have just Cut Their Own Throat." *Dailymail*. 15 Jan 2019. Web.

Morrow, Lance. "American is Addicted to Outrage. Is There a Cure?" *Wall Street Journal*. 30 November 2018. Web.

Mukherjee, Sy. "Obama care's Dreaded 'Death Panels' Won't be Triggered This Year." *Forbes*. 22 June 2016. Web.

Murphy, January. "Senators Call on Drexel to Fire Professor Over Social Media Post." *Penn Live Patriot-News*. 13 April 2017. Web.

Murthy, Dhiraj. "Twitter. Microphone for the Masses?" *Media, Culture & Society* 33, no. 5 (2011). 779–89.

Murrow, Glenn R. "Academic Freedom." *Bulletin of the American Association of University Professors (1915-1955)* 40, no. 4 (1954/1955): 529–35.

Myers, Frank. "Political Argumentation and the Composite Audience: A Case Study." *Quarterly Journal of Speech* 85 (1999): 55–71.

Nadkarni, Rohan, and Alex Nieves. "Why Missouri's Football Team Joined a Protest Against School Administration." *Sports Illustrated*. 9 November 2015. Web.

Naaman, Mor, Jeffrey Boase, and Chih-Hui Lai. "Is it Really About Me? Message Content in Social Awareness Streams." *ACM Digital Library*, 2010.

Nahon, Karine, and Jeff Hemsley. *Going Viral*. Malden, MA: Polity Press, 2013.

Nangia, Aditi. "Foreign Policy: The Truth About Death Panels." NPR. 10 September 2008. Web.

Nelson, Cary. *Israel Denial: Anti-Zionism, Anti-Semitism, & The Faculty Campaign Against the Jewish State*. Bloomington: Indiana University Press, 2019.

Newfield, Christopher. "Feeding a Dangerous Fiction." *Inside Higher Ed*. 19 October 2017. Web.

Nissenbaum, Helen. "Privacy as Contextual Integrity." *Washington Law Review* 79 (2004): 101–39.

Noguchi, Yuki. "#OkBoomer Vs. #OkMillennial: Workplace Nightmare, Or Just a Meme?" NPR. 18 November 2019. Web.

Nussbaum, Martha C. *Anger and Forgiveness: Resentment, Generosity, Justice*. New York: Oxford University Press, 2016.

Oakes, Penelope, Haslam, S. Alexander, and John C. Turner. "The Role of Prototypicality in Group Influence and Cohesion: Contextual Variation in the Graded Structure of Social Categories." In *Social Identity: International Perspectives*, edited by Stephen Worchel, J. Francisco Morales, Darío Páez, and Jean-Claude Deschamps, 75–92. London: Sage, 1998.

"Occupy Cal Makes Its Dramatic Entrance." *San Franciscan Bay Guardian Archive*. 11 November 2011. Web.

Obeidallah, Tammy. "Haiti Hypocrisy Hides Yet Another War Crime." *Intifada Palestine*. 26 January 2010. Web.

O'Gorman, Ned. 2005. "Aristotle's Phantasia in the Rhetoric: Lexis, Appearance, and the Epideictic Function of Discourse." *Philosophy and Rhetoric* 38, no. 1 (2005): 16–40.

O'Neill, Natalie. "Critics Blast 'A Charlie Brown Thanksgiving' as Racist. *New York Post*. 23 November 2018. Web.

O'Neil, Robert M. "Limits of Freedom: The Ward Churchill Case." *Change* 38, no. 5 (2006): 36–41.

"Of Slavery and Swastikas." *The Economist*. 30 December 2015. Web.

Ong, Walter. "The Writer's Audience is Always a Fiction." *PMLA* 90, no. 1 (1975): 9–21.

Palumbo-Li, David. "Why the 'Unhiring' of Steve Salaita is a Threat to Academic Freedom." *The Nation*. 27 Aug 2014. Web.

Perelman, Chaïm, and Lucie Olbrechts-Tyeca. *The New Rhetoric: A Treatise on Argumentation*. Notre Dame, IN: University of Notre Dame Press, 1969.

Perry, Dave. "The Computational Turn: Thinking About the Digital Humanities." *The Digital Humanities Beyond Computing*. Spec. issue of *Culture Machine*. Vol. 12. 2011 (n.p.).

Perry, David. "Don't Speak Out: The Message of the Salaita Affair." *Chronicle of Higher Education*. 20 Aug 2014. Web.

Palin, Sarah. "Statement on the Current Health Care Debate." *Facebook*. 7 August 2009. Web.

Plucinska, Joanna. "'Walter Palmer is Satan': Celebrities Rage Over Cecil the Lion's Killer." *TIME*. 30 July 2015. Web.

Prelli, Lawrence. "Rhetorics of Display: An Introduction." In *Rhetorics of Display*, edited by Lawrence Prelli, 1–40. Columbia: University of South Carolina Press, 2006.

Pernot, Laurent. *Epideictic Rhetoric: Questioning the Stakes of Ancient Praise.* Austin: University of Texas Press, 2005.

Peters, Mark. "Virtue Signaling and Other Inane Platitudes." *Boston Globe.* 24 December 2015. web.

Petronzio, Matt. "Cecil the Lion's Death Opens Question of Why Illegal Poaching of Protected Animals is Still So Common." *Mashable.* 1 Aug 2015. Web.

Pfister, Damien. *Networked Media, Networked Rhetorics: Attention and Deliberation in the Early Blogosphere.* State College: Penn State University Press, 2014.

Pearce, Matt. "Protesters Celebrate After Top University of Missouri Leaders Resign Over Racial Turmoil." *Los Angeles Times.* 9 November 2015. Web.

Politico. "IT Really is Different This Time." *Politico.* 4 June 20200. Web.

Popkin, Helen. "As Your Social Media Emotions Go Viral, Anger Spread the Fastest." *NBCnews.com.* 17 September 2013. Web.

Poster, Carol. "A Historicist Recontextualization of the Enthymeme." *Rhetoric Society Quarterly* 22, no. 2 (1992): 1–24.

Poulakos, Takis. "Isocrates Use of 'Doxa.'" *Philosophy and Rhetoric* 34, no. 1 (2001): 61–78.

"Proctor & Gamble Fighting Devil Worship Rumors." *Daily News.* 25 Jan 1982 (4).

Pygas, Mark. "'Rage Yoga' Involves Swearing and Booze Breaks." *Distractify.com.* March 2019. Web.

Quintana, Chris, and Brock Read. "Signal Boost: How Conservative Media Outlets Turn Faculty Viewpoints Into National News." *Chronicle of Higher Education.* 22 June 2017. Web.

Ray, Victor. "Weaponizing Free Speech." *Inside Higher Ed.* 30 June 2017.

Raymond, James C. "Enthymemes, Examples, and Rhetorical Method." In *Essays on Classical Rhetoric and Modern Discourse,* edited by Robert J. Connors et al., 140–51. Carbondale: Southern Illinois University Press, 1984.

Reider, Bernhard, Ariadna Matamoros-Fernández, and Óscar Coromina. "From Ranking Algorithms to 'Ranking Cultures': Investigating the Modulation of Visibility in YouTube Search Results." *Convergence: The International Journal of Research into New Media Technologies* 24, no. 1 (2018): 50–68.

Richard, Catharine. "McCaughey Claims End-of-Life Counseling Will be Required for Medicare Patients." *Politfact.com.* 23 July 2009. Web.

Riotta, Chris. "Does Donald Trump Have an Anger Problem? President Continues Erupting at His Closest Aides." *Newsweek.* 17 June 2017. Web.

Rizk, Philip. "Israel Plays God: Floods Gaza Strip." *Tabula Gaza.* 20 Jan 2010. Web.

"Ronald Reagan Speaks Out Against Socialized Medicine." *YouTube.* 13 December 2010. Web.

Rosenfeld, Steven. "4 Ways Google is Destroying Privacy and Collecting Your Data." *Salon.* 5 Feb. 2014. Web.

Rothman, Noah. "The Backlash Against Cop Shows is a Moral Panic." *Commentary.* 11 June 2020. Web.

Sacks, Brianna, and Albert Samaha. "Starbucks Won't Let Employees Wear Gear That Supports Black Lives Matter Because It Is Political Or Could Incite Violence." *Buzzfeed News.* 10 June 2020. Web.

Saidi, Janet. "University of Missouri Missed the Opportunity to Address 2015 Racial Protests Directly." *Kansas City (MO) Star*. 14 July 2017. Web.

Salaita, Steven. "Why I Was Fired." *Chronicle of Higher Education*. 5 October 2015. Web.

Sampson, Tony. 2012 *Virality: Contagion Theory in the Age of Networks*. Minneapolis: University of Minnesota Press.

Sanchez, Chelsey. "What Is #BlackoutTuesday? Here's Everything You Need to Know." *Harper's Bazaar*. 2 June 2020. Web.

Schonfeld, Erick. "Zuckerberg: 'We Are Building a Web Where the Default is Social'" *Tech Crunch*. n.d. Web.

Schreiber, Katherine. "Why Social Media is Making Us Miserable." *Cosmopolitan*. 23 March 2016. Web.

Schriebman, Susan, Laura Mandell, and Stephen Olsen. "Introduction." *Profession* (2011): 123–35.

Schwartz, Mattathias. "Pre-Occupied: The Origins and Future of Occupy Wall Street." *New Yorker*. 28 November 2011. Web.

Scott, Joan W. "The New Thought Police." *The Nation*. 15 April 2015. Web.

Shugerman, Emily. "Professor Fired After Saying Otto Warmbier was a 'Clueless White Male' Who 'Got What He Deserved.'" *The Independent*. 26 June 2017. Web.

Sini, Matthew. "The Purity of the Shitstorm." *Areo*. 3 July 2020. Web.

Sloterdijk, Peter. *Rage and Time*. Trans. Mario Wenning. New York: Columbia University Press, 2010.

Smith, Marion. "How Did Obama Forget What 'Socialist' Means?" *Politico*. 22 March 2016. Web.

Soave, Robby. "Drexel Professor Tweets 'All I Want for Christmas is White Genocide.'" *Reason*. 26 December 2016. Web.

———. "Kevin Hart Quits Oscars Hosting Gig Over Past Homophobic Tweets, Social Media Mobs Win Again." *Reason*. 7 December 2018 Web.

Sperry, Paul. "Obama's Final Days Show His True Socialist Agenda." *New York Post*. 12 June 2016. Web.

State, Bogdan, and Lada Adamic. "The Diffusion of Support in an Online Social Movement: Evidence from the Adoption of Equal-Sign Profile Pictures." *Proceedings of the 18th ACM Conference on Computer Supported Cooperative Work and Social Computing*. New York: ACM, 2015 (11741–1750)

Stetler, Brian. "Protest Puts Coverage in Spotlight." *New York Times*. 20 November 2011 Web.

Stewart, Kathleen. *Ordinary Affects*. Durham, NC: Duke University Press, 2007.

Stone, Geoffrey. "Academic Freedom." *Bulletin of the American Academy of Arts and Sciences*. Vol. 59 No 2. Winter 2006 (17).

Stripling, Jack. 2 February 2016. "Confronting Racial Divide, Missouri's Interim President Finds Anger, Finger-Pointing." *Chronicle of Higher Education*. Web.

———. "Scathing Report on UC-Davis Pepper-Spray Incident Faults Chancellor and Police." *Chronicle of Higher Education*. 11 April 2012. Web.

Sullivan, Dale. 1993. "The Ethos of Epideictic Encounter." *Philosophy and Rhetoric* 26, no. 2 (1993): 113–33.

Sunstein, Cass R. 2007. *Republic.com 2.0*. Princeton, NJ: Princeton University Press.

Sung, Morgan. "Boomers Getting Mad at Everyone Saying 'Ok Boomer' Makes It Even Funnier." *Mashable*. 4 November 2009. Web.

Taibbi, Matt. "The Press is Destroying Itself." *Pittsburgh (PA) Post-Gazette*. 21 June 2020. Web.

Tharror, Ishaan, and Nate Rawlings. "'The Whole World Is Watching': Occupy Wall Street Stares Down the NYPD." *TIME*. 14 October 2011. Web.

Thompson, Derek. Everybody's in a Bubble, That's a Problem." *Atlantic*. 25 Jan 2017. Web.

Todd Huston, Warner. "Drexel University Professor's Christmas Wish: 'All I want for Christmas is White Genocide.'" *Breitbart*. 25 December 2016. Web.

Turner, Julia. "The Year of Outrage." *Slate*. 17 December 2014. Web.

Tywoniak, Ed. "The Whole World is Watching: The SDS and Student Movement of the 1960s." In *Baby Boomers and Popular Culture: An Inquiry into America's Most Powerful Generation*, edited by Brian Cogan and Thom Gencarelli, 17–34. Santa Barbara, CA: Praeger, 2015.

Ubel, Peter. "Paying for Healthcare Is So Confusing, Patients Don't Know Who To Be Angry At." *Forbes*. 22 August 2016. Web.

"University of Missouri President Resigns Amid Campus Protests." *Foxnews.com*. 9 November 2015.

Vaidhyanathan, Siva. *Antisocial Media: How Facebook Disconnects Us and Undermines Democracy*. New York: Oxford University Press, 2018.

———. *The Googlization of Everything (And Why We Should Worry)*. Oakland: University of California Press, 2011.

Vivian, Bradford. "In Regard of the Image." *JAC* 27, no. 34 (2007):471–504.

———. "Neoliberal Epideictic: Rhetorical Form and Commemorative Politics on September 11, 2002." *Quarterly Journal of Speech* 92, no 1 (2006): 1–26.

Vavreck, Lynn. "American Anger: It's Not the Economy. It's the Other Party." *New York Times*. 2 April 2016. Web.

Walker, Jeffrey. *Rhetoric and Poetics in Antiquity*. Oxford, England: Oxford University Press, 2000.

———. "The Body of Persuasion: A Theory of the Enthymeme." *College English* 5, no. 1 (1994): 46–65.

Walsh, Paul. "Walter Palmer Speaks: Hunter Who Killed Lion Will Resume Bloomington Dental Practice." *Star Tribune*. 28 July 2018. Web.

Warzel, Charlie. "Facebook Doesn't Deserve Your Information." *Buzzfeed*. 12 October 2018. Web.

Watts, Duncan. *Six Degrees: The Science of a Connected Age*. New York: W. W. Norton, 2004.

Wayne, Teddy. "Clicking Their Way to Outrage." *New York Times*. 3 July 2014. Web.

Weinstein, Adam. "'We Are the 99 Percent' Creators Revealed." *Mother Jones*. 7 October 2011. Web.

Wellington, Elizabeth. "Think You're Angrier Lately? You Probably Are and Your Facebook Feed is to Blame." *Philadelphia Inquirer*. 1 May 2008. Web.

"White Genocide." *ADL.org*. n.d. Web.

"Why We Fight." *The History of Cal*. 2 March 2012. Web.

Wilhelm, Heather. "The Last Gasps of Outrage Culture?" *National Review*. 26 Jan 2018. Web.

Williams, Mary-Elizabeth. "The Geeky Triumph of Pepper Spray Cop." *Salon*. 23 November 2011. Web.

Williams, Stereo. "Dear White People: Blackface is Not OK." *Daily Beast*. 13 April 2017. Web

Williams, Zoe. "We Are All Angry on Social Media—At Least Try to Listen to the Rage of Others." *Guardian*. 9 October 2017. Web.

Williamson, Kevin. "A Herd Has No Name." *National Review*. 11 July 2019. Web.

Winderman, Emily. "Anger's Volumes: Rhetorics of Amplification and Aggregation in #MeToo." *Women's Studies in Communication* 42, no. 3 (2019): 327–46.

Wolchover, Natalie. "Why is Everyone on the Internet so Angry?" *Scientific American*. 25 July 2012. Web.

Zappen James P. "Digital Rhetoric: Toward an Integrated Theory." *Technical Communication Quarterly* 14, no. 3 (2005): 319–25.

Zelizer, Julian E. "How Medicare Was Made." *New Yorker*. 15 Feb. 2015. Web.

Zinn, Howard. "The Politics of History in the Era of the Cold War: Repression and Resistance." In *The Cold War & The University: Toward an Intellectual History of the Postwar Years*, edited by André Schiffrin, 35–72. New York: The New Press, 1997.

Žižek, Slavoj. *The Sublime Object of Ideology*. New York: Verso, 1989.

Index